ÁLVARO OBREGÓN

Alvaro Obregón

ÁLVARO OBREGÓN

Power and Revolution in Mexico, 1911-1920

By LINDA B. HALL

 TEXAS A&M UNIVERSITY PRESS   COLLEGE STATION

Library of Congress Cataloging in Publication Data

Hall, Linda B. (Linda Biesele), 1939–
    Alvaro Obregon: power and revolution in Mexico,
1911–1920.

        Bibliography: p.
        Includes index.
        1. Obregón, Alvaro, 1880–1928. 2. Mexico—Politics
and government—1910–1946.
        F1234.O2H34   972.08′22′0924   80-6110
        ISBN 0-89096-113-1   AACR2

Manufactured in the United States of America
First Edition

To the memory of
Rudolph Leopold Biesele, Sr.—
inspiring teacher,
meticulous scholar,
loving grandfather

Contents

List of Illustrations

x   Illustrations

List of Abbreviations

AAA-CDE	Archivo de Amado Aguirre: Centro Director Electoral, private collection, Professor Alvaro Matute, Mexico City
AAA-DT	Archivo de Amado Aguirre: Departamento de Telégrafos, private collection, Professor Alvaro Matute, Mexico City
AC	Archivo de Venustiano Carranza, Centro de Estudios Históricos–Condumex, Mexico City
AGES	Archivo General del Estado de Sonora, Hermosillo
AGO/VR	U.S. Adjutant General's Office: Villa's Revolution, National Archives, Washington, D.C.
AHES	Archivo Histórico del Estado de Sonora, Hermosillo
ASRE	Archivo de la Secretaría de Relaciones Exteriores, Mexico City
AZ	Archivo de Emiliano Zapata, Universidad Nacional Autónoma de México, Mexico City
Casa	Casa del Obrero Mundial
COHC	Columbia Oral History Collection, Columbia University, New York
Confederación	Confederación Revolucionaria
Constituyente	Constitutional Congress at Querétaro
C.R.O.M.	Confederación Regional Obrera Mexicana
DAAC	Archivo del Departamento de Asuntos Agrarios y Crédito, Mexico City

DLGA	Lázaro de la Garza Archive, Latin American Collection, University of Texas at Austin
DRM	Isidro Fabela, *Documentos de la Revolución Mexicana*
ELA	Enrique Llorente Archive, New York Public Library
HLS	Hugh Lenox Scott Papers, Library of Congress, Washington, D.C.
LMG/AHDN	Luis Muro, Guide to the materials in the Archivo Histórico de la Secretaría de la Defensa Nacional
MID	Military Intelligence Division, National Archives, Washington, D.C.
MPPP	Mexican Political Parties Propaganda Archive, Latin American Collection, University of Texas at Austin
PHO	Programa de Historia Oral, Instituto Nacional de Antropología e Historia, Museo de Antropología, Mexico City
PHS	Patronato de la Historia de Sonora, Museo de Antropología, Mexico City
P.L.C.	Partido Liberal Constitucionalista
P.L.M.	Partido Laborista Mexicano
P.L.N.	Partido Liberal Nacional
P.N.C.	Partido Nacional Cooperatista
P.R.F.R.	U.S. Department of State, *Papers Relating to the Foreign Relations of the United States, 1916*
TP	Sylvestre Terrazas Papers, Bancroft Library, University of California, Berkeley
USDS	U.S. Department of State, Records Relating to the Internal Affairs of Mexico, 1910–1929, University of Texas at Austin

Acknowledgments

The completion of this project was possible only with the generous help of many individuals and institutions. I owe special thanks to Eugenia Meyer, of the Archivo de la Palabra in Mexico City, who provided me with many of the interviews pertinent to Obregón's career in her extensive collection and who instructed me in oral history, and to Antonio Pompa y Pompa, director of the Biblioteca de Antropología e Historia, who guided me to the excellent microfilm archives of that institution. Alvaro Matute generously permitted me to use the private archive of Amado Aguirre, Obregón's close associate and director of his 1920 campaign for the presidency. Antonio Carrillo Flores presented me to a number of Obregón's colleagues. Fernando Torreblanca, who had served Obregón as private secretary, spent many hours with me recounting his memories of the revolutionary years and kindly introduced me to other individuals who remembered Obregón and who also shared their recollections with me.

My understanding of the Mexican Revolution and of Obregón's role in it has been greatly aided by conversations with Douglas Richmond, Don M. Coerver, Stanley Ross, Berta Ulloa, Jean Meyer, David Bailey, Friedrich Katz, Luis Martín, John Womack, Jr., Richard Sinkin, Hector Aguilar Camín, Peter Smith, Stuart Voss, Arnaldo Córdova, and others too numerous to mention. At various stages the manuscript has been read and criticized by Herbert Klein, Edward Malefakis, Douglas Chalmers, Lambros Comitas, Karen Spalding, and Peter Henderson.

All helped save me from errors of fact, interpretation, or emphasis. Any errors that remain are, of course, my own. Stuart Fagan and Michel Oksenberg helped me gain an enlarged understanding of politics and revolution.

Some of the material in this book has appeared in articles elsewhere and is presented here with the permission of the publishers concerned. Portions of chapters 7, 9, 10, 11, and 12 dealing with the development of political parties have appeared as an article in *Historia Mexicana* 116 (1980). Portions of chapters 7, 9, 11, and 13 have appeared as an article, "Alvaro Obregón and the Agrarian Movement 1912–1920," in *Caudillo and Peasant in the Mexican Revolution*, ed. David Brading (Cambridge: Cambridge University Press, 1980).

I am grateful to the Danforth Foundation, to the National Endowment for the Humanities, and to the Faculty Research and Development Council of Trinity University for the support provided to me at various stages of my research and writing. To my colleagues in the history department here at Trinity, and especially to Donald E. Everett, I owe a debt of gratitude for their unfailing help and good will. Lynn Brown, Cynthia Narciso, and Virginia Cabello cheerfully typed the many versions of the manuscript. The most important thanks of all go to my children, Leslie and Douglas Hall, who traveled with me, shared my interest in this project, and gave me the peace of mind necessary to complete it. Without their encouragement, this book would never have been possible.

ÁLVARO OBREGÓN

CHAPTER I

Introduction

The subject of revolution has intrigued historians, political scientists, and other social scientists for many years. Revolution as extreme social change, the rapid and violent change of elites and institutions, has offered in microcosm an opportunity to study individuals and societies going through transformations that ordinarily would take many more years. However, the focus of almost all of these studies has been concentrated on those forces which divide men and push them to violent action. Little consideration has been given to the process of recovery and reinstitutionalization, the process by which peace between men is reestablished and goals, values, leadership, ways of dealing between men, and the political rules of the game in a given society are or are not changed.

Within the context of the Mexican Revolution, Alvaro Obregón stood out in the mythology as the organizer, the peacemaker, the unifier. The way in which he accomplished this reunification, however, has not been studied in any detail. How he did it, whether or not institutions would have been different had he not directed his efforts toward unification, whether the reestablishment of peace was inevitable or was a result of his efforts or of a combination of historical circumstances, what factors made it possible for him to rise to power in the first place, what the nature of his support was, and how this support influenced the subsequent emergent institutions of modern Mexico are questions that have scarcely been raised. Even the theoretical literature gives little help to those who would study the renewal of peaceful relationships between men.

The literature of revolution, studied on a theoretical or a comparative basis, has been overwhelmingly directed toward the causes and motives, both conscious and unconscious, that drive men to violence against authority. Many studies of economics and class, following in the tradition of Karl Marx, have considered the structural development of society and proposed theories about what structures, inherently unsound or unfair, may precipitate or justify rebellion. Many of these not only give analyses of structures that lead to revolution but also contain normative arguments in favor of revolution and violence in certain circumstances.[1] Some studies, such as Hannah Arendt's *On Revolution*, name certain goals that justify or even define revolution—in Arendt's case "freedom."[2]

Other studies have been more concerned with what psychological conditions may prove a spur to rebellion. Notable among these is Ted Robert Gurr's *Why Men Rebel*, which outlines the theory of relative deprivation—that is, "the actors' perception of discrepancy between their value expectations and their value capabilities." In other words, if men receive less than they expect, either because they are receiving less than what they are accustomed to or because they are expecting improvement and their expectations are not fulfilled, their tendencies to violence and rebellion are increased. Chalmers Johnson, in *Revolutionary Change*, defines revolution as a drastic form of social change to remedy specific conditions within the social system. Revolution, according to Johnson, results from multiple dysfunctions in the economic and social order com-

[1]See the definition of revolution in the preface to Karl Marx, *A Contribution to the Critique of Political Economy*, pp. 10–13. V. I. Lenin, *State and Revolution*, reviews and interprets Marx's and Friedrich Engels' works on the subject. Lenin, following Marx, sees the only possibility for the transition period itself in the "revolutionary dictatorship of the proletariat" (see p. 71). He briefly discusses this transition period (p. 73), saying, "Democracy for the vast majority of the people, and suppression by force, i.e., exclusion from democracy, of the exploiters and oppressors of the people—this is the modification of democracy during the transition from capitalism to communism." However, he does not detail the specific relationships that would be necessary in such a period.

[2]Hannah Arendt, *On Revolution*, pp. 21–27.

bined with elite intransigence and various kinds of accelerators, including ideology, which for him is a necessary part of revolution. However, Johnson does not consider the course the revolution may follow and implies that the eventual outcome is in some way inherent in the revolution from the beginning. Yet again the process of ending the revolution is ignored.[3]

Other comparative studies have been interested in certain groups of people who have seemed to be more likely to rebel. In his *Primitive Rebels*, E. J. Hobsbawm has studied what he calls "archaic forms of social movement in the 19th and 20th centuries," concentrating primarily on rural movements, both of social bandits and millenarian groups, but also considering city mobs and early labor sects. Hobsbawm freely admits that his interest is in the "prehistory of modern labour and peasant movements," and therefore much predates the phase of institutionalization or even of marginal success. A more specific comparative study is Eric Wolf's volume *Peasant Wars of the Twentieth Century*. Yet again, his interest and his conclusions are more drawn to original causes than to final results. He sees peasant rebellions rising out of alienation from the customary "social matrix" caused by the introduction of capitalism into the countryside. Peasant rebellions are, for Wolf, "parochial manifestations of great social dislocations." As for the building of a new social order on the basis of peasant revolutions, Wolf can only offer the thought that the peasant effort to undo the present, however grievous that present may be, will only introduce an unknown future. He offers no analysis of how that future may develop or what steps or conditions might make possible the retention of revolutionary values after the violent phase.[4]

Yet another type of study may be found in Lewis Coser's *The Functions of Social Conflict*. Sociologist Coser emphasizes

---

[3]Ted Robert Gurr, *Why Men Rebel*, p. 24; Chalmers Johnson, *Revolutionary Change*, pp. 59–118. Johnson's chapter "The Future of Revolution," pp. 166–172, refers only to potential future revolutions, not to what happens beyond the violent stage of any given revolution.

[4]E. J. Hobsbawm, *Primitive Rebels*, p. 11; Eric Wolf, *Peasant Wars of the Twentieth Century*, pp. 279, 301–302.

the usefulness of conflict with other groups in promoting solidarity and identity within a group, but even more helpful for
a study of revolution and particularly the Mexican Revolution is his suggestion that conflicts with some produce coalitions
with others. Thus, in the Mexican Revolution, the winning
group eventually comprised many groups within the society:
agrarian and urban workers, miners, intellectuals from all classes,
artisans, middle-class farmers, and businessmen. Coser further
suggests that social systems that are flexible enough to tolerate
and institutionalize conflict between groups, readjusting their
structures and readdressing the balance of power, thus avoiding
later catastrophic breakdown, may use conflict as a powerful
stabilizing mechanism.[5]

These suggestions for the uses and institutionalization of
conflict are extremely useful for the study of the course of
the Mexican Revolution, especially after the military phase.
The ability to balance groups and the willingness to listen and
to sense grievances before they reached crisis proportions was
one of the qualities that helped Obregón consolidate power in
the years before 1920. The institutionalization of conflict was
an important factor in the stable political system that developed
in Mexico after the Revolution, and Obregón's inclusion in his
coalition of many groups that might have been expected to be
dissident was critical in his ability to achieve this goal.

Another and extremely influential discussion of revolution
is Crane Brinton's *Anatomy of Revolution*. Brinton compares
revolution to a fever and identifies four stages. The first is the
prodromal, the early signs of the coming disturbance. This
stage is marked by increasing social unrest, signs of breakdown
in the economic and political realms, and the "desertion of the
intellectuals." In the second stage, the stage of disease, the full
symptoms are disclosed, a crescendo of protests and then actual
violence ensue, and finally the revolutionists topple the old
regime. After a short "honeymoon" period of revolutionary
unity, factionalism divides the revolutionists, and the most violent group takes over in a "Reign of Terror." Finally, in ex-

[5]Lewis A. Coser, *The Functions of Social Conflict*, pp. 151–155.

haustion, the society lapses into a period of convalescence, during which it recovers from the illness and emerges, perhaps strengthened, but by no means wholly changed.[6]

Brinton claims the universality of this "Thermidorean reaction." Although later revolutions have shown that this period is not universal, that there are any number of possibilities at this stage, such as a return to violence and chaos, Brinton's suggestion that a strong central ruler will emerge at this point to "handle centralized power when the mad religious energy of the crisis period has burned itself out" is provocative.[7] It is open to question whether this central ruler will govern through consent or force, a problem Brinton does not consider at any length, and whether his rule will or will not be accompanied by the return to importance of traditional institutions such as the church.[8]

Indeed, this latter stage of some revolutions during which the violence ends and the society establishes new ways of carrying out its tasks has been very little studied. This phase, not as dramatic and not as given to the creation of heroic legends, has proved less interesting to historians and social scientists than the phases during which violence is turned either against the former authority or against other revolutionary factions. This generalization has proved true for the case of the Mexican Revolution.

Most studies have concentrated on the military phases of the Revolution and the Constitutional Congress of Querétaro in 1917 and have then jumped a gap of several years into the 1920's, leaving the transitional phase unexplored.[9] Nevertheless, the transitional phase is important in setting the patterns of

[6]Crane Brinton, *The Anatomy of Revolution*, pp. 17–18, 41, 71, 95.

[7]Ibid., p. 218. For a potential revolution that did not follow Brinton's pattern, consider the case of the widespread agrarian movement in Colombia, which degenerated into the endemic and psychopathic violence called *La Violencia*. In the political realm, in Colombia a "controlled democracy" led by the two major political parties emerged, rather than strong, one-man rule. Nevertheless, power was centralized during this period in a striking manner.

[8]See Brinton's discussion, ibid., pp. 226–231.

[9]The major literature on the Mexican Revolution is discussed in the bibliographic note in this book.

political institutionalization. The first step in understanding this transition, it seems to me, is in understanding the major figure, Alvaro Obregón, and the way in which he himself in the years 1911 to 1920 developed the power and authority to play this transitional role and then began to exercise his influence, even before he became president. This, then, is the task of the book that follows: to examine Obregón's rise to power and prominence between the years 1911, when he first became politically active at the local level, and 1920, when Obregón became President of Mexico with the overwhelming support of the Mexican people. It is a story that must be viewed from both political and military perspectives, as these two aspects of his rise are mutually interdependent and each strongly influences the other. Further, it is a story of the way in which his political and military successes led to a national, rather than local, political power base and a national, not exclusively local, heroic image identified directly with the goals of the Revolution as they had emerged during this period. Lastly, it is the story of the way in which Obregón translated this power base and popular support into his successful campaign for the presidency in 1919–1920 and the way in which this national power base and national image of Obregón within the image of the Revolution helped establish a basis for the institutionalization of the modern Mexican state.

A further work of conceptualization and analysis must be mentioned, as it has contributed a great deal to the work that follows. This is S. N. Eisenstadt's edited volume of Max Weber's work *On Charisma and Institution Building*, which shows that charisma, which would seem to be the opposite of the rationality needed for the reestablishment of order and the creation or re-creation of institutions, may under certain conditions foster such rationality. As Eisenstadt points out, "such extension of rationality may indeed be very often the outcome of charismatic activities of personalities and groups who evolve new conceptions of order and goals and who are able to routinize these charismatic qualities and orientations through the crystallization of new social centers and institutional frameworks."[10] The key to the creation of order mediated through charisma would seem to be the nature of the charismatic leader himself, in this case Obregón, and the groups of followers who surround him. Weber's ideas, and how Obregón fits in with them, permeate the entire book.

As for Obregón's early role in the process of political consolidation and reunification, there are a number of prior questions that must be answered. First of all, it is important to know how Obregón got into a position to be influential at all. Second, it is important to know how he acquired the popular support and legitimacy he had in 1920 and why President Venustiano Carranza lost it. Third, the way in which he built an actual political organization to support his drive for legitimacy must be analyzed. Then it is possible to consider the various groups that constituted his political support, the ways in which these groups articulated and overlapped with one another, and the way in which they formed a base that would permit political stability and modernization within a new framework of ideals and goals, with a new and much wider group of participants in the political system.

Thus, the pages that follow describe and analyze the political rise of one man and the way in which this rise fits into the social and political developments of the period 1911–1920 to end the violence of the Revolution and to reestablish unified government in Mexico.

[10]S. N. Eisenstadt, Introduction to *On Charisma and Institution Building*, by Max Weber, p. liii.

CHAPTER 2

The Sonoran Background

The state of Sonora would have a major impact on the Mexican Revolution. It would be the site of many important revolutionary events, it would furnish the leaders who would consolidate power in 1920 and thus make possible the post-revolutionary institutionalization, and it would affect the way those leaders approached and solved problems. Indeed, it would determine in many cases what they defined as problems and how they viewed revolutionary goals and began their implementation.

Alvaro Obregón no less than the other Sonoran leaders who surrounded him would reflect his Sonoran background in his actions and policies, both during and after the Revolution. Further, it was the Sonoran social, economic, and political milieu that initially permitted his rise to prominence, although he had achieved power on the national level before he and his associates controlled his own state. It is therefore important to consider what Sonora was like at the outbreak of the Revolution and how Alvaro Obregón fit into the Sonoran context.

Sonora had developed almost in isolation from the rest of the Mexican nation, in great part for geographical reasons. As the state was cut off from the center of Mexico by mountains, the only easy access to Sonora was through its ports, notably the port of Guaymas. However, the border with the United States was relatively unobstructed, leading to a great deal of interchange across the frontier, especially with the state of Arizona. Indeed, during the last years of the nineteenth century, many U.S. citizens, frustrated by the closing of the frontier in their own country, turned their eyes southward for both land and investment opportunities. Some large fiefs were carved out in both mining and ranching, the holdings of William Greene being the most notable. Large U.S. land companies, such as the Compañía Constructora Richardson, took advantage of favorable concessions from the Porfirio Díaz government to buy land, irrigate it, and then sell it to settlers, frequently from the United States, at a large profit. In 1905, more than 200 U.S. companies of varying sizes were operating in the Hermosillo consular district alone.[1]

In the political realm, Sonora had never been securely controlled by Díaz. Although Díaz eventually resurrected the office of vice-president for a Sonoran, Ramón Corral, opposition groups at a number of levels had existed in the state ever since Díaz had overthrown Sebastian Lerdo de Tejada to take power himself. Even the Sonoran elite had never been united behind Díaz. Opposition formed behind wealthy landowner José María Maytorena and grew stronger after the institution of such Díaz policies as the wholesale removal of the Yaqui Indians, supposedly as a measure of "pacification," seriously affected the labor supply in this sparsely inhabited area.[2]

Sonora's isolated position made political opposition somewhat safer than in other areas, and the proximity of the U.S. border furnished a haven for those on whom Díaz did focus. It was perhaps Díaz' concern with Sonora's relatively independent position within the Mexican nation that caused him to choose a native Sonoran as his last running mate. Unfortunately for Díaz, this measure did not assure that Sonora would support him. During the presidential campaign of 1910, many prominent Sonorans supported opposition candidate Francisco I. Madero, and Adolfo de la Huerta, of a prominent Guaymense

---

[1]See David M. Pletcher, *Rails, Mines and Progress: Seven American Promoters in Mexico, 1867–1911*, pp. 219–259; Luis L. León, interview, July 18, 1974; Francisco Almada, *La Revolución en el estado de Sonora*, pp. 24–25; U.S. Department of State, Dispatches from U.S. Consuls in Hermosillo, 1905–1906, microfilm, University of Texas at Austin, nos. 10–11.

[2]See John Kenneth Turner, *Barbarous Mexico*, pp. 27–34, for a description of the exportation.

family, served as secretary of the Guaymas Club Antireeleccionista.[3]

In 1911, when armed rebellion by the Maderistas broke out, Governor Luis Torres called a meeting of the important men in the state to rally support for President Díaz. However, a number of members of this Junta de Notables, among them Benjamín Hill, Ignacio Pesqueira, and Flavio Bórquez, were supporters of Madero. Hill and Bórquez returned to Alamos to lead that district into the armed uprising against Díaz which was beginning all over the state.[4] After Madero's triumph, José María Maytorena, son of the nineteenth-century oppositionist leader, was elected governor, and de la Huerta, running on the same ticket, was elected state congressional delegate from Guaymas.[5] Unlike some other parts of Mexico, Sonora saw constitutional government established fairly easily under Madero.

Sonora was different from the rest of Mexico in other respects as well. In this overwhelmingly Catholic country, most Sonorans were not religious and many were rabidly anticlerical.[6] Again, its isolated position and the difficulties of travel within the state as well as its widely scattered population had made it difficult for the church to gain a firm grip. Moreover, the Indians of Sonora, as contrasted with the Indians of the central part of the country, were difficult to control and met encroachments on their land and liberty with violence. The only substantial efforts toward conversion were made by the Jesuits, particularly in the late seventeenth and eighteenth centuries, but the settlements they had begun largely languished after the Jesuits were thrown out of the Spanish realm in 1767. The appearance of a *Padre* in many areas of Sonora was a rare and surprising occasion, even in the early years of the twentieth century.

Economically, Sonora was different from the rest of the

[3]Antonio G. Rivera, *La Revolución en Sonora*, p. 176.

[4]Ibid., pp. 184, 200–201. Others who joined the movement actively at this time were Juan Cabral, Salvador Alvarado, Pedro Bracamontes, Arnulfo R. Gómez, and Francisco R. Manzo.

[5]Ibid., p. 238.

[6]Gilberto Valenzuela, interview, July 11, 1974, for the Programa de Historia Oral, Instituto Nacional de Antropología e Historia, Museo de Antropología, Mexico City (program cited hereafter as PHO), 4/42.

country. In agriculture, problems of water were paramount, but wherever water was available or irrigation provided the land was rich. Agriculture, however, was in many cases geared to the export market, as communication with the rest of Mexico was difficult and with the United States, easy. Cattle and hides were shipped in significant quantities to the United States, and the quality of the garbanzos grown in the area, famous throughout the Spanish-speaking world, gave them ready markets in Cuba, Spain, and even New York. During the last years of the Porfiriato, agricultural exports to the United States were increasing rapidly.[7] Moreover, the products of Sonora's silver and copper mines were almost entirely exported, and most of the major mines were owned by foreigners. A frequent pattern was the opening of a mine by a group of local Sonoran capitalists with the idea of selling it at a considerable profit to foreign interests when it came into production. Even those mines operated by Mexicans obtained much of their working capital from the United States.[8]

The orientation of Sonora to the United States rather than the rest of Mexico was enhanced by easy rail connections to the north and the lack of a complete line to Mexico City. In fact, at the time of the outbreak of the Mexican Revolution, the concession to provide the last link in the chain of railroads from Sonora to the capital had been given to the company that had done most of the development of the Sonoran railroad system. However, those involved preferred to finish certain feeder lines within Sonora itself before starting the second project, although these lines were frequently harassed by marauding Yaqui Indians.[9]

[7]For example, the value of garbanzos exported to the United States from Guaymas was $54,408 (U.S.) in 1908 and increased to $331,613 in 1909. The value of fresh tomatoes exported from the same port in 1908 was $15,537 and in 1909 was $47,559. See U.S. Department of Commerce and Labor, Bureau of Manufactures, *Commercial Relations of the United States with Foreign Countries 1909*, p. 541.

[8]Ibid., p. 539. See also the report of the director of the Compañía Unión Minera de las Prietas to the Asamblea General, reported in *El Comercio* (Guaymas), January 19, 1898.

[9]Contract between Joaquín D. Casasús as representative of the Compañía de Ferrocarriles del Sud-Pacífico and Secretaría de Comunicaciones y Trans-

The social configuration of Sonora differed considerably from that of the rest of the country, at least partly as a result of the small size of the population. The state contained both large and small landholdings, but many kinship ties connected those of the landowners who were white, respectable, and otherwise considered *gente bien*, literally, "good people." The range of these relationships extended to northern Sinaloa as well, and helps explain a certain political and economic mutuality of interest in the two states. During the Revolution against Huerta, Sonora sent men, weapons, and ammunition to help in the Sinaloan campaign, paying the costs of this help from state rather than national resources. Throughout the Revolution the two states were usually involved in a joint effort, and many of Obregón's strongest supporters were Sinaloans.[10]

Furthermore, landowning, though still important within Sonora, was becoming only one source of social, economic, and political status. A rising group of entrepreneurs, coming from the lower, and sometimes from the upper, strata of "good people," was providing a new model of success. Typically, these men were involved in many activities in the late nineteenth and early twentieth centuries, acting as commission agents in export-import transactions; operating as minor capitalists in light industry, particularly distilleries and other food-processing units; providing banking services such as letters of credit for import-export operations; selling maritime and cargo insurance; providing local outlets for powder, dynamite, and other mining supplies; and in general taking advantage of every business opportunity that came their way.[11]

---

portes, November 3, 1910, Archivo de la Secretaría de Comunicaciones y Transportes, no. 6/132–1. Also see Fred Wilbur Powell, *The Railroads of Mexico*, pp. 161–162.

[10]Hector Aguilar Camín, *La frontera nomada: Sonora y la Revolución Mexicana*, pp. 19–69, offers an excellent discussion of southern Sonora. See also Bernardo Gastélum, interviews, July 17 and 25, 1974, PHO/4/43. See chapter 3 for additional details about the cooperation between the two states and Sinaloans' support of Obregón.

[11]The newspapers of the period are full of descriptions of these activities. See, for example, *El Comercio* (Guaymas), March 23, 1898.

Moreover, the growing commercial activity had led to a very active Masonic movement, which by the 1890's was adding to the anticlerical atmosphere of the state sufficiently to call down the wrath of the Bishop of Sonora in a pastoral letter. One of the Guaymas newspapers, significantly named *El Comercio*, published the Masonic Code on the front page, inviting Sonoran society to judge for itself whether the tendencies of the said institution deserved to be treated in such a harsh manner by this prelate.[12]

Moreover, high wages in the mines were contributing to Sonoran prosperity generally and even permitting some talented and lucky individuals to rise from the lower to the middle class. The availability of high-paying mine jobs offset the low wages of agricultural workers, and a fairly common pattern was for a man to leave his family at home, migrate temporarily to a mining area, and return with considerable savings several months later.[13]

The same pattern applied to occasional trips across the border to the United States for a similar purpose: the accumulation of a certain amount of savings. While agricultural wages were frequently fifty centavos a day or less, even the least skilled jobs in the mines paid three pesos a day, and salaries ranged up to eight pesos for more skilled or more arduous jobs. These alternatives to agricultural employment gave the Sonoran workers an independence that was lacking in other parts of Mexico, where many workers were tied through a system of debt-peonage to large haciendas. Obviously, some workers were similarly tied in Sonora, but nevertheless the pattern was different from that in the rest of Mexico. Moreover, the proportion of small holdings in northern Mexico had been increasing, contributing to the slow growth of a rural middle class.[14]

[12]*El Comercio* (Guaymas), December 10, 1897.

[13]Valenzuela, interview, July 11, 1974, PHO/4/42.

[14]Esteban Baca Calderón, *Juicio sobre la guerra del Yaqui y génesis de la huelga de Cananea*, p. 18; Eric R. Wolf, *Peasant Wars of the Twentieth Century*, p. 19; François Chevalier, "Survivances seigneuriales et presages de la revolution agraire dans le Nord du Mexique," *Revue Historique* 222 (1959): 2, 5, 16–17; idem, *Land and Society in Colonial Mexico*, p. 150.

Although the figures for the entire state are considerably skewed by the presence of four large concessions of "public" land, amounting to over two million hectares, the figures for land distribution during the late Porfiriato are instructive. In the state as a whole, there were only 77 properties of over 1,000 hectares, and this in a state where average rainfall is less than ten inches annually and large holdings for the purposes of cattle-raising would be expected. Three hundred and ten properties were classified as *haciendas*, most under 1,000 hectares; 1,286 were shown as *ranchos*, most of them quite small. There were 279 *labores* (small, incompletely organized holdings) and 398 *congregaciones*, mostly of Mayo, Yaqui, Pima, and Opata Indians in the districts of Alamos, Guaymas, Arizpe, and Magdalena, further skewing the statistics, as most of their land was held in common. The large holdings were mostly desert; the small farms were along the rivers where irrigation was possible. The rural population amounted to 218,563, which was 82.7 percent of the state total, and this population was scattered. Of 43,912 heads of families in 1910, 1,875 owned their own land, with perhaps 10,000 more holding communal lands. More than 30,000 heads of families were thus left to support themselves as mining, agricultural, and industrial laborers. Still, the labor pool was relatively small in proportion to demand.[15]

The existence of the mines had other important consequences as well. A significant labor movement was taking root in the mining areas during the early years of the twentieth century, and the proximity of the U.S. border permitted the penetration of ideas from outside the country as well as access to the newspapers published by Mexican labor leaders, such as Ricardo and Enrique Flores Magón, in exile in the United States. Many teachers, such as Epifanio Vieyra of the Colegio de Sonora in Hermosillo, were followers of the Flores Magón brothers. It is interesting to note that it was Ramón Corral, Díaz' vice-president, who had fostered the development of the Colegio de Sonora. Vieyra was later forced to flee Hermosillo and take

---

[15]George M. McBride, *The Land Systems of Mexico*, p. 149.

refuge at one of the mines when his radical ideas came to the attention of state authorities.[16]

Moreover, the presence of workers from the United States at the mining sites gave Mexican workers further incentive to form unions. The difference in pay scale between the two nationalities was immediately noticeable and the cause of great friction between U.S. employers and Mexican employees. Despite earning relatively high wages in relation to the rest of Mexico, the Sonoran miners wanted to be recompensed at the same level as their North American counterparts. In June, 1906, at the mining town of Cananea, site of the operations of the Cananea Copper Company, workers attempted to organize to bargain collectively with the owners of the company. After the workers had peacefully presented their demands, the owners countered by emphasizing to the workers that they were getting higher wages and more company services than workers in the rest of the country; they even had recreation centers and other facilities unlikely to be duplicated elsewhere in Mexico. The workers were unimpressed. They wanted status and salary equal to that of the U.S. workers and would not settle for less. Therefore, the strike began and was put down in a bloody fashion by the authorities. The governor of Sonora even wired Washington for help in maintaining order. To help put down the strike, a group of Arizona citizens supposedly acting as individuals but commanded by Colonel Thomas Rynning crossed the border at Naco.[17]

Needless to say, the governor's call for help enraged many, both in Sonora and outside of it, and provided a nationalistic rallying point for a future move against the Díaz government. Moreover, the Cananea strike furnished an early opportunity for leadership to Sonorans who would later be crucial to the revolutionary movement: Manuel M. Diéguez and Esteban B. Calderón, both members of the Unión Liberal Humanidad,

[16]Valenzuela, interview, July 11, 1974, PHO/4/42; Rivera, *La Revolución*, pp. 122–123, 164.

[17]Manuel González Ramírez, *La revolución social de México*, 1:65; Rivera, *La Revolución*, pp. 142–160.

both commissioners for the strikers in presenting demands to management, and both later military commanders under Obregón.[18]

The organization of labor was also furthered by contact between migratory workers who worked for a time in the United States and members of the Industrial Workers of the World, the so-called Wobblies. The IWW encouraged material improvements attractive to the Sonorans, such as land reform and social organization based on the voluntary association of labor unions, village communes, and other small groups.[19] At the same time they were hostile toward institutionalized authority, be it state or church, and again their ideas struck a chord with the migrants. Land reform and anticlericalism were to become especially important in the actions of future Sonoran leaders, especially Obregón and Plutarco Elías Calles.

A further element in the social equation was substantial groups of Indians, particularly Yaqui and Mayo, who had traditionally had their lands in the richest agricultural areas, the valleys of the Río Mayo and the Río Yaqui. The constant attempts, frequently in the guise of irrigation projects, to deprive these Indians of their land had led to warfare throughout the nineteenth century. It was by no means over at the beginning of the Revolution against Díaz. In 1880 a private concession had been granted by the secretary of development to one Charles Conant to irrigate and colonize the area along the Fuerte, Mayo, and Yaqui rivers. This concession was reduced to the Río Yaqui, and the Sonora and Sinaloa Irrigation Company was formed. It became the property of the Compañía Constructora Richardson at the beginning of the twentieth century.[20]

The Compañía Richardson thus gained an enormous area of Sonoran territory and furnished the basis for continued problems with the Yaquis. In 1911 Madero had come to an agreement to restore to the tribe all the traditional Yaqui lands north

---

[18]Rivera, *La Revolución,* pp. 142–160.

[19]Paul Friedrich, "Revolutionary Politics and Communal Ritual," in *Political Anthropology,* ed. Marc J. Swartz et al., p. 206.

[20]Almada, *La Revolución en el estado de Sonora,* pp. 24–25.

and northwest of the river, and Obregón ratified this agreement after he became president in 1921, although litigation over land and water rights is still going on. Moreover, the Compañía Richardson was only the largest among many land companies, whether Mexican or North American owned, flourishing in the area during the Díaz period and threatening the Indian lands.[21]

Out of this social and economic milieu, a number of men emerged who were to be important leaders in the Revolution: labor leaders Manuel M. Diéguez, Esteban Baca Calderón, and Juan José Ríos; the future leader of the Partido Liberal Constitucionalista, Benjamín Hill; the man who was to become the radical governor of Yucatán, Salvador Alvarado; and future presidents Obregón, Adolfo de la Huerta, and Plutarco Elías Calles. Obregón would emerge as the most powerful of these leaders, although he did not have the social position of de la Huerta and Hill, the carefully fostered support of labor that Diéguez, Calderón, and Hill enjoyed, or the extensive family connections that Calles, though himself illegitimate, was able to call on. Surprisingly, however, Obregón was able to secure the help of men from many social groups: upper-class land-owning families such as the Pesqueiras came to support him, the rising middle class represented by Calles and others felt him to be more trustworthy than other potential leaders such as Pancho Villa, those who desired land were promised it in return for their military and political support, labor groups gave him their backing, and his own principal military support in the early part of the armed movement against the usurper, Huerta, came from Mayo and Yaqui Indians.

Obregón had been born on February 17, 1880, the son of Fernando Obregón and Cenobia Salido de Obregón, on a farm in the district of Alamos, Sonora. He was the youngest of eighteen children, and through his mother's family, the mar-

[21]Randall George Hansis, "Alvaro Obregón, the Mexican Revolution, and the Politics of Consolidation, 1920–1924," p. 295, Expediente 276.1/3029, and Expediente 4670, both in Archivo del Departamento de Asuntos Agrarios y Crédito, Mexico City (archive cited hereafter as DAAC). See a discussion of land company activity in U.S. Department of Commerce and Labor, *Commercial Relations 1909*, p. 541.

riages of his brothers and sisters, and other kinship ties he was related to members of the better class of Sonoran society, although he could certainly not be described as upper class in any economic sense. His own family was relatively low on the economic scale, although his father did own his own land. One report indicates that Fernando Obregón had been a man of some means, with properties in Mexico City, Cuernavaca, and Siquisiva, during the middle part of the nineteenth century, but that because his partner in business had been a supporter of the emperor Maximilian, all their joint properties were confiscated in the 1860's with the reestablishment of the Juárez government. In any case, when Obregón was small his father's holdings in Siquisiva, near the Río Mayo, were ruined by a disastrous flood and then by a Yaqui attack, in which all his cattle were stolen and his house burned to the ground. Shortly thereafter his father died, and Obregón was raised in Huatabampo, also near the Río Mayo and the port of Guaymas, by his mother and especially three of his older sisters.[22]

His home was near a pueblo of the Mayo tribe, and, as his childhood companions were mostly Mayo, he spoke Mayo as well as he spoke Spanish. His sisters served as schoolteachers for the Mayo children, and he developed a strong bond with the group. Obregón was not a well-behaved child, and a possibly apocryphal story recounts that one day he was flailing in the air with a sword, which he had made from a branch. One of the Mayo children, startled, asked Obregón what he needed it for. "To defend us," he answered. Later the Mayos were to form a major portion of his troops against Pascual Orozco, and in gratitude Obregón would restore some of their native lands in Huatabampo as a communal holding during his presidency and would name one of his sons Mayo.[23]

Obregón's education came principally from his sisters, who had themselves been more formally educated during better

[22]Gastélum, interview, July 17 and 25, 1974, PHO/4/43; E. J. Dillon, *President Obregón—A World Reformer*, pp. 32–34; Richard H. Dillon, "Del rancho a la presidencia," *Historia Mexicana* 6 (October–December, 1956): 256–259; Juan de Dios Bojórquez, *Obregón: Apuntes biográficos*, p. 12; Feliciano Gil, *Biografía y vida militar del General Alvaro Obregón*, p. 3.

[23]Luis L. León, interview, July 30, 1974.

times. He also studied for a while at the official school in Huata-bampo, where his brother José was in charge. For the most part, however, Obregón was self-taught. In the process he developed a prodigious memory, which was to stand him in good stead on the battlefield. He also developed a keen interest in other people, their hopes, motives, and behavior patterns, which he used to help him gather friends and defeat enemies.

Because of the difficult economic circumstances in which the Obregón family found itself after the death of the head of the family, Obregón went to work as a journeyman in a machine shop, working at least part-time under a North American manager.[24] Although he was only ten or eleven at the time, he showed considerable talent as a mechanic. It was about this time that he began to study in the regular school at Huata-bampo, which was directed by his brother José J. Obregón, described by one who knew him as a "rank agnostic." This schoolmaster taught the children to observe, compare, and criticize, encouraging in them a propensity for independent judgment and a distrust of authority. Among Alvaro's friends in school was Jesús Abitia, who was to travel with Obregón through many of his campaigns and who was to provide many extraordinary cinematographic records of the Revolution.[25]

Obregón not only showed an early facility for mechanical work but also began to function as an entrepreneur on the Sonoran model, engaging in many scattered enterprises. At the age of thirteen he acquired a small plot of land on which he grew tobacco, harvesting it himself, drying it, and making it into cigarettes. As the product was not of a particularly high quality, there was little demand for it, so he sent his friends around to the various small shops asking for his Americas-brand cigarettes. The shopkeepers, interested, did purchase some of his product, although eventually the manipulation failed and the enterprise itself did not last long. Again in Sonoran fashion, Obregón registered his company legally and employed his brother to work for him, paying him in the product of the

company. Other early money-making enterprises he under-
took were the formation of an orchestra with members of his
family, who reportedly constructed the instruments themselves,
and other odd jobs around the village such as painting, car-
pentry, barbering, blacksmithing, and photography. In short,
he tried a little bit of everything and was particularly interested
in things mechanical and new.[26]

Shortly thereafter, he left Huatabampo to work at the flour
mill at the Hacienda de Tres Hermanos in Camoa near Navojoa,
Sonora, where he had charge of keeping the machinery in
working order. In 1898 he went to Sinaloa, where he worked in
the sugar mill of Navolato, again as a mechanic. The owners
of the mill were Jesús and Jorge Almada, and Laura Salido de
Almada, Jesús' wife, was a relative of Obregón's mother. This
relationship served to get Obregón the job but not much prestige within the mill itself. However, although he was working
as a mechanic, he was accepted within polite society in the
region, mostly at the insistence of his employer's wife. Bernardo
Gastélum, who became a close friend and then undersecretary
of education during Obregón's presidency, remembered seeing
him for the first time inside one of the sugar vats that was being
repaired.[27]

During the few years he was there he was given more and
more important jobs, although he never rose to the level of foreman, and his status with the Almada family was that of a poor
relation. He was remembered within the mill as an entertaining
companion and as an excellent poker player. In fact, the owner
of one of the local gambling houses is reported to have given
him money not to play. His poker playing was undoubtedly
helped by his shrewd judgment about human character and his
amazing memory. Many observers have recounted his favorite
trick of looking through a shuffled card deck and then repeating
the order of the cards from memory.[28] The same capacity was

[26]Ibid. See also Bojórquez, *Obregón*, p. 12.

[27]Gastélum, interviews, July 17 and 25, 1974, PHO/4/43; Antonio G.
Rivera, "Apuntes sobre la vida de Alvaro Obregón," p. 2; E. J. Dillon, *President Obregón*, p. 44.

[28]Ignacio Ramos Praslow, interview, November 16, 1972; Fernando
Torreblanca, interview, November 15, 1972.

of use to him in his military campaigns, as after looking at a
potential battlefield he had an almost photographic remem-
brance of its topography, including rocks, trees, gulleys, and
any other potentially useful features.

His experience as a mechanic at the Navolato mill made
it possible for him both to identify with the frustrations of
industrial workers and to recognize them as a possible future
political force. A story he was fond of recounting to friends
described his disgust at the workers' having to eat their meals
without having an opportunity to wash their hands. As tortillas
rather than utensils were used, part of each meal would get
covered with grease and would have to be discarded. Both the
waste and the indignity offended him. One lunchtime he remarked to a companion named Camacho that when he was
president things would be different and they would be avenged.
Later, when he did become president, he invited Camacho to
Mexico City, where he spent several months as a presidential
guest.[29] In any case, Obregón himself had strong feelings, based
on experience, for the rights of labor, along with an ambivalence
about his own position and a desire to be accepted in the upper
echelons of society. His own ambiguous position between two
segments of society contributed to his concern with these problems and to his commitment to social change. It also gave him
a sense of what a powerful political tool the workers' sense of
rage could be.

Not satisfied with his position at Navolato, Obregón held
various jobs during the years before 1904, working as a traveling shoe salesman out of Culiacán and even teaching school for
awhile in Moroncarit, Sonora. Finally he was able to rent a
piece of land from the Valderrain family on the hacienda El
Naranjo, employing laborers to help him work it, and in 1906
he was able to buy about 180 hectares of land in Huatabampo,
reportedly from the federal government. He named this small
holding La Quinta Chilla, which in local Sonoran parlance
means Dead-Broke Farm. He began to grow garbanzos, a cash

[29]Torreblanca, interview, November 15, 1972; Rubén Romero, "Alvaro
Obregón," in *Obregón: Aspectos de su vida*, p. 17.

crop principally for the export market, and in 1909 he invented a garbanzo seeder, which was eventually produced and sold by the Fundición de Sinaloa in Mazatlán and adopted for use by most producers along the Río Mayo.[30]

By the time of the Madero revolution, Obregón had become a fairly prosperous member of the community and was continuing to rise through a combination of efforts: his agricultural activities, his mechanical inventions, and his contracting efforts in the extension of railroad lines and irrigation works near his area in Sonora. However, his wife had died in 1907, leaving him with two small children. He therefore, by his own admission, put the personal interests of his family before the interests of the Revolution and stayed home.[31] He was to suffer considerable criticism for this decision later.

Within the context of early twentieth-century Huatabampo, it is not difficult to see how he was able to be elected *presidente municipal* after Madero became president. Although he was far from being one of the wealthier citizens of the town, he had lived there off and on since he was a child, and he had been able, despite adverse circumstances, to amass enough capital to buy a small farm and to establish himself economically in other ways. Moreover, his family had occupied a position of respect if not wealth within the society there, with his brother and sisters serving as schoolteachers and his brother being for a time municipal president himself. Since his early manhood he had been acquainted with Adolfo de la Huerta, of the neighboring port of Guaymas, who was installed as the Guaymense delegate to the state congress under Madero. In 1910, he had risked the ire of the local leader, José T. Otero, by refusing to sign a statement supporting Díaz. In 1911, Obregón had run for office, that of alternate deputy from his district to the state congress, but he had been defeated by Rodolfo Cárdenas by a

[30]Bojórquez, *Obregón*, pp. 3–13.
[31]*El Monitor Republicano* (Mexico City), March 29, 1920; Alvaro Obregón, *Ocho mil kilómetros en campaña*, p. 4.

vote of 2,009 to 1,481.[32] Nevertheless, he entered the race for municipal president of Huatabampo shortly thereafter.

Obregón's opponent in this race was Pedro Zurbarán, also a Maderista, who had attended the Junta de Notables in Hermosillo in January of 1911 and who had distinguished himself by insisting on giving the people the right to vote for which they had been fighting. During the election, almost the total population of the town of Huatabampo voted for Zurbarán, whose earlier political stands made him a very attractive candidate. Zurbarán also had the support of the old *cacique* ("political boss"), José T. Otero. Obregón, however, received the larger total number of votes with a combination of Mayo votes delivered by their leader, Chito Cruz, and votes from peons on several haciendas.[33] The election commission awarded the victory to Zurbarán, on the grounds that the Mayos were illiterate and therefore not entitled to vote. Obregón took the controversy to the congress of the state, and in the election commission, composed of three deputies, including Adolfo de la Huerta, a number of charges and counter-charges were sorted out. Among these were the claim that José J. Obregón, who had been acting as interim municipal president during the election, had used the town police to campaign for his brother, that peons from other municipalities had been brought by the *hacendados* to vote illegally for Obregón, and that children below the age of sixteen had voted.[34] However, de la Huerta energetically supported Obregón's claim, and the commission decided in his favor.

Once in office, he moved quickly to institute a number of programs, particularly in the areas of public education and public works. By November, 1911, he had seven rural schools

[32]Valenzuela, interview, July 11, 1974, PHO/4/42; Gastélum, interviews, July 17 and 25, 1974, PHO/4/43; Archivo Histórico del Estado de Sonora, Hermosillo (cited hereafter as AHES), Congreso del Estado de Sonora, Tomo 190, Carpeta 2.

[33]Rivera, *La Revolución*, p. 247.

[34]AHES, Congreso del Estado de Sonora, Tomo 190, Carpeta 2, Acuerdo #25.

operating in the *municipio* and had opened two additional schools in Huatabampo, despite having to nag the state government to send more teachers and books.[35] His municipal budget, published on November 28, 1911, reveals that the major changes he made from the plans his brother had proposed were a rise in the tax on bars, the elimination of the tax on irrigation canals, and an addition to the amount of money allocated for rural schools. He was particularly interested, as well, in the construction of a municipal waterworks. Of the 20,040 pesos in his budget, exactly half was reserved for public education and material improvements—4,020 pesos for the former, 6,000 pesos for the latter.[36] His interest in education and in public works, particularly in the area of water supplies and irrigation, would continue into his presidency.

He seems to have established his authority in Huatabampo very quickly, for in 1912, when the Maderista revolution was threatened by a violent uprising led by Pascual Orozco, Obregón was able to organize and lead an irregular battalion to defend the state of Sonora from the invading Orozquistas. His successes in this endeavor were to bring him to the attention of the highest authorities in his state and to give him statewide renown that would lead in time to his being named head of the revolutionary forces of Sonora.

[35]The books Obregón requested from the state government seem to reveal that many of the individuals enrolled had not had an opportunity to study before, although they also reflect, no doubt, a large primary-school dropout rate. One hundred and fifty books were ordered for first grade, 100 for second grade, and 40 for third grade. The state also furnished pencils, crayons, and notebooks (Obregón to Secretario del Estado, November 18, December 27 and 29, 1911, January 1, 1912, in the Archivo General del Estado de Sonora, Hermosillo [cited hereafter as AGES], Tomo 2688).

[36]Alvaro Obregón, "Plan de propios y arbitrios; presupuesto de egresos; y ordenanzas municipales, formado por el ayuntamiento de Huatabampo," pp. 13–18; Adolfo de la Huerta, *Memorias de Don Adolfo de la Huerta*, p. 29.

CHAPTER 3

Obregón versus Orozco:

Beginnings of Acclaim

The government of President Francisco I. Madero was in difficulties from its inception, and problems with erstwhile Maderista Pascual Orozco in Sonora gave Obregón his first opportunity to achieve military renown and a place of his own within the Revolution. Obregón's participation in the fight against Orozco's rebellion provided him with recognition for his skill as a military leader, admiration for his audacity, and a wider circle of friends and potential military and political supporters, won over by his charm and his ability. During the fight against Orozco, he became known throughout Sonora and on the U.S. side of the border as well, and he came vividly to the attention of Sonora's Maderista governor, José María Maytorena.

It is significant to recognize that Obregón began his military career in support of Madero, not in opposition to a constituted government. This circumstance differentiates him vividly from other revolutionary leaders, such as Pancho Villa, Emiliano Zapata, or even Venustiano Carranza, and provides a clue to his motivation. He was seeking a place within a movement that had already started and achieved a certain tenuous success, a movement that was already socially acceptable within the Sonoran context. Still, he felt that military participation was a validating experience within the context of the Revolution, and he had felt considerable shame in his failure to take part in the earlier phase of the struggle against Díaz. In future years, he would be critical of, when not actively hostile to, civilians who had failed to put their lives on the line at the time of crisis and who, after the danger had passed, wanted to choose the goals and form the new institutions that would guide the Mexican nation.

He expressed his feelings about his failure to join the Maderista phase of the Revolution in his autobiography:

The revolution broke out. . . .

Then the Maderista or Anti-reelectionist Party divided into two groups: one composed of men submissive to the call of Duty, who abandoned their homes and broke the ties of family and interest to take up rifles, pistols, or the first arm that they encountered; the other, of men heedful of the mandates of fear, who did not find arms, who had children who might be orphaned if they died in the struggle, who had a thousand more ties that Duty cannot suppress when the specter of fear has taken possession of men.

I am ashamed to say that I belonged to the second of these groups. The war continued. . . .

We inactive Maderistas contented ourselves by making cowardly and cunning rationalizations. We continued to be the object of oppressions, soothing ourselves by saying, "Soon they will pay for this."[1]

He also spoke of being profoundly moved when the Sonoran Maderista revolutionaries arrived in Huatabampo from Navojoa in 1911: "I began to feel myself possessed by an intense impression, which little by little degenerated into shame. . . . I felt that each one of these men was superior to me."[2]

His opportunity to redeem himself was almost immediate. Madero's installation as president in Mexico City on November 6, 1911, had by no means pacified the country, especially the north. Sonora particularly had been faced by threats from the supporters of the Flores Magón brothers, who had been engaged in their own battle against the Díaz regime and who set up a base of operations in Baja California to oppose the new Madero government. However, the most serious threat came from Chihuahua, where Madero had enjoyed his strongest support before coming to power. Madero's leadership had been challenged by the younger Pascual Orozco during the campaign against Díaz,

[1]Alvaro Obregón, *Ocho mil kilómetros en campaña*, pp. 4–5.
[2]Ibid., p. 6.

and Orozco had even threatened Madero's life after the revolutionary forces had taken Ciudad Juárez. In March, 1912, Orozco declared against the Madero government, and the federal forces in the state were unable to contain his movement.[3] General Victoriano Huerta, who had served under Díaz, was appointed to lead the forces of the Madero government against the rebellion. Nevertheless, Orozco quickly threatened the neighboring state of Sonora.[4]

The Orozco threat was not entirely unwelcome in Sonora, however, as the Maderista governor, José María Maytorena, had burned himself politically in his own state by overspending state funds during a four-month visit to Mexico City. The irritated Sonoran legislators expected a report on his expenditures, which had not been forthcoming. Maytorena used the expedient of the outside threat from Orozco to rebuild his damaged prestige and take attention off his own unauthorized expenditures.[5]

Taking note of the rapidly spreading Orozco rebellion, Maytorena sent a circular to all municipal presidents in Sonora inviting them to organize forces to help put it down. Obregón was in Alamos when the circular came out and went immediately to Navojoa, where he spoke with Vice-Governor Gayou about raising a force from Huatabampo. By mid-April he had three hundred men ready and proceeded north to Hermosillo, where he was given arms, ammunition, equipment, and a title:

[3]Stanley R. Ross, *Francisco I. Madero: Apostle of Mexican Democracy*, p. 145. Rumors that Orozco would rebel had been circulating for several months, and by February, 1912, governors of other northern states had been warned to be prepared (González Garza to Maytorena, February 27, 1912, Patronato de la Historia de Sonora, microfilm, Museo de Antropología, Mexico City [cited hereafter as PHS], Roll 48).

[4]It is possible that Orozco and Huerta had actually come to some sort of anti-Madero agreement between themselves. Both were opposed to the Maderista governor of Chihuahua, Abraham González, and both had approached the wealthiest landowning families, the Terrazas and the Creels, in search of possible support. Madero himself had vacillated between González, his governor, and Huerta, the military leader in the state, when problems between them had come to his attention (Madero to González, July 20, 1912, and Madero to Huerta, July 20, 1912, both in Archivo de Francisco I. Madero, microfilm, Museo de Antropología, Mexico City, roll 12).

[5]Antonio G. Rivera, *La Revolución en Sonora*, pp. 252–254.

lieutenant colonel of the Fourth Irregular Battalion of Sonora.[6] Nevertheless, it took more than two months to get the battalion into battle in Chihuahua. Not until June 26 did the Sonoran troops join General Agustín Sanginés' column at the Hacienda Ojitos, guarding the Cañon del Púlpito, the major pass between Sonora and Chihuahua, against invasion by the Orozquistas.[7]

Before the battle, as Obregón was speaking to the men of the Fourth Battalion to get them ready for the fight, a projectile fired from one of the enemy cannon fell within a few feet of Obregón, who waited serenely for it to explode. Fortunately it was a dud, but Obregón's military career had come close to ending before it had even begun.[8] Such narrow escapes were to occur a number of times in the future and would help to build his reputation for calm in a crisis as well as the myth of his indestructibility. In the battle that followed, cavalry led by Obregón pursued retreating Orozquista artillerymen and captured three cannon, several carts, and various supplies. As he was about to return to his own lines with the captured materiel, an Orozquista column appeared to his rear. Stationing his men around the ranch El Cuervo, he sent out two men to talk to the Orozquistas, who believed that Obregón and his men were cohorts of their own. As the Orozquistas approached El Cuervo, "in complete disorder and without even taking out their arms," as Obregón described it, Obregón's men waited until they were almost upon them and then began to shoot. The Orozquistas fled, without attempting any further resistance, and Obregón returned to Ojitos with his spoils.[9] Sanginés was impressed with his initiative and military shrewdness.

A few days later, General Huerta, who within a few months would overthrow Madero and perhaps conspire in his murder, passed through the territory controlled by Sanginés' troops on his way to take charge of the fight against Orozco in

[6]Maytorena to Obregón, April 7, 13, and 14, 1912, and Obregón to Maytorena, April 1 and 13, 1913, PHS/49; Obregón, *Ocho mil kilómetros*, p. 9.

[7]Rivera, *La Revolución*, p. 258.

[8]Antonio G. Rivera, "Apuntes sobre la vida de Alvaro Obregón," p. 30.

[9]Obregón, *Ocho mil kilómetros*, pp. 18–19.

the name of Madero's government. At a stop at Estación Sabinal, Sanginés introduced him to Obregón, whom he described as one of his coming young officers. Huerta replied of the man who was later to defeat him in battle, "I expect this young leader will be a hope for his country."[10]

Obregón's first major action on his own occurred in September of 1912. The Orozquistas had by this time entered Sonora, were menacing Agua Prieta, and had taken possession of the mine El Tigre. Obregón, whose Fourth Irregular Battalion consisted of 150 men, all on foot, and one machine gun, had been sent to reinforce the town of Nacozari, site of a mine belonging to Phelps Dodge, which might become a target for the Orozquistas. On hearing that the Orozquistas, under José Inés Salazar, had set up a major encampment at Hacienda San Joaquín, 120 kilometers north near the town of Fronteras, he decided to move his troops to Fronteras and to attack from there. He was accompanied by Edward Larocque Tinker, the young Phelps Dodge lawyer, who had been assigned to find someone to protect the Nacozari mine. Tinker was impressed with Obregón, whom he described as bigger and stronger than the usual Mexican, as well as courageous and straightforward. The young lawyer reported back that he both liked Obregón and believed that he would defend the mine and the railroad line. There was even a rumor in Nacozari that Obregón was the grandson of the Irish foreman of the railroad company that had built the line to Hermosillo. Presumably this information, had it been fact, would have convinced the Americans that Obregón had a special fondness for railroads and their preservation, as well as making him somehow more trustworthy than the average Mexican.

Obregón's troops at this point were ragged at best; Tinker reported that the only thing they had in common were their Mausers. The troops traveled in open steel ore cars, and a machine gun in the charge of the half-German, half-Mexican Maximiliano Kloss was mounted on the roof of the caboose. As they traveled, Kloss regularly tested the gun, adding to the excitement.

[10]Ibid., pp. 20–21.

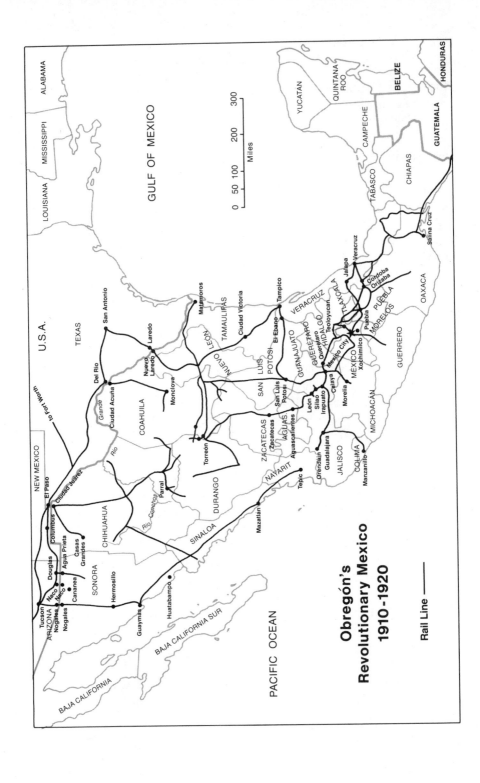

Obregón's
Revolutionary Mexico
1910-1920

Rail Line ——————

The train stopped at Fronteras for breakfast, and when one of the troops asked for beer, the owner of the cantina where they were eating refused, saying that the beer was only for the officers. The soldier, incensed, attempted to shoot the bartender, but someone struck the barrel of his gun, and the bullet hit a mirror behind the bar. Breakfast continued with no further incidents.

As there had been a report that the Orozquistas were coming across the mountains, Obregón had taken the precaution of sending out spies. One of these reported that he had seen five hundred men coming across the tracks ahead, so Obregón ordered immediate preparations for the advance. The train caboose, complete with machine gun, was then switched front, the ore cars with the troops put in the middle, and the engine was put behind to push the train. Obregón made his usual stirring appeal to the troops, saying that they were going into a dangerous battle, that all who wanted could return to Nacozari, but that he would continue even if he had to go on alone. Tinker remarked that he was a "real leader." Obregón then asked all those who would follow him to take a step forward. As Tinker put it, "Every Indian did; those Mayos love to fight." As the train pulled out again, the men began to shoot in the air as though at a Fourth of July celebration. Tinker was now riding on top of the caboose with Kloss and was afraid that they might be shot off by mistake.

As the train got out of town into the open countryside, Tinker saw about one hundred horsemen coming toward them. The troops lay down in the train so that it would appear to be engaged in the ordinary activity of carrying ore. Then, pulling opposite the Orozquista cavalry, they jumped up, piled out of the ore cars, and rolled under the barbed wire protecting the train, shooting all the time. They pursued the cavalry, who immediately began retreating, and Tinker followed for a while taking pictures. Then, as he commented, he let them go on since it was not his war anyway. Obregón's men were all on foot, including the officers, but Obregón himself remarked later that this was an advantage during the battle, as the countryside was full of bogs and wire fences, which caused trouble to the men on horseback.

Later Tinker heard the troops returning mounted. Obregón had pursued the Orozquista cavalry right back into their own camp, where four or five hundred more enemy cavalry were having lunch while their horses grazed unsaddled after the tough mountain crossing. The advance guard had plowed right through the others and had thrown all into confusion. Obregón's men were pleased with the victory; most of those who had gone on foot returned mounted. Obregón reported that they had captured more than 200 horses, a machine gun, and 150 rifles.

Tinker helped treat the wounded and watch the prisoners when they returned to the train, which took them back to Fronteras. Kloss, the machine gunner, had been shot through the knee, and Tinker remembered getting him a bottle of beer and discussing the battle. The next day he and Obregón went back to the battlefield, where Tinker took pictures of Obregón standing in front of his orderly, who was playing the "Diana," the signal of victory.[11]

The battle of San Joaquín illustrates many of the characteristics of Obregón's approach to military action. First of all, Obregón knew what his own resources were, and he had good information on the Orozquistas before starting out. During the actual confrontation, Obregón was already using the techniques of surprise, bluff, and superior knowledge of the enemy to his own advantage. He was audacious when it was to his advantage to be so. Moreover, he was able to use his victories as a lever to obtain help from the North Americans, who were eager to protect their mines.

The early battles against the Orozquistas were also important in pointing out to Obregón the need for medical support for his troops. Tinker, who had helped with the wounded, reported that at the time of the battle of San Joaquín there was

[11]Edward Larocque Tinker, interview, 6–14, Columbia Oral History Collection, Columbia University, New York (collection cited hereafter as COHC). Other details of the battle are in Obregón, *Ocho mil kilómetros*, pp. 21–25.

no regular medical staff at all, and it seems likely that many perished or their wounds were so badly treated that they could not return to action. Obregón began to organize such support, and by the time of the battles against Villa in 1915 he had a well-organized medical corps.

Tinker's approval of Obregón evidently resulted in some support for his military effort from the companies Tinker was representing, as, later, officials of the El Paso and Southwestern Railroad and the Nacozari mine gave the young lieutenant colonel a testimonial dinner at the Gadsden Hotel in Douglas. The possibility that the support was financial is reinforced by the fact that Obregón in the latter part of 1912 had $2,000 (U.S.) in the First National Bank of Douglas, Arizona, a convenient place to have it when he was in the market for guns and ammunition. Another report of the good opinion held of Obregón by American firms came from the Cerro de Plata Mining Camp. The informant indicated that the camp had had problems with "bandits," by whom he meant the men of Orozquista leader Emilio Campa, but that there were a few good federal officers in the area helping to control the depredations, notably one Colonel Obregón operating below Douglas.[12]

The danger from Orozco having lessened considerably, Obregón briefly returned to Huatabampo, but by November of 1912 the continuing disorders in the north caused the Sonoran governor, Maytorena, to order him to reorganize his Mayo forces and return to Agua Prieta, just across the border from Douglas.[13] He was to remain more or less in a state of military readiness, except for occasional trips home, until the assassination of Madero and the outbreak of the second phase of the Revolution, the fight against the usurper, Huerta.

One friend later recalled that he had first met Obregón in Hermosillo at about this time, striding rapidly through town wearing a "Texas" or ten-gallon hat with two stars on the

[12]Tinker, interview, 6–14, COHC; Report, August 4, 1912, Archivo de la Secretaría de Relaciones Exteriores, Mexico City, 119, L-E-728, Leg. 63-R (archive cited hereafter as ASRE); Report, September, 1912, from Cerro de Plata Mining Camp, PHS/51.
[13]Gil to Maytorena, November 15, 1912, PHS/52.

front designating his rank. Later the friend heard about his triumphs against Oroczo.[14] By this time, Obregón was well known by name, at least within his native state, and a number of informants mention that it was at this time that he first came to their attention.[15] He was lauded to the congress of the State of Sonora by no less than the governor himself, and despite Obregón's later difficulties with Maytorena it was Maytorena who was at this time most impressed with his capabilities and willing to give him more responsibility. It was, of course, to Maytorena's advantage to focus attention on Sonoran military successes and not on his as yet unexplained expenditures in the capital.[16]

Thus, by the end of 1912, Obregón was known for his military prowess and his reliability within Sonora and had established himself as a protégé of Governor Maytorena. Further, he was becoming known within the federal army at large, as his commanding officer and others who had dealt with him remained impressed, and his fame was spreading across the border into the United States. He was gaining confidence, acquiring the charismatic appeal of a military hero, and establishing the rudiments of a power base. In addition, he was already acceptable as a leader to many segments of Sonoran society— the upper class, by virtue of his family connections, indigenous groups such as the Mayos, with whom he had grown up and whose language he spoke, and laboring and middle-class groups, with whom he was identified by economic status and experience.

Yet he was a strange kind of revolutionary, entering the Revolution only after it had been established. He had already developed a pattern of political and military activity within a framework of an existing government, even while espousing principles that he and those around him regarded as revolutionary. At no time would he initiate a movement against an authority generally recognized as legitimate, and when forced

[14]Juan de Dios Bojórquez, *Obregón: Apuntes biográficos*, p. 9.
[15]For example, see ibid., pp. 8–9; Gilberto Valenzuela, interview, July 11, 1974, PHO/4/42.
[16]Informe presentado por el Gobernador José María Maytorena ante la XXIII Legislatura del Estado de Sonora, September 23, 1912, PHS/50.

to choose between opposing authorities he would opt for the one that most clearly represented links with the earlier Madero movement. Not until 1920 would he be forced into open opposition to a constituted government, and even then others would begin the military effort. Indeed, Obregón seems to have seen himself much more as a civilian who took arms to protect revolutionary gains than as a radical dedicated to a violent military struggle against authority.

CHAPTER 4

Development of the
Revolutionary Triangle

The disintegration of Francisco Madero's revolutionary government during 1912 and 1913 profoundly affected the political situation in the state of Sonora and in northern Mexico in general. With the collapse of the Madero regime in February, 1913, the stage was set for the emergence of three leaders from the north: Obregón, Venustiano Carranza, and Francisco Villa. Carranza, Maderista governor in Coahuila, maintained an aura of legitimacy and assumed the title of first chief of the Revolution, thus permitting revolutionary forces to rally around him. Obregón in Sonora and Villa in Chihuahua, however, became the major pillars of the military effort. While considerations of power might have led to problems among the three in any event, differences in personalities, backgrounds, and goals made these problems inevitable and devastating. The combined struggle against presidential usurper Victoriano Huerta gave way to a factional struggle between Villa on the one hand and Obregón and Carranza on the other; the triumph of Carranza and Obregón led in turn to a political battle between them. The seeds of the problem were developing even before Madero's death.

Carranza, the elder statesman and father figure of the revolutionary movement, had risen to prominence in the Díaz administration, serving as a senator and as governor. He had literally fought his way into the Díaz government in an armed revolt against the Porfirian governor of his home state and had later joined fellow Coahuilan Madero in his revolution against

Díaz.[1] He was twenty-one years older than Obregón and far more secure, both economically and socially. Though not exceptionally wealthy, he was an *hacendado* in his home state, and his early revolutionary activity seems to have been directed against the dictator Díaz rather than in favor of any far-reaching revolutionary changes that would favor the masses.

Obregón's background was more complex. His family's connections had helped him get jobs and maintain himself economically, but he was always cast in the role of a poor relative with all the humiliations that implied. His was a childhood and young manhood filled with ambiguities: bicultural and bilingual, lacking money but possessing a tenuous claim to social status, fatherless but part of a family of older (some much older) siblings, who remembered the family in better times, and a mother who had married beneath herself and had suffered for it when her husband's fortunes failed.[2] It is not surprising that he emerged driven and ambitious. Nevertheless, he did not become militarily involved in the early Madero movement.

Villa, of course, was far different still. From a poor background, he had become an outlaw, and the most common story is that he had killed a man who had violated his sister. A natural leader of men, either as bandits or as revolutionaries, he had joined the Madero movement under the aegis of his mentor, Abraham González, who would later serve as Maderista governor of Chihuahua. Mercurial, audacious, sometimes cruel, and sometimes charming, he was, thanks to his military genius, indispensable to Carranza for a time. He distrusted Carranza from the beginning and would quickly become jealous of Obregón. The control of the Revolution would ultimately be determined by the struggle among these three men of the north.

[1]Douglas W. Richmond, "Venustiano Carranza's Rise to Power, 1893–1915" (Master's thesis, University of Washington, 1971), pp. 15–16.
[2]Harold Lasswell has indicated the revolutionary potential of men whose families have lost money and status and has stressed the importance of the cases in which the mother survives to instill her expectations of restoration in her son ("The Political Personality," reprinted in *Personality and Politics*, ed. Gordon J. DiRenzo, p. 42).

One of the most startling occurrences during the 1912–1913 period was Obregón's own emergence from obscurity into a position of national military power. His initial military successes brought him to the attention of Sonoran political leaders, but although he became commander of the Sonoran forces he was not able to dominate the state politically until years later. Nevertheless, he was able to use his military success as a springboard to national power. Leaving behind the tangle of opposing political forces in Sonora, he carried his military victories into the capital of Mexico to achieve a national political position that eventually permitted him to control his own state. In much the same way in which he would bypass minor military objectives that he judged to be of less value than the effort needed to achieve them, he bypassed the horizontal political struggles in Sonora to move vertically into the national leadership. Although the political division in Sonora eventually contributed to a split in Constitutionalist ranks, Obregón's powerful position at the national level then made it possible for him and his associates to dominate Mexico, including most particularly the Mexican northwest.

Critical in this rise, of course, was Carranza's recognition of his military ability and therefore his usefulness to the cause of the Constitutionalists, as those in opposition to Huerta designated themselves. And it was the political and military situation in Mexico and especially Sonora in 1913 that permitted Obregón to come to Carranza's attention.

In February, 1913, Madero was overthrown in Mexico City, and his place as president was taken by General Huerta, the same general who had led the troops against the Orozco rebellion earlier. Sonoran Governor Maytorena vacillated, although he had called Obregón and others to confer with him about the danger to Madero's government several days before the assassination. Maytorena at that time had approached Obregón to run on his own ticket as a deputy for the Sonoran congress. Obregón, according to his own account, had refused, maintaining that he wished to remain independent politically.[3]

---

[3]Alvaro Obregón, *Ocho mil kilómetros en campaña*, p. 26.

Apparently he judged that Maytorena's popularity was on the wane. Obregón had then returned to Huatabampo, only to be recalled to Hermosillo almost immediately, when the news of Madero's death reached the Sonoran capital.

Significantly, Maytorena called on those military chiefs and political prefects in the state who had taken part in the fight against Orozco. These were the leaders on whom he felt he could depend in this crisis. The governor, however, was not ready to follow through and declare against the Huerta government.

The northern governors feverishly consulted among themselves about how to react to the events in Mexico City. As early as February 11, when the first word of the anti-Madero movement reached the north, governors Venustiano Carranza of Coahuila and Abraham González of Chihuahua were in contact with Maytorena, urging the maintenance of constant communication and the readiness for concerted action in the crisis. González even asked the Sonoran governor for arms, which Maytorena denied having.

Meanwhile, popular demonstrations in support of Madero began to take place throughout the state of Sonora, including a large one in front of Maytorena's residence in Guaymas. By February 15, he was also in communication with Felipe Riveros, the governor of Sonora's neighboring west-coast state Sinaloa, and was able to wire Madero that the governments of Sonora, Sinaloa, and Chihuahua were ready to support his government in the emergency. Maytorena then issued a manifesto to the Sonoran people in support of Madero on February 16. On February 18 he received Huerta's telegram from Mexico informing him that he had assumed the executive power of the nation, authorized by the Mexican Senate. It was at this point that Maytorena called on the military and political leaders of the state to come to Hermosillo to decide on a plan of action against the coup.[4]

[4]The account of these northern reactions relies on Informe del Gobernador de Sonora, Serie Sonora, microfilm, Museo de Antropología, Mexico City (archive cited hereafter as SSMA), roll 9.

Maytorena, however, was more and more frightened.
Coahuila and Chihuahua, led by Carranza and González, seemed
likely to stay in line against Huerta, but Riveros in Sinaloa was
already sliding toward his eventual recognition of the new government. Moreover, Maytorena's friends within Mexico City
informed him that the cause was lost and that Huerta was
firmly in control. When Obregón went to the governor to
offer his help in the military declaration he expected against the
Huerta government, the governor replied that he needed a
peacekeeping force rather than an army.[5]

Despite the attempts of Obregón and others to convince
Maytorena to take military action to support Madero, Maytorena continued to stall. He did, however, name Obregón
head of the armed forces in Hermosillo in place of an officer
whose loyalty to Madero was in doubt. Even after the news
of Madero's assassination on February 22, Maytorena was unwilling to accept the responsibility for challenging Huerta. He
quickly requested a leave of absence on the grounds of ill health;
the Sonoran congress granted it on February 26, and he left
immediately for the U.S. border. Ignacio Pesqueira, from another prominent Sonoran family, was named interim governor
in his place.[6]

By this time, the revolt was beginning throughout the
state. On February 23, Maderistas in the town of Fronteras, a
station on the railroad line between the capital and Agua Prieta,
which was across from Douglas, Arizona, had risen against the
federal garrison in their own town, taking most of the federal
soldiers prisoner. They had obtained information about events
in the Mexican capital through communications sent to the
Americans in charge of the railroad line and of the Moctezuma
Copper Company, both at their offices in Douglas.[7] In Agua
Prieta itself, the chief of police Plutarco Elías Calles secretly
left town to begin to recruit troops and support in the nearby

[5]Alfredo Breceda, *México revolucionario*, 2:60–61; Obregón, *Ocho mil kilómetros*, p. 28.

[6]Obregón, *Ocho mil kilómetros*, p. 29.

[7]Ibid., pp. 30, 32. Antonio G. Rivera, *La Revolución en Sonora* (p. 287), gives the date as February 26, 1913.

areas. The town of Ures was taken for the Maderistas and became a point of transit for troops crossing the state. In the mining town of Cananea, the municipal president, Manuel M. Diéguez, who had led the strike in 1906, and his labor associates Juan José Ríos and Esteban B. Calderón positioned themselves with their armed contingents of miners at the Estación del Río of the Nogales-Cananea-Naco railroad, ready to join the fight. In Alamos, the friends of Benjamín Hill and Obregón's brother José J. Obregón began the organization of troops to defy the federal forces. In Sahuaripa, near the Sierra Madre, the municipal prefect organized a contingent of forces.[8]

With the entire state aroused, it was only a matter of days before the new Sonoran governor sent to the thirteen members of the Sonoran congress his declaration refusing to recognize the Huerta government, and it was approved on March 5, 1913. The congress also ordered that the flags in Hermosillo were to fly at half-mast in mourning for the deceased Madero and his vice-president. Governor Pesqueira then proceeded to appoint Obregón chief of the military section, with the state divided into three military zones: the north, commanded by Juan Cabral, the center, under Salvador Alvarado, and the south, under Benjamín Hill.[9] The northeast under Plutarco Elías Calles was to report directly to the governor himself. On March 6, Obregón marched toward the border to meet the enemy. A parade preceded the departure for the frontier, and the occasion furnished Obregón an opportunity for a dramatic manifesto, saying in part: "We will smother them in their own thirst for blood, and we will then be worthy of the land which gave us birth."[10]

Despite the rhetoric, the military and political situation for the Constitutionalists was far from good. Only the governors of Coahuila, Venustiano Carranza, and of Chihuahua, Abraham González, and Pesqueira, now interim governor of Sonora, were

[8]Rivera, *La Revolución*, pp. 290–292.
[9]XXIII Congreso de Sonora, sesión permanente del día 5 de marzo de 1913, SSMA/9; Breceda, *México revolucionario*, 2:94–95; Obregón, *Ocho mil kilómetros*, p. 33.
[10]Obregón, *Ocho mil kilómetros*, p. 34.

left to fight against Huerta. González, who had warned Madero about Huerta's intentions and who was viewed by Huerta as a dangerous enemy, was captured by federal forces and reportedly thrown under a moving train. In any case, he was killed, and it was his death perhaps more than Madero's that brought Pancho Villa so strongly into the Revolution. The last remaining holdout among Madero's governors was therefore Venustiano Carranza, who issued the Plan of Guadalupe from his Hacienda de Guadalupe on March 26, 1913.

This plan, drawn up by a small group of conspirators, had no more power than that which the armies that would gather behind Carranza could give it. He could count on the Sonorans, however, in Maytorena's absence, and Cabral and Obregón had already attacked and taken Nogales, giving the Sonorans a border outlet to the United States. The plan did gain acceptance by most revolutionaries, including Villa, and Carranza assumed the title *Primer Jefe del Ejército Constitucionalista* ("First Chief of the Constitutionalist Forces"). Adherents to his movement were known as Constitutionalists from that time on.

The Plan of Guadalupe was not a social document. More than anything else, it was a call to revolution against the assassin of Madero. Carranza already had at his disposal a small contingent of troops under Pablo González, and the forces of Sonora soon joined his movement. Governor Pesqueira immediately sent his brother, Roberto V. Pesqueira, and Adolfo de la Huerta to assure Carranza of Sonoran support. Carranza thus gained a number of able military leaders in the Sonoran group, including Obregón himself, Benjamín Hill, Plutarco Elías Calles, Salvador Alvarado, and Juan Cabral. Four future presidents of Mexico were now involved in the Revolution: Carranza, Obregón, de la Huerta, and Calles—and three of them were Sonorans.

Pancho Villa, of course, became the leader of the Constitutionalist forces in Chihuahua. The alliance between Villa and Carranza was destined to be a stormy one and redounded to Obregón's benefit as Carranza used him as a counterpoise to Villa's power. Villa, of course, had lived outside the law most of his life and was a very poor military subordinate. He frequently disobeyed orders, a habit distressing to Carranza, an admirer of German military discipline. Villa's own experience of imprisonment under Madero at the instigation of Huerta had not made him less suspicious of those with whom he was fighting. He was bitterly aware that loyalty was not always rewarded and that allies could quickly become enemies. He had learned to read and write long after childhood, and he was little impressed with questions of legality. He was loyal to the memory of Abraham González and to the ideas of Madero despite his imprisonment, and this loyalty and his hatred for Huerta furnished his impetus in the war that followed Madero's death. He and Carranza disliked and distrusted each other almost immediately.

Meanwhile, Obregón was establishing himself more firmly as head of the military forces in Sonora. He had not won this position unchallenged. Although he was the obvious man to take command, just having returned to public acclaim in Hermosillo from the fight against Orozco, both Salvador Alvarado and Juan Cabral felt that they, as old Maderistas, had a better claim to the position. Benjamín Hill also had a right to consideration, but he immediately offered to march south to secure his own home district of Alamos and was named chief of the southern zone of the state. Pesqueira seems originally to have envisioned a rotating command among the other three, depending on who was attacking where, but Obregón established his preeminence when Cabral wired from his command asking for reinforcements. Obregón and his troops joined him, and Obregón seems to have taken over direction of the entire operation rather smoothly. In any case, by the end of March he was clearly preeminent in the military hierarchy, so much so that Pesqueira feared for his own authority and attempted to make Cabral's position somewhat stronger.[11]

Pesqueira's problems were intensified by the reappearance of the ubiquitous Maytorena. Maytorena had been living in Tucson, where he was approached both by Huerta emissaries seeking accord and by revolutionaries, including Pancho Villa,

[11]Cabral to Gobernador del Estado, March 6, 1913, PHS/54.

who remembered him from the early days of the Maderista movement. To make matters worse, he returned to Sonora in late April and early May, after the Sonoran forces had taken several border towns, and then returned to Tucson again, apparently still nervous about the Huertista threat but eager to return and take over should victory appear imminent.[12] Finally, in July, he met with Venustiano Carranza, with whom he had been in constant contact during his exile, and then decided to return to Sonora again to take up his duties as governor. Sonoran military successes had improved his health.

Of the major Sonoran military leaders, the only one who really supported Maytorena's return was Obregón, and it was he and Governor Pesqueira who met Maytorena at Nogales when he returned. Obregón seems to have had several motives. First, Pesqueira seemed a little unsure of giving Obregón unqualified command of the Sonoran armies and tried to divide the command. In fact, he had for a time tried to name Juan Cabral as chief of the armed forces in Obregón's place. Secondly, Pesqueira had refused to punish an officer who had threatened Obregón's life during the early part of the anti-Huertista campaign.[13] Obregón had threatened to resign if the man was not punished, but Pesqueira neither accepted his resignation nor punished the offender. Thirdly, Maytorena represented legitimacy, as one of Madero's own governors. Fourthly, it was Maytorena who had initially rewarded and elevated Obregón in rank and prestige, and it may be that Obregón felt a certain loyalty, even if he did not have much personal respect for the man. In the fifth place, it seems likely that he thought Maytorena would be easier to manipulate than Pesqueira and would give him a freer hand in the exercise of military power. A sixth possibility is suggested by Carranza's secretary, Alfredo Breceda, who claimed that Obregón thought Pesqueira and Maytorena would neutralize each other, leaving Obregón preeminent both militarily and politically in the state.[14]

[12]Informe del Gobernador de Sonora, SSMA/9.

[13]Breceda, *México revolucionario*, 2:179–181; Rivera, *La Revolución*, p. 347.

[14]Breceda, *México revolucionario*, 2:185–186.

The return of Maytorena was not accepted tranquilly by the other Sonoran leaders, and a junta was called in Nogales for July 28. Attending were Hill, Calles, Roberto Pesqueira, Breceda, who attended as a representative of the first chief, and other political and military leaders. Pesqueira probably could have maintained himself in power had he insisted upon it, but it was instead Maytorena who was insistent. Finally those present decided to cede the governorship to Maytorena to avoid further friction, especially since it was Carranza himself who actually held power over the Sonoran forces and would direct their move on Mexico City. Control of the day-to-day military situation in Sonora remained effectively in Obregón's hands, despite Maytorena's pretensions.[15]

During this time, Sonora was becoming the center of the Revolution in more than just a military sense. Finding a ready welcome behind the lines of the victorious Sonoran forces, revolutionaries and intellectuals from all over the country had come to Hermosillo. Among them were Juan Sánchez Azcona, the journalist who had been Madero's private secretary, General Felipe Angeles, who had fought for Madero and who would become Villa's principal military adviser, and Aarón Sáenz, a law student sent to Obregón by Carranza and destined to become Obregón's chief of staff and even his secretary of foreign relations when Obregón became president.

It had become obvious that Carranza would also have to come to Sonora. Thus, even before Maytorena's return, Obregón, sending the former law student Sáenz as his representative, took the initiative of inviting Carranza to take refuge behind his lines. Obregón pointed out that in Sonora Carranza would have the opportunity to organize his forces with strong supply lines to the United States for arms and other materiel, and the movement from north to south could be organized on a firmer basis.[16] Obregón would later be in San Blas, Sinaloa, to meet Carranza when he arrived after a three-month trip across the

[15]Diebold to Secretario de Relaciones Exteriores, August 5, 1913, ASRE-119, L-E-776R, Leg. 27, 6.
[16]Aarón Sáenz, interview, in *Testimonios del proceso revolucionario de México*, ed. Píndaro Urióstegui Miranda, p. 389.

mountains and to accompany him to Hermosillo, thus stealing a march on Maytorena, who had hoped to set up a power base in Sonora and was making claims of his own to leadership of the Revolution. This invitation was a stroke of political genius on Obregón's part, as it established both his military control and his stance as protector of the legitimate Revolution in Carranza's eyes.

By the time Carranza arrived, the Constitutionalists held Sonora, with the exception of the port of Guaymas, which was still in the possession of federal forces. The Sonoran group had therefore responded to pleas for help from the neighboring state of Sinaloa. The former governor of Sinaloa, Felipe Riveros, had meanwhile accepted Huerta, had been removed by him and jailed, had escaped, had contacted Carranza, and had reinstated himself as the Constitutionalist governor. He was working with the revolutionary forces in the state under Ramón Iturbe, a Maderista of unquestioned credentials. Obregón had at first objected to Riveros' return, reminding the Sonoran authorities pointedly of his original vacillation and cowardice.[17] Maytorena, on the other hand, was eager to have his old friend back in office. Additionally, the charge of cowardice cut no ice with Maytorena; he was inclined to look on the original acceptance of Huerta as prudence.

Nevertheless, Obregón and Maytorena had had a fairly close working relationship until the arrival of Carranza in Sonora, at which time Obregón began to work much more directly with the first chief. Moreover, as early as May, 1913, Obregón was in contact with Governor Riveros in Sinaloa, but he and Maytorena negotiated through August with Riveros before sending him significant help. The negotiations were complicated by the fact that various individuals floated back and forth between the two states, looking for personal advancement with one or another revolutionary leader. Riveros more than once warned Maytorena of accepting men who had left his camp or of negotiating with unauthorized representatives. Nevertheless, by August, the Sonorans were supplying the

[17]Obregón to Pesqueira, May 31, 1913, PHS/55.

Sinaloans with ammunition, and a tentative arrangement had been worked out for a pact of alliance between the two states. Sonora would agree to send enough help to eliminate "traitors," that is, federal troops, from Sinaloa, and Sinaloa would recognize Obregón as chief of the armed forces in Sinaloa pending a decision by the first chief on the command of the west-coast armies. Obviously, with such an arrangement in force, the chances of Obregón's being named commander would be greatly enhanced, and presumably the position of Sonora as benefactor to other revolutionary states would enhance Maytorena's political position as well.[18]

The Sonoran governor, unable up to this time to do much about establishing his own claim to leadership, was eager to ingratiate himself with Carranza. It was Obregón, however, who took advantage of events and went to Sinaloa to meet the first chief when he emerged from the Sierra Madre after his arduous trip across northern Mexico. Obregón knew that the federal forces at Guaymas were planning to send a column to disembark at the Sinaloan port of Topolobampo and thence to march to San Blas, where Sinaloan general Ramón Iturbe had his headquarters. As this action would menace the first chief on his arrival in Sinaloa, Obregón sent a column of 600 men under Hill, still operating in southern Sonora, to reinforce San Blas. Obregón retired from directing the siege of Guaymas to accompany Hill, and they arrived at San Blas on September 13. Obregón continued on to El Fuerte, where Carranza had arrived with an escort of 150 men.[19]

On September 14, Obregón met Carranza for the first time outside the tiny town of El Fuerte, and they proceeded the next day for San Blas. During the fourteenth and fifteenth, a minor scuffle took place in Naranjo, close to the port of Topolobampo and on the road to San Blas. Although Governor Riveros reported to Maytorena that it had been of little importance and

[18]Obregón to Riveros, May 31, 1913, Expediente Obregón, Serie Sinaloa, microfilm, Museo de Antropología, Mexico City; Obregón to Riveros, September 2, 1913, and Riveros to Maytorena, August 25, 1913, both in PHS/56.

[19]Maytorena to Obregón, September 12, 1913, and Obregón to Riveros, September 13, 1913, both in PHS/56; Obregón, *Ocho mil kilómetros*, p. 82.

had involved only an advance patrol of federal forces, Carranza was very worried and asked for reinforcements.[20] Obregón's arrival and quick transporting of the first chief north to safety reinforced his image as the older man's, and thus the Revolution's, protector.

As Obregón and Carranza proceeded north by horse and train, Maytorena was making frantic efforts to prepare Hermosillo for a proper welcome and to get to Carranza himself as quickly as possible. Despite Maytorena's attempts to get together a band, obtain a cinematographer from El Paso or Los Angeles, and properly outfit an escort for Carranza, Obregón had already established himself in Carranza's mind as the man in control of the situation on the west coast. The governor was even hampered in his attempts to get a car to take Carranza over the areas where he could not travel by train, because, as Maytorena plaintively reported, the only automobile available was out of commission and a mechanic could not be found to repair it in time. Finally, by the eighteenth, Maytorena had gotten himself together sufficiently to meet them in Cruz de Piedra, Sonora, on the railroad line for Hermosillo.[21]

The reception that awaited Carranza in the Sonoran capital was one of delirious enthusiasm, but Maytorena was unable to capitalize on it, and from the time of Carranza's arrival in Sonora his own star sank rapidly. Obregón, on the contrary, was immediately named chief of the Army of the Northwest, with command of the campaign in Sonora, Sinaloa, Chihuahua, Durango, and Baja California.[22] He had already become a national rather than a local figure.

Certain problems were inherent in Obregón's sudden rise to prominence, however. First of all, the first chief had placed under Obregón's command the forces of Pancho Villa, operat-

[20]Maytorena to Obregón, September 13, 1913, and Maytorena to Carranza, September 13, 1913, both in PHS/56.

[21]Maytorena's frantic efforts are recorded in Maytorena to Joffrey and Levine, September 13, 1913, Maytorena to Obregón, September 16, 1913, Sánchez Azcona to Obregón, September 12, 1913, and Villaseñor to Maytorena, September 17, 1913, all in PHS/56.

[22]Breceda, *México revolucionario*, 2:196.

ing in Chihuahua. Secondly, Maytorena did not view with contentment the rise to power of his former protégé. Both circumstances would later lead to disastrous dissension. Carranza had driven a wedge of jealousy between two of his principal military commanders, Obregón and Villa, by making Obregón at least nominally Villa's military superior. He thus made division almost inevitable within Sonora, the state in which the position of the Revolution was established most firmly. The stage was set for a strategic alliance between Maytorena and Villa against Obregón and Carranza and the subsequent breakup of the revolutionary forces into factions following the defeat of Huerta.

Carranza came dangerously near to alienating Obregón as well, when in late October of 1913 he named Felipe Angeles secretary of war. Angeles had been a federal general before the Maderista rebellion, had joined Madero, but later had recognized Huerta after his takeover and had accepted a diplomatic assignment to Paris from the Huerta government. He had returned to Mexico to join the Revolution, but had been met by the suspicions of the Sonoran leaders, especially Obregón, who condemned him out of hand as an ex-federal. Maytorena, however, was not so unenthusiastic, seeing in Angeles a possible brake on Obregón's rise. Carranza was much taken with Angeles, who was courtly, intelligent, and a well-trained officer, differing in this latter respect from all the other major revolutionary leaders.

Meanwhile the Sinaloan campaign under Obregón and Iturbe, whom he had wisely taken as his second in command, was proceeding exceptionally well. It is not surprising, then, that the appointment of Angeles to the highest military command would infuriate Obregón, who was at that time moving on the Sinaloan capital, Culiacán. Moreover, two of the other principal Sonoran generals, Hill and Diéguez, threatened to resign if Angeles remained in that capacity. Obregón made a hurried trip to Hermosillo to protest to the first chief himself. Carranza attempted to calm Obregón by explaining that the actual conduct of the campaign would remain in the hands of the first chief and that Obregón would continue to have a free hand at the local level, but Obregón was not satisfied. He

returned to the campaign against Culiacán extremely dis-
gruntled.[23] Eventually the hostility of the Sonorans would force
Angeles to leave Hermosillo to join Pancho Villa as his principal adviser.

By November of 1913, Obregón's forces controlled Sinaloa
after the victory over federal forces at Culiacán. However, a
lack of railroad connections between Tepic and Orendáin cut
the line between the northwest and Mexico City at a point that
was very mountainous and thus difficult to cross. Worse, at this
time the northwest provided no consistent source of funds,
although the mines in northern Sonora continued to operate
during much of this period. In Chihuahua, Villa was able to
round up cattle belonging to wealthy landowners in the area,
especially the Terrazas family, and sell them across the border.
In exchange, he was able to buy arms and ammunition. It began
to look as though Villa might get to Mexico City first, and it
was quite likely that once there he would renounce the first
chief. Therefore, Carranza resolved in early 1914 to go to
Chihuahua to keep an eye on Villa.

At about the same time, Angeles decided to resign as secretary of war and to join Villa. Carranza was unwilling to cross
U.S. territory and therefore faced a long overland journey
through the Sierra Madre, but Angeles had no such scruples
and stepped across the border to go by train to El Paso and
Ciudad Juárez, arriving in Villa's camp several weeks before
Carranza.

Unfortunately for the Constitutionalist cause, Villa and
Carranza did not come to trust each other any more thoroughly
on close contact than at a distance, and Carranza did not stay
long before moving on to Coahuila. Carranza felt that Villa
would lend his support to the Constitutionalist effort only as
long at it suited his own ends. On May 16, 1914, according to
Obregón's account, Carranza communicated his suspicions to
Obregón, urging him to push toward the cities of the interior
because Villa and his adviser Angeles could not be trusted.[24]

[23]See Obregón, *Ocho mil kilómetros*, pp. 84–85.
[24]Ibid., p. 121.

Obregón therefore abandoned his plan to attack Mazatlán on the coast and decided to proceed immediately towards Guadalajara, beginning his advance on the principal city of Jalisco in June, 1914.

By this time, Obregón was making major decisions in the areas his armies controlled with no reference whatsoever to Maytorena, who was left behind in Sonora. On June 18, 1914, he named Manuel M. Diéguez, the Cananea labor leader and one of his principal generals, as governor and military commander of Jalisco without consultation with Maytorena but with the approval of the first chief.[25] The split among Sonoran revolutionaries was widening, but Obregón was beyond their quarrels and had become a national leader of considerable power.

The relationship between Villa and Carranza had meanwhile been gravely exacerbated by a dispute between them over the battle of Zacatecas. Zacatecas was a major point of federal concentration on the way to Mexico City, and the general who took the city would be a hero of the Revolution. It was directly south on the railroad line from Torreón, where Villa was camped, and was a logical target for Villa's Division of the North. Carranza, however, in what seems to have been a deliberate move to weaken Villa and delay his progress toward the capital, ordered Villa to take Saltillo, the capital of Coahuila, almost directly to the east of his position. Saltillo was easily within the range of General Pablo González' operations in the northeast and would have been a logical target for him. Worse, a move east for Villa's troops would cause a breakdown in their lines of supply and communication from their Chihuahuan base. Nevertheless, Villa marched east to help the Army of the Northeast, returning later to Torreón to reestablish his supply lines from the north, which Pablo González had failed to protect.[26] Carranza was obviously acting against Villa's independent power position within the Revolution. Meanwhile, General Pánfilo Natera, who had been commanded to take Zacatecas,

[25]Diéguez to Maytorena, June 18, 1914, PHS/58.
[26]By far the clearest account of these difficulties from Villa's point of view may be found in the report by Felipe Angeles, 1914, PHS/59.

proved unequal to the task, and Villa stepped in with all his forces to win the battle, despite Carranza's opposition.

On June 25, as soon as the city was secured, Villa wrote to Obregón in the hope of an alliance against the first chief, describing all the difficulties that had been put in the way of his own military campaign and emphasizing his friendship for Obregón. Villa anticipated a meeting with the leaders of the Army of the Northeast and probably with Carranza himself. Villa urged Obregón to attend or to send a representative. Basically, he was seeking Obregón's help in forcing Carranza to supply his trains with coal, thus making it possible for Villa to take part in the military effort against Mexico City. If these supplies were denied, Villa warned, he would retreat to the north, leaving Obregón's troops isolated in their march southward against the capital.[27]

The strong implication in Villa's letter was that Carranza's political machinations were harming the military progress of the Revolution. While the letter was at once an invitation to Obregón to join him in taking power for the real military leaders of the Revolution, it was also a threat that Villa might refuse military aid to the cause, leaving Obregón overextended and alone facing Huerta's troops in the center of the country.

Obregón did not receive the message until July 2, at which time he was occupied with the march on Guadalajara. He had already had one encounter with a federal column, which had come out from that city to meet his forces, and he answered Villa that he could not possibly leave his division at that moment of the offensive. He urged Villa to present a united front against Huerta and to try to solve his differences with Carranza.[28] Obregón then pressed southward, and Villa and Carranza came to a temporary but not very solid agreement. Villa retired to consolidate his position in Chihuahua.

The city of Guadalajara was actually untouched by the fighting that was decisive in its fall. Obregón had been patiently moving up on the city for almost a month, the delay partly a

[27]Obregón, *Ocho mil kilómetros*, p. 132. Another, slightly different version appears in Martín Luis Guzmán, *Memoirs of Pancho Villa*, p. 246.
[28]Obregón, *Ocho mil kilómetros*, p. 133.

result of the difficulties of crossing the mountainous gap in the
railroad between Tepic and Orendáin, near Guadalajara. On
July 6 and 7, the federal troops came out of the city to meet
Obregón at Orendáin and were decisively defeated. Obregón
wired Alvarado and Maytorena on July 8 that the federal
column had been destroyed after a thirty-six hour combat.[29]

The federal army in Jalisco was never able to offer any
further organized resistance. Two thousand had perished, 6,000
became prisoners, and the rest of the 12,000-man federal army
fled in any direction and by any means available. Obregón
on July 8 wired Carranza asking for an elevation in rank for
six of the "heroes of Guadalajara": Brigadier Generals M. M.
Diéguez, Juan G. Cabral, Benjamín Hill, and Lucio Blanco, and
Majors Juan Mérigo and Francisco Serrano.[30] Four were Sonorans who had been involved in the anti-Huerta effort from the
beginning.

A *corrido* ("popular song") celebrating the victory was
published and distributed:

> Life to all the forces
> Of the courageous Maderistas!
> Death to the praetorians!
> Life to the Carrancistas![31]

Guadalajara was the last major battle in Obregón's drive
on Mexico City. By July 31, 1914, the vanguard of Obregón's
troops under Lucio Blanco attacked and captured the plaza of
Irapuato, a key point in his move to the capital.[32] Irapuato was
a major rail junction, the point at which the line from Guadalajara joined the Central Mexicano from Zacatecas, Torreón,

[29]Alvarado to Maytorena, July 8, 1914, and Obregón to Carranza, July
9, 1914, both in PHS/59.

[30]Charles C. Cumberland, *Mexican Revolution: The Constitutionalist
Years*, p. 139; Obregón to Carranza, July 8, 1914, PHS/59. See also *La Patria:
Organo de la División del Norte*, July 27, 1914, in Almada Papers, PHS/40.

[31]"La toma de Guadalajara: Entrada triunfal de las fuerzas carrancistas,"
in Mexican Political Parties Propaganda Archive, Latin American Collection,
University of Texas at Austin (hereafter cited as MPPP).

[32]Robert E. Quirk, *The Mexican Revolution, 1914–1915: The Convention of Aguascalientes*, p. 53.

and Chihuahua, the rail line by which Villa would have been able to move south. Thus either by luck or by design, probably the latter, Obregón contained Villa in the north and assured his own victory in the race to the capital. The forces of Pablo González and the Army of the Northeast held Querétaro, to the east of Irapuato, thus controlling the other rail line that could have facilitated Villa's southward movement.

Huerta had already fled the country and his representatives were negotiating with Carranza. Obregón therefore went immediately to Querétaro to confer with Pablo González, chief of the Army of the Northeast, about their advance on Mexico City. He and González met on August 1, but during the meeting a message from Carranza arrived urging them to press on to Mexico City, as his own negotiations with the Huertistas had broken down. Carranza instructed the two generals to take the capital by storm if necessary, completely ignoring Villa and the Division of the North. As early as July 25, 1914, Carranza had authorized Obregón to establish a basis for the surrender of Huerta's army with federal negotiators who had been attempting to contact him.[33]

By August 9, when Obregón arrived with the Army of the Northwest at Teoloyucan, twenty miles north of Mexico City, Carranza reiterated Obregón's authority to deal with the federal commanders.[34] From this time until the surrender of Mexico City, Obregón was the chief negotiator for the Constitutionalists.

The negotiations were completed in Teoloyucan on August 13, 1914. Francisco Carbajal had resigned from the interim presidency, had ordered the withdrawal of federal forces from Mexico City, and had left authority in the hands of the governor of the Federal District. The governor acted as one of the federal representatives, along with a representative from each of the federal armed forces. They agreed to a withdrawal of federal forces from the capital to an unspecified place and the immediate peaceful entrance of the Constitutionalists. The

[33]Carranza to Obregón, July 25, 1914, and Villa to Carranza, July 31, 1914, both in PHS/59.
[34]Quirk, *The Mexican Revolution*, p. 57.

command of the police force and the government of the capital would be surrendered by the governor of the district to the occupying forces, led by Obregón. The entrance was to be peaceful, and the responsibility for the maintenance of order fell on the Constitutionalists.[35] Thus the Treaty of Teoloyucan was completed and the stage set for the peaceful occupation of Mexico City.

On August 15, Obregón's troops marched into the capital. The city was put under martial law, and the death penalty was proclaimed as the punishment for the disturbance of public order or the committing of crimes such as "outrages" and robberies. The occupation was completed without major problems.

Carranza arrived in Mexico City on August 18, but immediately violated the Plan of Guadalupe by not assuming the office of provisional president. Carranza was playing his own game, going after the office of elected president. Presumably, had he become provisional president, he would have become ineligible for the office later under his slogan: Effective Suffrage, No Reelection. He therefore maintained the government in a preconstitutional, extralegal state. He did not recall the Congress of 1913, which had been dispersed by Huerta, nor did he pay any attention to foreign diplomatic representatives, particularly those who had recognized Huerta. His actions, designed to prevent any attempt to replace him as the leader of the Revolution, would contribute in major part to the inability of revolutionary leaders to establish a government peacefully at that time. Factionalism was growing throughout the country, especially in Sonora, and Carranza's intransigence would be an important factor in the divisions among the Constitutionalists.

Further, Obregón and Villa were both buoyed by their military successes and increasingly jealous of Carranza. Carranza, however, showed few signs of giving them political power commensurate with their military achievements.

Villa was increasingly alienated, and Obregón, eager to avoid further armed conflict and hoping that he could improve

---

[35]Obregón, *Ocho mil kilómetros*, p. 159; Quirk, *The Mexican Revolution*, p. 58.

his own political position, would try to become the mediator between the other two leaders. Ultimately he would fail, and the factional struggle would enter another military phase, with Obregón and Carranza on one side and Villa on the other.

CHAPTER 5

Collapse of the Revolutionary Alliance

The days from July through September were crucial for the future of the Revolution, as the alliance of northern leaders began to strain and crack. It was also dangerous for Obregón personally, and it was during this time that his attempts to reconcile the factions falling into line behind Villa and Carranza almost cost him his life. He would, however, come to know both Villa and Carranza much better during this time, sharpening his political senses for the showdown in October and November at Aguascalientes.

The political situation in Sonora was the most obvious problem, but even as Obregón was nearing Mexico City in the fight against Huerta factional strife was growing all over the country. Generals, governors, and other political and military leaders intensified their efforts to gain strong positions in the emerging power structure. The tug-of-war between Villa and Carranza was only the most visible struggle as political jockeying for position alternated with out-and-out violence while individuals and groups strove to establish themselves within the context of the new situation. The atmosphere of violence and distrust permeated revolutionary ranks. Sonora itself was filled with suspicions and open animosities.

Obregón had had constant problems within his own command, as well as outside it, and as early as the attack on Naco a subordinate had refused to obey his orders and had threatened his life. This attempt was the first in a series of challenges, both overt and hidden. Salvador Alvarado, who had never recovered from the blow of having Obregón named chief of the Sonoran forces in preference to himself, was always an unreliable subordinate, although Alvarado never came to support the man who would be the leader of the other Sonoran faction, José María Maytorena. Nevertheless, his constant political machinations against Obregón were common knowledge in Hermosillo for several months before Obregón entered the capital city with his troops.[1] Alvarado was charged with the direction of the siege of Guaymas as Obregón marched on the capital, but reports of his potential insubordination almost led Obregón to turn back in order to resolve the situation to the rear of his advancing army. However, he judged the march on Mexico City to be of more importance to the outcome of the Revolution and to his own political position than the resolution of political problems in his own state, and he therefore continued his drive on the capital.[2]

His difficulties were not confined to Sonoran military leaders. As he moved through other areas, he was faced with jealousies from other local leaders as well. A notable example was General Rafael Buelna, who was operating in the area of Tepic and who joined Obregón for the march on Guadalajara. Buelna at one point attempted to assassinate Obregón, but he chose to deliver a speech of justification to his intended victim before killing him, and this delay gave other military leaders time to rush to the scene and persuade Buelna to give up his plan.[3] Despite the fact that Obregón later permitted Buelna to join the vanguard of the troops moving on Mexico City, Buelna remained jealous and alienated from the military leader and later joined Villa when the revolutionary coalition blew completely apart following the Convention of Aguascalientes.

Within Sonora itself, Maytorena and other leaders who saw no prominent place for themselves in a government led by Ca-

[1]Alvaro Obregón, *Ocho mil kilómetros en campaña*, p. 51; Alfredo Breceda, *México revolucionario*, 2:187–192.

[2]José C. Valadés, *Las caballerías de la Revolución: Hazañas del General Buelna*, pp. 79–85.

[3]Ibid. Valadés, a personal friend and sympathetic biographer of Buelna, makes no attempt to gloss over this incident.

rranza and Obregón were moving closer to Villa. By the time Obregón had moved into Sinaloa, the political strains in Sonora were strikingly obvious even to recent arrivals.[4] By June, 1914, while Villa was having his altercations with Carranza over the reinforcement of Zacatecas, the Huerta consular representative in El Paso informed his chief that a split in the Constitutionalist ranks, spreading from Chihuahua to Sonora, was preventing the stable governing of the area and noted that "everyone fears everyone else." He was undoubtedly correct. He went on to say that a "counterrevolutionary group" under M. M. Diéguez, of Cananea fame and at that time one of Obregón's most trusted subordinates, was reported to have captured Obregón and to be holding him prisoner. This story, totally false, was typical of the wild rumors circulating at the time and well illustrates the atmosphere of suspicion. However, the consul did go on to report correctly that the Revolution in the west was continuing with Obregón as chief and Diéguez, Alvarado, Ramón Iturbe, Juan Cabral, Juan Carrasco, Lucio Blanco, Benjamín Hill, and Rafael Buelna functioning as his subordinates.[5] Of these men, Alvarado and Buelna had been at times openly hostile to Obregón. The difficulties of holding his army together in the march on Mexico City required all of Obregón's tact and diplomacy and was good training for his later problems in reunifying the strife-torn country under his presidency.

As the armies under Obregón's direct control continued to have difficulties, the Sonoran situation was quickly deteriorating into open warfare. By July of 1914, Calles was publicly recruiting men in the north of the state, principally in the towns of Agua Prieta, Naco, and Nacozari, although he was apparently experiencing some difficulty since Maytorena had considerable

[4]See, for example, Juan Barragán's first-hand account in *Historia del Ejército y de la Revolución Constitucionalista: Primera Epoca*, p. 30. Pedro Bracamontes, who had earlier tried to assassinate Obregón, had in fact joined Villa as early as January, 1914 (Obregón to Villa, January 9, 1914, in Sylvestre Terrazas Papers, Bancroft Library, University of California, Berkeley [cited hereafter as TP]).

[5]Elías to Secretario de Relaciones Exteriores, June 12, 1914, ASRE-119, L-E-776, Leg. 27.

support in the area.[6] A strike in the Cananea copper mines had exacerbated the strains within the state. As the revenues of the mines were important to the Constitutionalist cause as a source of funds for war materiel and supplies, such a strike was viewed by the Constitutionalist leadership, under Carranza, as virtual treason. Calles went in to calm the situation, which meant, in fact, that he took the town by force. Maytorena and a commission had attempted to go to Cananea to study the problem but had been stopped in Nogales by Calles. As it stood, Calles and the Carrancistas were dominant in the north, Maytorena in Hermosillo, and Alvarado, who was still playing his own rather obscure game, held sway in the south. Carranza, made aware of these various difficulties, wired Alvarado congratulating him on his steadiness and loyalty and urging him to replace any officers of whom he was suspicious, notably two Yaqui chiefs who were leaning to Maytorena, and to do whatever was possible to effect a change in the government of the state. Alvarado wired back that it was important to move slowly, as the two officers in question, Urbalejo and Acosta, would shoot him if he attempted to remove them, and that no overt action should be taken until Calles had two thousand men. He additionally requested that Alfredo Breceda, Carranza's own secretary, who was then in Sonora, be prevented from mixing in Sonoran affairs "because he is very indiscreet and dumb and will harm us."[7]

It was against this background of near warfare in Sonora that the Constitutionalists under Obregón moved into Mexico City in early August. Maytorena was bringing troops north to challenge Calles, who had reconcentrated his forces slightly east of Nogales in the hamlet of Naco, Sonora, directly across the border from Naco, Arizona.[8] Before the end of August, armed conflict would break out. The proximity of both forces to the

[6]Elías to Secretario de Relaciones Exteriores, July 4, 1914, and July 13, 1914, ibid.

[7]Intercepted telegrams, Carranza to Alvarado, June 16, 1914, and Alvarado to Carranza, June 18, 1914, ibid. The previous year, Breceda had declined to join Alvarado in a plot against Obregón.

[8]Antonio G. Rivera, *La Revolución en Sonora*, p. 418.

U.S. border and the danger of damage to the Arizona side further complicated the situation by raising the threat of North American intervention. Worse, Villa enjoyed considerable political support in the United States and was considered something of a Robin Hood by President Woodrow Wilson.[9] Maytorena was thus encouraged to move closer to Villa in the power struggle that was developing between Villa on the one hand and Carranza and Obregón on the other. Calles continued to support the first chief.

By the time Constitutionalists had taken Mexico City, Villa had completely lost faith in Carranza. He felt that the only hope for unity within the revolutionary ranks lay in an agreement between himself and Obregón, though he was not enthusiastic about even that prospect. Carranza, for his part, had almost resolved to take military measures to stop Villa's and Maytorena's threats, but Obregón insisted on trying to solve the conflict peacefully.[10]

Villa's concern about the problems had led him and his generals to send Carranza a telegram making the following points. First, they accused Carranza of supporting his own partisans in Sonora rather than the old Maderistas, a claim that was biased at best. Second, Carranza had aggravated the problem by giving the command in Sonora to Calles under the leadership of Obregón, both of whom were implacable enemies of Maytorena. The lack of support for Maytorena indicated, according to them, a lack of support for the men of the Division of the North. This telegram was signed by such Villista

[9]Both Villa and Carranza had agents in the United States working to gain the support of President Woodrow Wilson and the people of the United States (Sommerfeld to de la Garza, June 8, 1914, Sommerfeld Papers, Lázaro de la Garza Archive, Latin American Collection, University of Texas at Austin [archive cited hereafter as DLGA], Wallet V, Folder B, #26; Pesqueira to Obregón, July 5, 1914, in *Documentos de la Revolución Mexicana*, ed. Isidro Fabela [cited hereafter as DRM], 1:303–305). For further information on Villa's propaganda efforts, see the Enrique Llorente Archive, New York Public Library (cited hereafter as ELA). For a discussion of the situation in Naco, see Linda B. Hall, "The Mexican Revolution and the Crisis in Naco, 1914–1915," *Journal of the West* 16 (October, 1977): 27–35.

[10]Obregón, *Ocho mil kilómetros*, p. 167; Manuel González Ramírez, *La revolución social de México*, 2:485.

commanders as Thomás Urbina, Eugenio Aguirre Benavides, José Isabel Robles, and Felipe Angeles.[11]

Obregón therefore obtained permission from the first chief to go and confer with Villa in Chihuahua. Carranza was rightly concerned for the personal safety of his principal general but finally agreed to let him go. By the time Obregón left Mexico City, open warfare had broken out in Sonora. Maytorena's forces were already advancing against Calles. As close an observer as Luis Aguirre Benavides, one-time secretary to Villa and brother of one of his principal generals, reported that at that time Maytorena had in effect broken with the first chief at the encouragement of Villa.[12]

Villa was reluctant to receive Obregón, feeling that he might become compromised in the eyes of his own Sonoran followers. However, some of Villa's advisers, among them Villa's biographer Martín Luis Guzmán, urged Villa to see Obregón, making the point that the only way to avoid further bloodshed would be for the two military leaders to unite. Otherwise, Carranza would lead Obregón and Pablo González into war against Villa. Bowing to these arguments, Villa decided to receive him.[13]

Obregón arrived in Chihuahua on a special train on August 24, reportedly authorized by Carranza to make broad concessions to pacify Villa. Villa had also resolved to be amenable to any reasonable grounds for settling the difficulties. After deciding to go together to Sonora to try to determine the state of affairs and make peace, they discussed the future of the country under Carranza. Villa immediately expressed doubts about Carranza's intentions toward the poor. Obregón rather rashly assured him that Carranza would not betray the ideals of the Revolution. He also said that he and Pablo González, chief of the Army of the Northeast, would join Villa in asking Carranza

[11]Martín Luis Guzmán, *Memoirs of Pancho Villa*, p. 275.
[12]Luis Aguirre Benavides, *Las grandes batallas de la División del Norte*, p. 199.
[13]Guzmán, *Memoirs*, p. 269.

for a government of the people rather than the dictatorship of one man.[14]

Villa then suggested that the three of them, Obregón, González, and himself, unite behind one trustworthy candidate for president. According to Obregón, Villa again offered him the presidency, and according to Villa himself he suggested several candidates, among them Felipe Angeles, whom Obregón hated, and Obregón himself.[15]

Despite the outward amicability of these discussions, Obregón was well aware of the danger of alienating Villa, whom he described as "a man who has trouble controlling his nerves." He reported, "I could see without any effort that should he become suspicious my cause would be lying in the dust along with my head." He felt that Luis Aguirre Benavides was trying to prevent Villa's complete rupture with the first chief, but Angeles and Urbina, among others, were trying to provoke it. Obregón was aided in his attempt at unity by the friendships developing between his officers and Villa's and especially by the fact that one of his staff, Julio Madero, had a brother, Raul, in Villa's camp. Both, of course, were brothers of the dead revolutionary president, and their presence in both camps gave a symbolic unity to the two forces.[16]

On August 28, Villa and Obregón arrived together in Nogales, Arizona, having traveled for the most part on the U.S. side of the border. Villa reported that they were well received by the North Americans in El Paso as they crossed the International Bridge. Both the citizens who had come to observe and the authorities who had come to speak with them were friendly and encouraging. Villa felt that this reception

[14]Canova to Secretary of State, August 22, 1914, and Cobb for Carothers to Secretary of State, August 26, 1914, both in U.S. Department of State, Records Relating to the Internal Affairs of Mexico, 1910–1929, microfilm, University of Texas at Austin (archive cited hereafter as USDS), 812.00/12960, 13003; Guzmán, *Memoirs*, p. 290.

[15]Guzmán, *Memoirs*, p. 290; Obregón, *Ocho mil kilómetros*, p. 168.

[16]Obregón, *Ocho mil kilómetros*, p. 169.

reflected Washington's good feeling toward the revolutionary chiefs.[17]

By the time of the trip, Maytorena had advanced into Nogales, Sonora, which had been abandoned by Calles' troops to avoid bloodshed, probably at Obregón's request. The next day Villa crossed the border alone to speak with him and to assure Obregón's safety. Maytorena again vilified Obregón but agreed to a conference, and at noon Villa recrossed the border to bring the Sonoran general across the line.[18]

Despite warnings from friends throughout the state that Maytorena's jealousy would put Obregón's life in danger, Obregón and Villa, along with Luis Aguirre Benavides, crossed the line into Mexico at 2:00 P.M. and went to meet with the governor at his home. Obregón asked that they be joined by Colonels Urbalejo and Acosta, who had fought under his command and were now with Maytorena, and this request was granted. Upon their entrance, Obregón challenged Maytorena to substantiate the charges of treason and insubordination against him that he had been spreading, but Maytorena was unable to produce any evidence. He also asked the two colonels if they had ever witnessed any attempt by him to betray the governor in word or deed. They answered that they had not. An agreement was then reached with some dispatch, apparently because Maytorena was unable to stand up to Obregón face-to-face.[19]

Maytorena was given control of the armies in Sonora and recognized Obregón as his military chief, evidently not realizing that he had thus implicitly recognized his subordination to Carranza as well. Obregón and Villa then crossed again into the United States, but the next day Maytorena, discovering his mistake, issued a manifesto viciously attacking Obregón as a traitor and a "bastard son of Sonora." Obregón hoped that this overt act of hostility would lead Villa to abandon Maytorena, and Villa agreed that the manifesto was grossly unfair, but

17Guzmán, *Memoirs*, p. 292.

18Ibid., p. 293. See also "Informe rendido por el General Benjamín G. Hill," Documento #2, in Barragán, *Historia del Ejército*, 2:547.

19Obregón, *Ocho mil kilómetros*, pp. 169–171.

he was unwilling to sacrifice a potential supporter for an obvious rival for revolutionary preeminence in the north.[20]

However, in the face of the hostile document, Villa was compelled to acquiesce in Maytorena's removal from military command in Sonora, and he and Obregón agreed that Juan Cabral, a general of considerably less controversial character, should be brought back from outside the state to be military governor. Maytorena was allowed to keep the troops under his command, Calles' forces were to be passed to General Hill, and both groups were ordered to stay where they were for the time being.[21]

Obregón and Villa returned to Chihuahua, where they came to further agreements about the problem in Sonora. Calles' troops were to be moved to Chihuahua, where they would be under the general command of Villa, Maytorena's troops would be dispersed, and Cabral would be instructed to protect the person of Maytorena, who would leave the governorship. Municipal elections would be held as quickly as possible in order to restore constitutional government in the area.[22]

In a separate statement Villa and Obregón jointly petitioned Carranza regarding the future government of the country. At this time they were able to reach agreement on many questions. First of all, Carranza was urged to assume the title of interim president and to form a cabinet, thus ending the extralegal status of his government. He was asked to appoint judges to the supreme court as quickly as possible and to establish a civilian judiciary. Councils should be selected to govern the states, and after these councils had been chosen elections on the federal and local level should be held. The new federal congress would choose a civilian president and enact laws benefiting the poor. Officers in the "new National Army" would be

---

[20]Guzmán, *Memoirs*, p. 297; Obregón, *Ocho mil kilómetros*, p. 173; Luis Aguirre Benavides, *De Francisco I. Madero a Francisco Villa: Memorias de un revolucionario*, p. 182.

[21]Obregón, *Ocho mil kilómetros*, p. 175; Guzmán, *Memoirs*, p. 297.

[22]Bases para cambios político-militares en Sonora, September 3, 1914, PHS/59; Guzmán, *Memoirs*, p. 301; Aguirre Benavides, *De Francisco Madero*, pp. 183–184.

restricted from holding major civil offices, particularly those of president and governor. All men currently under arms would have to resign from the army at least six months before becoming candidates, which would exclude Villa and Obregón themselves, at least initially. A further point indicated that the interim president, that is, Carranza, would be prohibited from succeeding himself in office. Thus the door would have been opened for a compromise candidate.[23]

An interesting point in the agreement was the last clause, number nine, which dealt with the question of land distribution. Villa was well aware of the importance of the desire for land in the motivation of revolutionary troops, and Obregón, who would become the master of the immediate payoff in future dealings with revolutionary groups, was learning. The clause called for the interim governors of the states to name agrarian commissions as soon as they came into office. These agrarian commissions, with a representative from each district of the state, would study the "agrarian problem," that is, the land question, and would develop proposals for the new state congresses. These proposals would then be enacted into law.[24]

Thus, two of the major leaders of the Revolution came down strongly for immediate action on land as a reward for revolutionary service. Further, they were willing to consider the problem of separating the military per se from politics, when they asked that military men be prevented from holding major government offices at the national and state level. Thus, revolutionary leaders would have to choose between the institutional military, the "new National Army," and civilian politics. Obregón, who had never thought of himself as a military man, but rather as a citizen who had taken arms at a time of crisis, was already conscious of the dangers of a political situation in which military factions became arbiters. He was thus looking down the road to the establishment of a civilian government, but he would consistently support the right of the revolutionary army, those validated by the experience of revolutionary vio-

[23]Obregón, *Ocho mil kilómetros*, pp. 178–179.
[24]Obregón, *Ocho mil kilómetros*, p. 178; Guzmán, *Memoirs*, pp. 302–303.

lence, to set the initial framework of that civilian government.

Obregón, with this petition in hand, then returned to Mexico City. As might have been expected, Carranza did not agree to its terms despite Obregón's warning that a refusal would lead ultimately to a break with Villa. Carranza would not give up his claims to the elected presidency and would not put himself in a position in which he could not legally aspire to that office. Therefore, he wired Villa that he was willing to assume the interim presidency but would make no agreements limiting his own future political activity. Further, Carranza called for a convention of revolutionary leaders in Mexico City to consider the matter of the future government.[25] Villa was enraged, of course, and refused to come.

It is important to note that at this point Villa's distrust of Carranza had further jaundiced his relationship with Obregón. Obregón himself was careful to deal with Villa as an equal, always giving him the title of divisional general, although Carranza had never raised Villa to this rank. He also paid considerable attention to Villa's opinions on such matters as democracy and social change. Carranza himself, however, dealt with Villa as an unruly and unpleasant subordinate and was obviously afraid of Villa's power.

Moreover, it was plain to Villa's advisers and to Obregón during his first visit to Chihuahua that Villa was still opposed to Carranza and was willing to defeat him in arms if it was not possible to remove him politically. Villa's distrust of Obregón himself was fostered within his own circle of advisers. Some of Villa's lieutenants had been thrown out of Sonora during the early part of the Revolution. Obregón and Villa were clearly the preeminent powers in the north, both politically and militarily, and contending factions in that area were beginning to line up behind one or the other. It was to the advantage of many of these men to keep the two from reaching a permanent accord.[26]

[25]Guzmán, *Memoirs*, pp. 303–304.
[26]Obregón, *Ocho mil kilómetros*, p. 177; Aguirre Benavides, *Grandes batallas*, pp. 200–201; Charles C. Cumberland, *Mexican Revolution: The Constitutionalist Years*, p. 156.

Further, it was almost a foregone conclusion that May-torena, Calles, and Hill would not resolve their differences just because Villa and Obregón had worked out an agreement. In addition, in Obregón's opinion, Villa immediately violated the agreement himself by ordering Hill's forces to leave Sonora. Hill refused, of course, and Villa wired Obregón on the eighth of September complaining that Hill would not release the towns he held to Maytorena.[27] Villa believed that this refusal was made on Obregón's orders.

A further problem was caused by the presence of North American troops in Veracruz. Obregón had been opposed to their presence since their arrival, but Villa had vacillated. At that time he still maintained a good relationship with the United States, particularly the border authorities. When Obregón wired Villa for his support on the petition to Carranza asking him to demand the withdrawal of these troops, Villa initially agreed. After Villa reconsidered, he telegraphed Obregón asking him to withhold his name until he had thought it over. Villa claimed that the request was made because Woodrow Wilson, the U.S. president at the time, was disposed to remove the troops anyway. Obregón contended that it was because Villa hoped to obtain aid for himself from the United States. In any case, the story had already been released to the newspapers in Mexico City and published, and Villa was furious.[28]

Meanwhile, Obregón's own visibility in the United States was growing. Woodrow Wilson's special representative in Mexico City, Paul Fuller, was apprised of the Villa-Obregón agreement and took it upon himself to visit Obregón at his office. Fuller was looking for more information on the military situation in the north, which everyone recognized as crucial to the future of the Revolution, and wanted to learn more about this new leader who had emerged into prominence in the last year. By Obregón's report, Fuller suggested that Obregón maintain a representative close to the government in Washing-ton, but Obregón declined, indicating that he was a member of

[27]Obregón, *Ocho mil kilómetros*, p. 183; Guzmán, *Memoirs*, p. 314.
[28]Obregón, *Ocho mil kilómetros*, pp. 184–185; Guzmán, *Memoirs*, p. 307.

the Constitutionalist government, which already had a representative in the United States. Fuller went on to indicate that Villa had his own representative in the United States, but Obregón was not interested. Fuller then went to Carranza to urge adoption of the Villa-Obregón plan, emphasizing that the establishment of a viable government would be an important prior condition to the North American evacuation of Veracruz. Carranza was enraged and uncompromising.[29]

Carranza, though increasingly suspicious of Obregón, still needed his military support and thus discussed with him the possibility of his taking over the War Department at this time. Obregón declined, wishing to maintain his own freedom of movement, and another Sonoran, former governor Ignacio Pesqueira, was given the post. His title was only assistant secretary of war, however, as Carranza himself retained ultimate authority over Constitutionalist military activity.[30] Carranza would not offer Obregón so high a position again until forced to by circumstance. For the time being, Obregón remained free to mediate with Villa.

By this time, Obregón had given up hope of a lasting accommodation with Villa, and his second visit to Chihuahua was an attempt to win all the "good elements" among Villa's supporters to the Constitutionalist side. Obregón was sure that war between the Constitutionalists and the Villistas was inevitable. Further, he believed that there were many officers and men in Villa's Division of the North who felt "a natural repugnance for many of the actions of their chief" and who were thus ripe for conversion. However, arriving in Chihuahua on the sixteenth of September, he found many of Villa's subordinates so terrified that they would not speak to him. On the other hand, José Isabel Robles and Eugenio Aguirre Benavides, two of the most important generals under Villa's command, seemed to be strongly discontented by Villa's intransigence, and Obregón saw them as potential allies. Contacts with

[29]Obregón, *Ocho mil kilómetros*, pp. 180–181; Larry D. Hill, *Emissaries to a Revolution: Woodrow Wilson's Agents in Mexico*, p. 242.
[30]Obregón, *Ocho mil kilómetros*, p. 182.

individuals in Villa's camp had to be very careful, however, as Obregón knew that "should the least suspicion fall on us, we would be erased from the list of the living."[31]

Nevertheless, Obregón, who had been feted constantly during his earlier trip to Chihuahua, responded to these earlier invitations by planning a dance in honor of the Division of the North to be given by his staff. This event was scheduled for the second day of his visit. However, while he was lunching that day with Raul Madero, another potential ally, Villa called him to his house. On arrival, he found Villa in a fury over a message from Maytorena that announced that he was being attacked by Hill and Calles. After insisting that Obregón send a telegram to Hill and Calles to ask them to stop the attack, to which Obregón acquiesced, he turned irately to an aide and asked him to summon a squad of his elite troops, the Dorados, to execute Obregón as a traitor. This order was received with dismay by some and delight by others, principally one man who had earlier been expelled from Obregón's camp in Sonora. Villa then reacted with disgust and anger at the bloodthirstiness of this man and shouted at him to leave the room. Meanwhile he began pacing up and down the room, continuing to yell threats at Obregón. Obregón, deciding that the only way to slow him down was to make him believe that he would be giving the opposing side an advantage, said, "Well, personally, you'll be doing me a favor, because this death will give me a stature I don't actually have, and the only one injured will be yourself."[32] By this time, the firing squad had arrived, and Obregón's officers had been confined to Obregón's room. Meanwhile, the men of the Division of the North began to gather and argue both pro and con, while Leon Canova, President Wilson's representative, arrived to talk to Villa but was forced

[31]Ibid., pp. 199–200.

[32]Ibid., pp. 202–204; Guzmán, Memoirs, p. 316. See similar telegram quoted in Carranza to Aguilar, September 17, 1914, Archivo de Venustiano Carranza, Centro de Estudios Históricos—Condumex (archive cited hereafter as AC).

to go away without being received. Villa meanwhile left the room, retiring to the interior of the house.[33]

An hour later, Villa returned, called the guard away from the door, sent the firing squad away, and invited Obregón to sit by his side. As Obregón described it later, "Never have I accepted an invitation more eagerly." Then Villa repentantly told him that he did not shoot defenseless men, much less a guest. Later they went in to dinner. Meanwhile, Obregón's officers had been released and continued preparations for the dance, which took place after dinner, as scheduled. Obregón danced all night. Villa did not attend, having lost his taste for merrymaking, but Obregón's sangfroid impressed many.[34] However, the situation was still so tense that Obregón sent a messenger to Hill in Sonora, instructing him to ignore any orders in his name issuing from Villa's headquarters. He included a sum of money to be distributed to the families of his personal staff in the event that they should be murdered along with him. The messenger, unable to leave temporarily, spent a nervous night in Canova's room.[35] The next day, Villa permitted Obregón to leave for Mexico City but called the train back to Chihuahua almost immediately.

Meanwhile, Carranza was making active preparations for war. On receiving word from Hill in regard to the telegrams that were issuing from Chihuahua in Obregón's name, he congratulated Hill on refusing to obey them and instructed him to continue in this policy until word that Obregón was safely out of Villa's clutches should be received. He further ordered Hill to use such means as necessary to force Maytorena to submit to order, a difficult job as Maytorena's forces were far stronger than Hill's, and stated that he was sending troops and ammunition from the south to reinforce Hill. He also instructed Hill

---

[33]Obregón, *Ocho mil kilómetros*, p. 204; Canova to Secretary of State, September 11, 1914, USDS 812.00/13323.

[34]Obregón, *Ocho mil kilómetros*, pp. 204–205; Guzmán, *Memoirs*, p. 318; Victor Anda, interview, PHO/1/46, p. 31.

[35]Obregón, *Ocho mil kilómetros*, p. 205; Canova to Secretary of State, September 25, 1914, USDS 812.00/13326.

to request Juan Cabral, who was to have taken over as governor of Sonora, to return to Mexico City immediately. Cabral, however, sickened by the political intrigues in progress, crossed the border to El Paso, Texas, announcing that "following the dictates of my conscience I will not participate any further in the coming factional struggle."[36]

Carranza also alerted leaders in other parts of the country that yet another fight was upcoming. For example, he wrote to Pánfilo Natera in Aguascalientes, a major point Villa might be expected to take in a drive on Mexico City, that Villa was proceeding in bad faith and was continuing to import arms with the intention of rebelling against the first chief's government. Further, he accused Villa of fomenting rebellion in Sonora, of sending Felipe Angeles to Baja California to maintain Villista power there with federal troops, and of sending forces to Durango to threaten the Arrietas. He warned Natera, who would later support Villa, to be alert for an invasion or attack by Villa's troops. Natera replied that he would try to prevent the advance of Villista troops but insisted on further consultation with the first chief in the hope of solving the difficulties.[37] Natera was already wavering.

On the same day, Maytorena in Sonora publicly withdrew his recognition of the Carranza government, and Villa announced his own withdrawal of support because of indignities that the Division of the North had suffered at the hands of Carranza. In a letter from Villa to the Arrietas in Durango, he stated, "We have decided to fight only against the personality of Venustiano Carranza, without any intention of threatening or molesting the other leaders who have fought for the defeat of the usurper's government. . . ."[38]

On the evening of this eventful day, Obregón again started south by rail. This time Roque González Garza, Villa's close

[36]Simpich to Secretary of State, September 22, 1914, USDS 812.00/13249; Cabral to Carranza, September 23, 1914, PHS/59.

[37]Carranza to Natera, September 22 and 23, 1914, and Natera to Carranza, September 23, 1914, all in PHS/59.

[38]José María Maytorena, Manifesto, September 23, 1914, and Villa to Arrietas, September 23, 1914, both in PHS/59.

and trusted adviser, went with him. Almost immediately, Villa wired ahead for a train to stop Obregón at an intermediate point between Chihuahua and Mexico City. However, probably by pure luck, Obregón's train continued on through the night, passing the train instructed to stop him, which had pulled over onto a siding to await daybreak. Villa then wired instructions to Obregón's train to return. Obregón refused, and his train continued south.

Fortunately for Obregón, Villa's telegram had also been picked up farther down the line by the telegraph station serving Eugenio Aguirre Benavides' and José Isabel Robles' commands. These two men, though supporters of Villa, would not acquiesce in the assassination of Obregón and sent their own train to meet Obregón's and to bring him safely through the lines.[39] Thus accompanied, Obregón made his way through hostile territory and back to Mexico City.

Therefore, while Carranza was calling for a meeting of revolutionary leaders in Mexico City to map out future plans for the governance of the country, one of his two major subordinates was threatening the life of the other. Obregón's peace missions seemed to have failed, although he would make one more major effort. However, Obregón's visits to Villa had given him certain benefits for the struggle to come. First, he knew and understood Villa better, having had the opportunity to size him up as an opponent. Second, he had gained insight into the motivation of Villa's forces and particularly was coming to understand the importance of land in return for revolutionary support. In the third place, he was able to meet the men of the Division of the North face-to-face, and the impression that he had left with many of them was good. Thus, they became potential allies in the years to follow. Finally, he was becoming vividly aware of the near impossibility of the reestablishment of the orderly functioning of government in a country in which a number of separate leaders controlled their own armed forces.

[39]Obregón, *Ocho mil kilómetros*, p. 214; Canova to Secretary of State, October 9, 1914, USDS 812.00/27411.

CHAPTER 6

The Convention of Aguascalientes

Given the events of August and September, 1914, it was evident that the Convention of Aguascalientes was never destined to be a meeting between united leaders to map out a common future course for revolutionary Mexico. On the contrary, factions had already developed, new alliances were being strengthened, and all sides were preparing for war. Even in August, the most that might have been hoped of the Convention was the working out of a peaceful modus vivendi between antagonistic leaders, but by October such an accommodation had already become impossible. The differences and mutual suspicions between Carranza and Villa, exacerbated by the open warfare in Sonora between Maytorena on the one hand and Hill and Calles on the other, doomed the Convention as a peacemaking body from the start. Given the open splits in the Constitutionalist ranks, it is easy to understand why no progress was made in the rebuilding of the destroyed political institutions of the country or in the effective introduction of any of the social changes for which they had ostensibly been fighting. The fact that all major groups that had participated in the defeat of Huerta attended the Convention has given the appearance of a unity and a will to cooperate for the good of the country that never existed. No group that attended the Convention was willing at that time to make major concessions to preserve peace.

The question, then, is not why the Convention failed but how it ever came to be held at all. The answer, perhaps, is that the various factions came to view it as a forum before the

Mexican people, as well as foreign powers, which might concede recognition to one group or another. The group gaining control of the Convention would also gain an aura of legitimacy within the Mexican nation. But although Villa and Zapata were to gain control of the Convention, they were ultimately to lose control of the Revolution itself, as much because they were unable to cooperate between themselves as because they were defeated in battle by Obregón and Carranza. Obregón, for his part, had badly misjudged the effect the Convention would have on Villa's image. He assumed that Villa would be exposed as unreasonable and bloodthirsty, but Villa on the contrary gained through his control of the Convention a legitimacy that would have been impossible for him to obtain in any other way. Nevertheless, Villa's inability to use effectively the power he had gained and Zapata's own growing distrust of Villa led ultimately to the discrediting of the Convention government itself.[1] Therefore, Obregón, in leaving the Convention and by making a decision to join the apparent loser, in fact became the ultimate winner. Carranza, moreover, would have been unable to retain power without Obregón's military help.

Before the Convention, Obregón had felt that it might be possible to form a group of revolutionary leaders who would be willing to forsake both Villa and Carranza in favor of a government directed by themselves as independents.[2] His experience with Villa in Chihuahua had shown him that even in the Division of the North there were moderates who favored revolutionary unity, notably Eugenio Aguirre Benavides and José Isabel Robles, who had helped him escape from Villa. Within the Constitutionalist ranks, he felt that he could find many leaders who would be willing to do without Carranza. It seems clear that even before the Convention, Obregón con-

---

[1] For a discussion of the problems, both practical and ideological, between Villistas and Zapatistas in the Convention, see Luis Fernando Amaya, *La Soberana Convención Revolucionaria 1914–1916*, especially pp. 187–190, 212–222.

[2] See Amado Aguirre, *Mis memorias de campaña: Apuntes para la historia*, p. 70; Juan Hurtado Olín, interview, PHO/1/30, p. 41; Alvaro Obregón, *Ocho mil kilómetros en campaña*, pp. 216–218.

templated the eventual removal of both leaders, which would improve the chances for unity among the other revolutionary elements while bettering his own position within the Revolution. He had come to hate Villa, having narrowly escaped assassination at his hands, and he was distrustful of Carranza, who had refused to go along with the political measures that he and Villa had suggested. Therefore, he himself took the initiative in arranging for a meeting of revolutionary leaders from all camps.

Leaving Mexico City almost immediately after his eventful return from Chihuahua, he returned north as far as Zacatecas to confer with Robles and Aguirre Benavides as well as Pánfilo Natera, who later was to be responsible for assuring neutrality at the Convention. During these meetings, it was agreed that a convention of revolutionary leaders should meet at Aguascalientes, an area under the control of Natera, who was nominally neutral.[3] In fact, Aguascalientes was always vulnerable to military pressure from Villa's Division of the North, which was close at hand. In any case, Carranza did not sanction this convention and called his own meeting of revolutionary leaders to start October 1, 1914, in Mexico City.

Although those attending this early meeting resolved almost immediately to go to Aguascalientes, despite Carranza's opposition, it was important in exposing Obregón's own concerns and ambivalences about military versus civilian rule. Though he already feared the dangers of military factionalism, it was his clear tendency to favor members of the revolutionary army as valid decision makers for the country. The question of who should attend Aguascalientes emerged early, as Obregón's Sonoran friend Roberto V. Pesqueira was suggested as a delegate to the Convention. Obregón insisted that the agreement with Villa provided only for military men at the Convention, while civilian Luis Cabrera pointed out that many civilians had served the Revolution equally well. After a secret meeting between

---

[3]Obregón left Mexico City on September 27, 1914, only four days after his life had hung in the balance in Chihuahua. He was accompanied by Francisco R. Serrano, his chief of staff, and Captain Jesús M. Garza, both of whom were to play major roles in his rise to the presidency (see *Nueva Patria* [Mexico City], September 28, 1914).

Obregón and other military delegates, it was decided to restrict attendance along military lines, except for those who attended as representatives of military leaders. Obregón, who had not made the proposal himself, said that though it was a "crime" to exclude those civilians who had served the Revolution well, he supported the resolution on the basis that the military phase of the Revolution was not yet over.[4]

Cabrera, however, continued to defend his own right to attend the Aguascalientes conference until October 5, when he challenged Obregón's position, saying that of 14 million Mexicans, only 150,000 would be represented at an exclusively military meeting. Obregón, furious, replied that 14 million Mexicans had voted unanimously for Madero and had let him be assassinated. The civilians had vacillated, failing to revenge themselves on his successor. He then stated: "We intend to return their liberties to those 14 million and we will try to better their social condition. . . . Señor Cabrera, do you believe that if we give them peace and liberty, these 14 million inhabitants will protest because only we represent them?" The final decision of the assembly was to permit Cabrera to attend as a special exception, an honor he finally declined.[5]

A further unsettling consequence of the Mexico City conference arose from the acquainting of the delegates with the events that had taken place in Chihuahua and Obregón's narrow escape. Many of these leaders, both independents and those closely associated with Carranza, were then afraid to attend the Convention in person so close to Villa's troops. Instead, they sent representatives, who could not have been expected to be as forceful as their chiefs.[6] Villa himself did not attend, although he did visit the Convention briefly to sign the revolutionary flag, but his presence was strongly felt by the other delegates. Obregón himself was the only major leader who did attend as

[4]Florencio Barrera Fuentes, ed., *Crónicas y debates de las sesiones de la Soberana Convención Revolucionaria*, 1:35, 37–38.

[5]Ibid., pp. 62–63.

[6]Ibid., p. 29; Amaya, *La Soberana Convención*, p. 171. A good summary of the entire proceedings of this preliminary meeting may be found in *El Demócrata* (Mexico City), October 7, 1914.

a functioning delegate, and although he was eager to bring the various factions together, minus Villa and Carranza, this task proved impossible.

The Convention that ensued was a debacle, and what resulted was neither reactionary nor progressive but simply chaotic. The meeting gave birth to a government of democratic appearance, directed by two men, Villa and Zapata, who were able to govern their own areas but had little in their experience to aid them in the task of governing a country. As a result, the government was headless, decisions were made by accommodation of the two chiefs until the tacit defection of Zapata, and the Convention itself never furnished viable direction for the country.[7]

As we have seen, Carranza himself was by no means reconciled to the Convention of Aguascalientes and had no intention of entering any arrangement that would include Pancho Villa as a principal power. He told Obregón before Obregón's departure for the north that he would not sanction any arrangement that would turn the country over to "a man like Villa."[8] Carranza himself refused to attend, feeling that the situation was hopeless and ultimately would be resolved by military means.

Villa, also reluctant to attend in person, nevertheless sent his representatives in full force. His own one-day appearance in Aguascalientes was emotional, however. He and Obregón, on the podium together, embraced in a gesture of revolutionary solidarity. Then Villa, looking at Obregón, said: "I have received various telegrams asking me if I will be the Pascual Orozco of the north. History will decide who Mexico's true sons are." Obregón answered, "Precisely, sir."[9] Still, Villa was

[7]See comments by Luis Cabrera, "The Mexican Revolution—Its Causes, Purposes, and Results," *Annals of the American Academy* 69, 1st supplement (January, 1917). The newspapers in Mexico City during the Convention period are filled with reports of the chaotic conditions there and the Convention government's attempts to deal with them. See, for example, such Conventionist publications as *El Norte, El Renovador,* and *Los Sucesos.*

[8]Obregón, *Ocho mil kilómetros,* p. 218. Villa, on his part, continued to fulminate against Carranza (see *Dallas Morning News,* October 11, 1914).

[9]*Nueva Patria* (Mexico City), October 18, 1914.

clearly unwilling to accept any arrangement that provided for Carranza's continuance as chief executive, by whatever title, and Carranza would accept no alternative.

The conflict between the various factions was so serious that order and personal safety were major problems from the beginning of the Convention. Villa prudently stationed his men in Guadalupe, 100 miles north of Aguascalientes on the railroad lines.[10] His troops hung like a specter over the heads of the delegates, but even closer were Pánfilo Natera's men, the group responsible for keeping order in the city of Aguascalientes itself. It is not insignificant that this general owed a considerable debt of gratitude to Villa, who had relieved him at the battle of Zacatecas. Among many reported incidents of violence, Obregón's own car was fired upon in the city during the Convention.[11]

The Mexico City newspapers frequently described the pressure and harassment directed against the delegates, and Carranza remained hostile to the Convention's deliberations. As early as October 17, 1914, just seven days after the Convention had opened and while Obregón was working hard to maintain a spirit of unity in the mutually suspicious members of the assemblage, *El Liberal*, a pro-Carranza paper, carried a bitter editorial by Heriberto Barrón, claiming that the treasonous intention of the Convention was to disown Carranza. Obregón and Eduardo Hay, both delegates, wrote immediately to *Nueva Patria*, another Mexico City daily more favorable to the Convention, protesting that this type of editorial was damaging the chances for future peace in the country.[12] However, Obregón himself never felt safe in Aguascalientes, and on October 19 he and three other leaders asked the Convention to take measures to insure the neutrality of the town and the safety of the delegates.

[10]Robert E. Quirk, *The Mexican Revolution, 1914–1915: The Convention of Aguascalientes*, p. 103. See also *San Antonio Express*, October 21, 1914.

[11]Antonio I. Villarreal, "The Real Story of the Aguascalientes Convention," in *Immediate Causes of the Present Conflict in Mexico*. See also *Dallas Morning News*, October 21, 1914; *New York Times*, October 21, 1914.

[12]*El Liberal* (Mexico City), October 17, 1914; *Nueva Patria* (Mexico City), October 19, 1914.

Roque González Garza, the principal Villa delegate, and Antonio Villarreal, the head of the convention's governing board, agreed to reduce their own armed escorts and to ask other leaders to do the same.[13] However, nothing came of such requests.

The mutual suspicions of the delegates, almost all men accustomed to violence, made the situation potentially explosive. Moreover, most of the delegates and their escorts were constantly armed, despite agreements to the contrary.

Villa, of course, stayed with his troops rather than attend as a functioning delegate; he permitted his adviser, Roque González Garza, to look after his interests. Villa had lost considerable prestige as a result of the incidents with Obregón, and Villa's absence contrasted unfavorably with Obregón's presence, particularly since the Convention was held within easy range of the main body of Villa's troops. Nevertheless, González Garza, a skilled and strong-minded negotiator, carefully protected and enhanced Villa's interests. He maintained a position of sweet reasonability, knowing all the while that he had the power of the Division of the North behind him. Meanwhile, the troops that had been directly under Obregón's command were being disbanded in Mexico City.[14] It is possible that this move was deliberate on the part of Carranza, who obviously feared betrayal by the Convention, or it may have been mere coincidence.

With all of these factors in the background, the wrangle over the credentials of the delegates was just as bitter as might be expected. The Convention opened in the Morelos Theater in Aguascalientes on October 10, and the assembled delegates immediately declared themselves to be a new Convention, not a continuation of the meeting in Mexico City. Moreover, they declared themselves to be sovereign in the country. Antonio Villarreal, a Carrancista but a known radical, was chosen president of the governing board and the two vice-presidents were Pánfilo Natera, whose troops were "assuring the neutrality" of

[13]*Nueva Patria* (Mexico City), October 19, 1914.
[14]Canova to Secretary of State, October 10, 1914, USDS 812.00/27411; Quirk, *The Mexican Revolution*, p. 120.

Lieutenant Colonel Obregón with Captain Antonio Guerrero (*left*) after the battle against the Orozquistas in Ojitos, Chihuahua, 1912. *Casasola, INAH*

From left: Sonoran governor Jose María Maytorena, First Chief Venustiano Carranza, and General Obregón in front of artillery taken from federal forces during the battles of Santa Rosa and Santa María, 1913. *Casasola, INAH*

Left: Yaqui Indian, fighting under Obregón's command, 1913. *Library, Universidad de Sonora. Upper right:* Yaqui chieftain Luis Bule, who fought for Obregón, with one of his sons, ca. 1913. *Fondo de Cultura Económica. Lower right:* Train seized from the federals in the Battle of Orendáin, Jalisco, 1914. *Library, Universidad de Sonora*

Foreground, left to right, starting in center: Obregón, photographer Jesús Abitia, and Captain Francisco Serrano, ca. 1913. *Fondo de Cultura Económica*

ADOR GUSTAVO SALINAS PREPARANDOSE
EFECTUAR UN VUELO SOBRE MAZATLAN SIN.

Aviator Gustavo Salinas, preparing to fly over Mazatlán, Sonora, in one of the first planes used for military reconnaissance, May, 1914. *Library, Universidad de Sonora*

Obregón (*center, wearing white*) giving orders for the attack on Guadalajara, 1914. *Casasola, INAH*

From left: Obregón, First Chief Carranza, and General Pablo González triumphantly entering Mexico City, August 20, 1914. *Casasola, INAH*

Obregón and Carranza (*second and third from left*) standing in front of
the Presidential Chair in Chapultepec Palace in Mexico City, September,
1914. *Brown Bros.*

Obregón's first visit to Chihuahua to confer with Pancho Villa, August, 1914. Present were General John Pershing (*second from left*), Obregón (*third from left*), Rodolfo Fierro (*center, in white hat and suit*), Carothers, who was Woodrow Wilson's special emissary to Villa (*leaning on pole at right*), and Villa (*immediately to Carothers' right*). *International*

Obregón and Villa on their way to interview Governor Maytorena in Sonora, 1914. *Front, from left*: Obregón, Villa, and Pershing; *second row, from left*: Villa's aides Julio Madero (*between Obregón and Villa*) and Luis Aguirre Benavides (*between Villa and Pershing*) and Pershing's aide George Patton. *Casasola, INAH*

Eulalio Gutiérrez (*left foreground, in business suit*) and Obregón (*center*) arriving at the military Convention of Aguascalientes, October, 1914. *Casasola, INAH*

Left: Obregón (*left*) and Cándido Aguilar at a banquet for Carranza after the break-up of the Aguascalientes convention, November, 1914. *Casasola, INAH. Right*: Obregón aide Francisco Serrano (*left*), Obregón, and unidentified aide at Hotel Saint Francis, Obregón's headquarters after he retook Mexico City, late January, 1915. *Casasola, INAH*

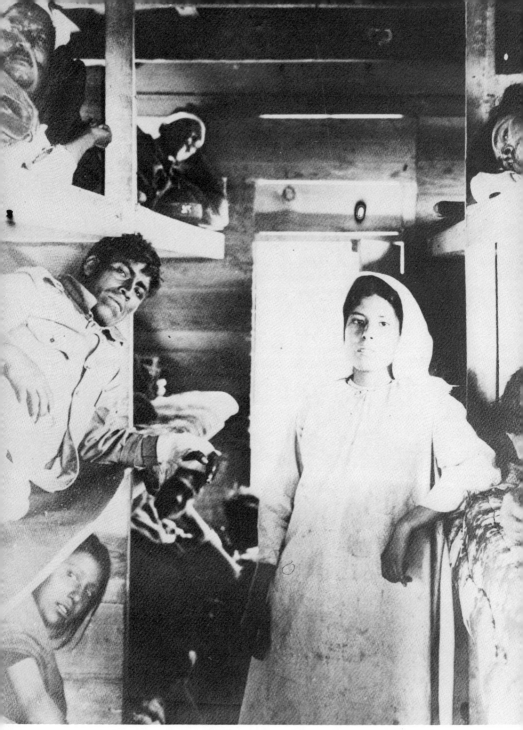

Hospital car for Obregón's forces during Battle of León against Villa, May, 1915. *Library, Universidad de Sonora*

the meeting, and José Isabel Robles, the Villista general who had helped save Obregón's life. Thus a Carrancista became chairman of the meeting, but two potentially pro-Villista generals sat on the governing body as well.[15]

The day of the selection of Villarreal as president was the most tense, with most delegates expecting trouble. One Villista later reported that their contingent had gone to the meeting armed and ready and had spread out around the hall in strategic positions. Depending on the situation, they were instructed to fire in a particular way at an agreed-upon signal, which, luckily for all, was never given. He went on to say that the same day a discussion had arisen about withdrawing recognition from both Villa and Carranza, and the argument had gotten hot and heavy, "horribly ugly." He commented that had the shooting started no one would have come out alive, as all the various generals had their own men stationed around the hall as well. Fortunately things calmed down. Another Villista, looking back on the Convention, called it a *cena de negros*, a "chaotic brawl" in local parlance. At the time, this same man had considered Obregón an enemy because he was an enemy of Villa's. Later he felt that Obregón had been the only reasonable voice at the Convention.[16]

After the installation of Villarreal, there was a moment of peace as each delegate went forward to swear allegiance to the Convention and to sign his name to the Mexican flag on the stage. From this point forward, the Convention went considerably less smoothly.

The qualifications for being seated as a representative at the Convention had been set some time before by Villa's and Carranza's representatives. They had decided that only military men would be represented, each chief being accepted if he had commanded at least a thousand men and had entered the Revolution before the Battle of Zacatecas, back in the days when the success of the Revolution was still in doubt. However, González

[15]Barrera Fuentes, *Crónicas y debates*, p. 14; Quirk, *The Mexican Revolution*, p. 101.
[16]Gilberto Navas Presa, interview, PHO/1/26, pp. 20–23; José de Baez, interview, PHO/1/34, pp. 7–8

Garza, as Villa's representative, favored the widest possible representation. He suggested in an early speech that each one thousand men be represented by one vote, a somewhat different interpretation of the early agreement, which would have included only recognized military leaders who had more than this number of men. Obregón and some other leaders opposed González Garza's position strongly, insisting that only generals of recognized service be allowed to participate.[17] Villa was hoping to pack the assembly, and Obregón knew it.

An example of the "leaders" that Villa attempted to seat in the assembly was the owner of a San Antonio bar. This individual had taken $6,000 of revolutionary funds and had gone to the United States to buy armaments for the troops. However, he had decided instead to purchase the bar, and he had stayed in San Antonio out of harm's way until the fighting was over. The delegates, after Obregón's protest, refused to seat him.[18]

These wrangles continued for two or three days, until at last Obregón rose to make a major speech. His topic was revolutionary disunity. He declared that he had feared the growth of factionalism as early as August, 1914, when his troops first entered Mexico City. At that time he already foresaw "a dark cloud rising in the North, . . . a dense cloud rising in the South, and a bolt of lightning that announced the storm to come." He told of his visits to the north, the suspicions that men on both sides had tried to sow in his mind about the good faith of the other, and the doubts cast on his own mission. He denied that he had been anything less than open with both sides: "I did not betray Carranza; . . . I did not betray Villa, . . . I did not betray my country, and I will live my life in its service." He then called again for unity, and for a short time the Convention worked in relative harmony.[19]

[17]Roque González Garza, "Discurso leido por el C. Coronel Roque González Garza en la solemne apertura de la Convención Militar Revolucionaria de Aguascalientes, la noche de 14 de octubre de 1914," p. 6; Barrera Fuentes, *Crónicas y debates*, p. 96.

[18]Barrera Fuentes, *Crónicas y debates*, p. 133.

[19]Ibid., pp. 234–235. See also Federico Cervantes, *Felipe Angeles en la Revolución Mexicana*, p. 113.

But by the next day, the wrangling had begun once more. The problems in Sonora, which had occupied Obregón and Villa, had broken out into open warfare and led to the usual name-calling, charges, and counter-charges.[20] Obregón asked that the delegates cease discussing personalities and get on with the business of planning the peace. After one delegate had denounced Plutarco Elías Calles, leader of Carranza's supporters in Sonora, as being of "infamous memory," Obregón in exasperation called for the delegates to forget the past and decide instead what should be done in the future.[21]

The Zapatistas, who had been invited by Villa's emissary, Felipe Angeles, arrived on October 26, adding another dimension to the factionalism of the Convention. From the beginning of their participation it was obvious that they had no interest in revolutionary impartiality. On the contrary, they intended to make the Convention the political vehicle of a Villa-Zapata alliance. This design was clear from the time of the first speech, when the leader of the Zapatista delegation, Paulino Martínez, took the rostrum. It was emphasized even more strongly, one might even say wildly, with the speech by Antonio Díaz Soto y Gama, a radical young lawyer in Zapata's service. He denounced the Mexican flag, as well as Carranza, whose resignation he demanded, and insisted on the complete adherence of the Convention to the Plan of Ayala, Zapata's own plan for the future of the country, with its heavy agrarian content. His speech was seconded by Villa's representative, Roque González Garza, who insisted that the Convention adopt the plan.[22]

Of course, there was resistance to such a move, and Díaz Soto y Gama's fiery and insulting speech had caused enormous turmoil among the delegates. Obregón, who was visibly agitated by the two speeches, asked González Garza whether he spoke for the whole Villista delegation. In a dramatic gesture, Gon-

[20]For U.S. accounts of the Sonoran fighting, see for example Bliss to Secretary of War, October 18, 1914, U.S. Adjutant General's Office, National Archives, Washington, D.C.: Villa's Revolution, #2212358 (archive cited hereafter as AGO/VR), Box 7642.

[21]Barrera Fuentes, *Crónicas y debates*, p. 269.

[22]Quirk, *The Mexican Revolution*, pp. 109–111.

zález Garza asked all the Villista representatives who did not support the plan to remain seated. All rose to their feet in a block. It was a striking demonstration of the unity of the Villistas with the forces from the south.[23] Obregón himself must have been vividly impressed.

It was not easy, however, to force the Convention down this particular path. Confused and heated debates raged for two days until at last, on October 26, the delegates agreed to accept most of the articles of the Plan of Ayala "in principle."[24]

Meanwhile in Mexico City, Carranza, his civilian advisers, and the Mexico City newspapers were becoming daily more hostile to the Revolutionary Convention. Early in the Convention a delegation, including Obregón, had been sent to the first chief, inviting him to attend. He had refused and had given Obregón a secret communication to read in the event that it became necessary. This letter was addressed to the governing board and sent in a sealed envelope. As the wrangles about the Plan of Ayala and how much of it to accept continued on October 29, Obregón, apparently under instructions from Carranza, rose to read the communication. He began to read from his chair, but the delegates, sensing the importance of the moment, called out for him to ascend the rostrum.[25]

In this letter, Carranza attacked his opponents, specifically Villa and Zapata, saying that they, in their ignorance, had been led astray by reactionary influences. Carranza himself, therefore, had become too radical for them. Thus Carranza turned the tables on these men who distrusted his wealth and aristocratic background by telling them that they were, in fact, the ones who served privilege and wealth. Nevertheless, he said that he was willing to step down himself if it would serve the revolutionary cause. However, he set several strong conditions on his resignation: that a preconstitutional government supported by the Constitutionalist Army be established to carry out necessary social and political reforms until a full Constitu-

23Ibid., p. 112.
24Ibid., p. 114; John Womack, Jr., *Zapata and the Mexican Revolution*, p. 218.
25Barrera Fuentes, *Crónicas y debates*, p. 646.

tional government could be established; that Villa renounce not his aspirations to the presidency or vice-presidency, which nobody had offered him, but his chieftaincy of the Division of the North and leave the country; and that Zapata renounce his command and all pretensions to political posts, both local and national, and likewise leave the country.[26]

Carranza accused the other generals, namely Zapata and Villa, of wanting to use their military power, with or without the title of president, to dominate Mexico. He himself, he indicated, had not attended because he wished to keep Villa away as well, feeling that only in Villa's absence would democratic proceedings be insured. His conviction that proceedings were in fact not at all democratic was obvious throughout his message.[27]

As Obregón finished reading, hysteria and wild accusations of bad faith burst forth from the delegates. González Garza was heard to declare that since the first chief was so blatantly uninterested in the welfare of the Convention, henceforth the delegates would be uninterested in him. After this outburst, chaos reigned. Obregón, finally able to be heard, moved that the session close and suggested a private meeting to try to agree on a formula for peace. On that note, the stormy session ended.[28]

From this point forward, Carrancistas were making preparations for breaking away from the Convention. It was clear that only a stroke of luck would prevent an open rupture, and it is likely that further negotiations were carried on by the adherents of the first chief only to gain time.

Meanwhile Villa received a wire from Felipe Angeles telling him that Carranza had agreed to resign conditioned upon Villa's own withdrawal. Villa's reaction upon seeing the wire was to reply to Angeles: "I propose not only that the Convention retire Carranza from his post in exchange for retiring me from mine but that the Convention order both of us shot."

[26]Ibid., p. 645; "Reply of Carranza to the Convention," in *Historia documental de México*, ed. Ernesto de la Torre Villar et al., p. 477.

[27]"Reply of Carranza," in *Historia documental*, ed. de la Torre Villar et al., p. 477.

[28]*La Convención*, December 14, 1914–January, 1915, article reprinted in Barrera Fuentes, *Crónicas y debates*, p. 649.

Villa's delegates were greatly upset by this reply, not being altogether sure what he was proposing. They wired him for confirmation, and he indicated that he would stick by his offer to resign. Therefore, his delegates drew up a formal act to this effect.[29]

The session of the following day, October 30, was as stormy as the previous one, but the delegates were able to agree overwhelmingly to accept the resignations of both Carranza and Villa. Carranza, of course, had not really submitted his resignation, but that was a point they chose to overlook.[30]

Carranza and Villa were by no means alone in the attacks upon them by delegates. A rumor was widely circulated that Maytorena, the governor of Sonora with whom Obregón had had so much trouble, had made a pact with members of the old Díaz regime, the *científicos*, and had accepted 600 federal forces to add to his military contingent. Moreover, Zapata himself was accused of not observing the armistice and of continuing his depredations in order to improve his bargaining position.[31] In other words, nobody trusted anybody.

On the next day, a great mob was swirling around the Morelos Theater as early as nine in the morning, trying to gain access to the building. Their entrance was prevented by a strong military guard, but some journalists, in their enterprising fashion, were able to sneak in. The arguments began almost immediately and were now principally between the Carrancistas and the Zapatistas. The Villistas were apparently willing to sit back and let things develop for a while.

Obregón rose to try to clarify the status of the southern delegates. He asked them to present a complete list of their demands, be they fifty or five hundred or twenty thousand, so that the Convention could consider all their proposals at once without being constantly threatened.

Díaz Soto y Gama rose, but not to present a list of consolidated demands. Instead, he began to vilify Carranza. Obre-

---

[29]Martín Luis Guzmán, *Memoirs of Pancho Villa*, p. 349.

[30]Quirk, *The Mexican Revolution*, pp. 115–116.

[31]*El Liberal* (Mexico City), October 31–November 1, 1914, articles reprinted in Barrera Fuentes, *Crónicas y debates*, p. 655.

gón called on him to stop discussing personalities, since it was issues that were important. (He was quite wrong on this point: at this time the course of the Convention turned on personalities.) Díaz Soto y Gama began to stamp around the hall, ranting about the slights and injuries he and the Zapatistas had suffered. Obregón sharply attacked him for using language and posturings appropriate only to an actor of the theater. He accused Díaz Soto y Gama of hypocrisy when he said that if the Convention didn't do this or that he would go back to the mountains to fight. He further attacked Díaz Soto y Gama for never having taken up a rifle to defend the Revolution and for having no intention of doing so in the future. Díaz Soto y Gama huffily admitted that in fact he had no intention of taking up a rifle, but instead served the Revolution in an intellectual capacity.[32] Obviously, Obregón was exasperated by the whole proceeding, but the danger of an outbreak of war between military factions was never far from his mind. Therefore, he made one more attempt to unify military forces and bring them under central control.

On November 2, he signed a report, which was issued by the Joint Committee of War and Interior. It was described by U.S. observer Leon Canova as "able, just and politic." Among the seven provisions, which requested the simultaneous resignations of both Villa and Carranza and the naming of a provisional president by the Convention, an article was included abolishing all of the army corps and making all divisions, including Villa's, subject to the War Department, which would be set up by the Convention. The Convention approved the report, 112 to 17, to a storm of cheers.[33]

As the session continued, a stalemate developed over the selection of a replacement for Carranza. Obregón took the initiative in calling a recess, as the session had become so acrimonious that any agreement was impossible. During the interval, he prevailed on the delegates to select a compromise candidate:

[32]This account of the morning's session is from ibid., p. 656.
[33]Canova to Secretary of State, October 30, 1914, USDS 812.00/13658; Schmutz to Secretary of State, November 2, 1914, USDS 812.00/13659; Silliman to Secretary of State, November 2, 1914, USDS 812.00/13660.

Eulalio Gutiérrez, a Constitutionalist general who by some miracle had failed to offend any of the various factions.[34]

Gutiérrez was a colorless and, it developed, a politically ingenuous individual. He had joined the Revolution under Madero, which gave him a certain stature, and as there had been few federal forces in his area he had not lost many engagements. His principal duty in the defeats of both Díaz and Huerta had been blasting railroad bridges and trains rather than leading great bodies of men. It quickly became evident that he was not likely to become a leader, either.[35]

Nevertheless, the delegates were delighted at finally having decided something. When Gutiérrez' election was announced, the cries exploded: "Viva Villa! Viva Carranza! Viva Zapata! Viva la Revolución Mexicana!" The delegates embraced Gutiérrez, and then they surged out onto the street. It was midnight, but the bells were ringing, locomotives were whistling, the delegates cheering. The townspeople as well began to shout "Vivas" for Gutiérrez, and he was accompanied to his hotel by the surging mob.[36]

It was not long, however, before the joy wore off and the wrangling began again. Villa, in a step that removed all doubt about his intention to dominate the Convention by force if necessary, moved several thousand troops from Zacatecas to just north of Aguascalientes.[37] The die was cast.

On November 3 it was decided to send a delegation to Carranza to tell him that he had been removed as first chief. He was perfectly aware of this already, as it had been reported widely in the Mexico City newspapers, and it was the subject of an acid letter that he sent to the Convention pointing out that he had never resigned but had only submitted his conditions for resignation. Nevertheless, an official delegation including Obregón was sent to inform him that he had been replaced. It is likely that the delegates welcomed the opportunity to get

---

[34]Quirk, *The Mexican Revolution*, p. 118.

[35]Ibid., pp. 118–119, 145.

[36]*El Liberal* (Mexico City), November 2–3, 1914, articles reprinted in Barrera Fuentes, *Crónicas y debates*, p. 673.

[37]Quirk, *The Mexican Revolution*, p. 118.

safely away from Aguascalientes, and only one ever returned behind Villa's lines.[38]

Meanwhile, Carranza had left Mexico City, ostensibly on a sight-seeing tour of the pyramids, leaving the capital in the charge of General Lucio Blanco. He did not return to the capital for months. He had felt insecure in Mexico City where he was surrounded by troops of at best doubtful loyalty. By the time Obregón left the Convention to deliver to Carranza the news of his replacement, the rest of Carranza's civilian cabinet had begun to leave the capital. Carranza reunited his advisers temporarily at Puebla, where Obregón wired him that he was bringing a message. Carranza replied, putting him off, still quite unsure of Obregón's loyalty. He then moved on to Córdoba, where on November 8 he published an answer to the ultimatum of the Convention. He ordered all his supporters to withdraw from Aguascalientes by the evening of November 10.[39]

Nevertheless, as late as the tenth of November, a few Constitutionalist leaders were still making efforts to reconcile their differences with the Conventionists peacefully. Villa, however, was rapidly moving his troops into combat position south of Aguascalientes, effectively cutting off from Mexico City those still present at the Convention. Eduardo Hay, one of the negotiators who had been sent to try to arrange terms with Carranza, wired Eulalio Gutiérrez from Silao, directly on the rail lines between Aguascalientes and Mexico City, that Villa had now taken that town without the permission of the Convention. Villa had also promised to support the Convention by force of arms, which in itself implied a violation of the agreements of the Convention. Further, the Convention was continuing to discuss Carranza's resignation without waiting for the commission to deal with Carranza himself. Hay urged that the Convention wait ten days before discussing Carranza's resignation and that the Convention move to Mexico City, where the forces of Obregón (those that still remained) and Blanco might guaran-

[38]Ibid., pp. 119–121.
[39]Juan Barragán, *Historia del Ejército y de la Revolución Constitucionalista*, 2:113; Quirk, *The Mexican Revolution*, p. 123.

tee the personal safety of the delegates. He warned that failure to take these measures would mean inevitable bloodshed.[40]

The next day Obregón, having arrived in Mexico City, wired Carranza in Córdoba that he was informing Villa that he knew of his troop movements south of Aguascalientes. He asked Villa to prove that he was a patriot by removing his troops, resigning from his command, and leaving the country temporarily. Carranza would then resign on November 20, leaving the government of the country in the hands of the Conventionists. Obregón indicated to Carranza that he thought Villa would agree to this plan if he and Carranza would stick together on the offer, and he warned that the consequences of failing to come to an agreement would be anarchy or even intervention. Obregón sent copies of the telegram to Pablo González, chief of the Army of the Northeast, Eulalio Gutiérrez, president of the Convention, Manuel M. Diéguez and Benjamín Hill, his own subordinates in the Army of the Northwest, and a number of other revolutionary generals.[41] Unfortunately, the time for either Carranza or Villa to back down had passed, since both felt that any concession would simply give power to the other.

Of course, if Villa and Carranza had resigned, Obregón would have been the most politically powerful figure left in the arena, a fact that was obvious to all three men. However, if Villa and Carranza came to blows, Obregón would be in the weakest position, both politically and militarily. Villa still had the loyal and strong Division of the North, while Obregón's troops had been considerably dispersed. Carranza had the prestige of being the first chief and the legitimacy of being regarded by most as Madero's political heir, while Obregón had only the much less tangible political power afforded him as an effective and popular general and an ardent but not very effective peacemaker. Thus Villa would be preeminent militarily, Carranza politically, and Obregón would be faced with joining one or the other. Therefore, he had personal reasons, in addition to his no

[40]Hay to Gutiérrez, November 10, 1914, ASRE-119, L-E-841R, Leg. 2.
[41]Obregón to Carranza, November 11, 1914, ibid.

doubt genuine desire for peace, to inspire his efforts to prevent a resumption of hostilities. Should fighting break out again, it was foreordained that he would choose Carranza in the face of Villa's obvious jealousy and personal hostility. Moreover, he realized that the forces of Villa and Zapata could not effectively govern the country, although they might be able to control the country militarily for a period of time.

As a last attempt at a political solution, Obregón and several other military chiefs had wired Gutiérrez that if Villa was dismissed from his post as head of the Division of the North, they would adhere to the Convention. If not, they would fight. Gutiérrez wired back that Carranza was considered to be in rebellion and that Villa had been restored to his old post. In fact, Villa had been made chief of military operations under the Convention. This arrangement was completely unacceptable to Obregón, and he therefore went on to join Carranza, who was still nervous about his loyalty. Carranza again wired the Convention that he had not resigned, his hand much strengthened by Obregón's adherence. On the twelfth he wired all military and political leaders throughout the country who he felt might remain loyal, reporting messages from Pablo González, Antonio Villarreal, Obregón, and others, condemning the "shocking conduct" of Eulalio Gutiérrez as president of the Convention and announcing their continued support of the first chief and their willingness to combat the usurping "bandits."[42]

The debacle between the Constitutionalists, under Carranza and Obregón, and the Conventionists, under Villa and Zapata, was about to erupt. Obregón had been caught between Villa and Carranza, had been forced to make a choice, and had finally made it. Military necessity required Carranza to accept him. However, Obregón's willingness to see the first chief resign had permanently damaged his relationship with Carranza, and Carranza's lightly veiled hostility toward the man who would lead his Constitutionalist forces into battle against Villa would be a problem for Obregón from that time forward. Carranza,

---

[42]Obregón, *Ocho mil kilómetros*, p. 224; Carranza to Jefe de Armas, Gobernadores, etc., November 12, 1914, ASRE-119, L-E-841R, Leg. 2.

feeling that Obregón had betrayed him at Aguascalientes, henceforward tolerated him only as a military leader and began to move to check any growth of his political power and influence. Obregón, on his own part, recognized the importance of such power and was moving to gain political supporters, a constituency of his own. His visibility, as a political figure at Aguascalientes and as a military figure in the subsequent fight against Villa and the Convention, would help make it possible to build such a constituency.

The Aguascalientes Convention not only increased Obregón's political contacts, it also had a significant effect on his thinking about a number of issues. First of all, the importance of the land question was brought still more vividly to his attention. The attendance of the Zapatistas, who had been the first to come up with a coherent statement on the principles of agrarian reform, forced Obregón to focus on this issue. Though he was at that time negatively impressed with one of their major spokesmen, Antonio Díaz Soto y Gama, he was nevertheless made aware of their ideas.[43] In the future, the appeal of the land reform program in gaining supporters for the Constitutionalist military effort would never be far from his mind.

Even clearer to Obregón was the near impossibility of attempting to establish peace in a country in which there were large numbers of armed men still operating under military *caudillos*, each with his own ideas for the country and his strong concern for his own power and political position. Thus, though he remained committed to the formation of the new government by those who had participated in the military struggle, he would be concerned with the eventual subordination of the military to the new civilian leadership of the country. And, of course, he himself intended to be a major part of that new civilian leadership.

[43]Alvaro Obregón, "El problema agrario," p. 20.

CHAPTER 7

The Constitutionalist Recovery

Aguascalientes had been a disaster for the Constitutionalists. Pancho Villa had gained significant advantages: he had acquired an aura of legitimacy, and he had made an important alliance with the Zapatistas. Obregón, on the other hand, had suffered major setbacks; in hoping to prevail over both Villa and Carranza, he had, in fact, been caught in an untenable position in the middle. However, he had learned a great deal, and he would make great efforts in the future to avoid being caught in the same way.

Most importantly, he was acutely aware of the need to develop a power base of his own. From this time forward, he was constantly looking for ways to improve his own independent position: developing linkages with other leaders through his contacts in the revolutionary army; making himself accessible to emerging social groups, especially organizing labor and the agrarian movement, and acting as their champion in contacts with First Chief Carranza; and even making an effort to develop a quasi–political party, the Confederación Revolucionaria, to improve his position vis-a-vis Carranza and to help him press for a Constitutionalist stance on social issues, which would make it possible for him to recruit the lower classes into his armies for the coming fighting.

Further, it was after the debacle at Aguascalientes and during the fight against Villa and the Conventionists that Obregón's reputation as the preeminent popular military hero of the Revolution was established. His contacts with other members

of the Constitutionalist revolutionary army were greatly increased as he led a coordinated national military effort as contrasted with the more local campaign he had led down the
northwest coast against Huerta. These contacts, many of which
had begun at the military conventions in Mexico City and
Aguascalientes, would serve him well in forming the nation-
wide linkages that would increase his political power and influence.

In addition, his administration of the areas he controlled
and especially his defiance of the Mexico City elite during the
Constitutionalist occupation of the capital established his reputation as the champion of the popular classes. His belligerence
toward the uncooperative foreign community in Mexico City
enhanced his image as a defender of his country, despite his
earlier willingness to accept help from the more amenable U.S.
interests in Sonora. That he was able to achieve all of these
ends despite the weakened condition of the Constitutionalist
Army after Aguascalientes, despite the aura of legitimacy Villa
had acquired from the Convention, and despite his continuing
problems with the suspicious Carranza is a tribute to his military
talent and to his political acumen.

At the moment of the split with the Convention, Obregón
and Carranza were faced with a situation in which they lacked
troops and organization. The Villistas and Zapatistas had never
lost their combat readiness. Villa and Zapata quickly moved
into Mexico City in the absence of any resistance, but they were
not to be there long. As the Constitutionalist forces were built
up, the Conventionist forces suffered attrition. As the Carranza-
Obregón organization began to move, the Villa-Zapata axis
began to disintegrate.

By November 16, Obregón was in direct contact with Carranza, making plans to combat Villa and Zapata. Aarón Sáenz,
Obregón's chief of staff, had been acting as an emissary between
them, bringing Obregón Carranza's orders. In a remarkably
prescient telegram, Obregón responded to Carranza's instructions, warning that it was not a good idea to evacuate the
capital immediately. He proposed instead a plan of operations
that would have permitted Villa to enter the capital in about

forty days, by which time Obregón and his forces would have established themselves on a line along the Pacific coast from Salina Cruz to Manzanillo to Guadalajara. General Iturbe of Sinaloa and General Hill of Sonora would be able to combat Maytorena in the northwest. Obregón was therefore in favor of establishing the Constitutionalist line of attack in the area he knew best, much of which he had traversed in his original drive on Mexico City. Such a plan would have implied defeating Zapata in the south first, before making a move against Villa. Carranza, however, ordered immediate evacuation, fearing isolation of his forces in the capital, with Villa to the north and Zapata to the south. Obregón complied.

The most interesting part of Obregón's telegram contained a prediction for the political future of the country. Obregón speculated that the forces of the Convention would divide into three groups after taking the capital. The first group, composed of ex–federal army officers, *científicos*, and other supporters of the former dictator Díaz, would be led by the personally ambitious Felipe Angeles. The second, under Villa and Zapata, would be composed of bandits. The third, honorable men, would come to recognize Villa and Zapata for what they were—that is, bandits. Villa and Zapata would defeat Angeles, and then Villa, separated from the men who had been able to combat his more feral impulses, would misuse his power so severely that he would lose his false prestige and his undeserved reputation for being both politically able and a man of honor. Therefore, Obregón concluded, "we will have triumphed morally, and as for material triumphs, perhaps there will be no necessity for prolonged battles." He then went on to urge Carranza to issue a manifesto or a new plan that would be a real guarantee for the social goals of the Revolution.[1]

Although his predictions for the future of the Revolution were not precisely correct, strains within the Conventionist camp quickly became evident. Villa did become suspicious and

[1]Obregón to Carranza, November 16, 1914, quoted in Luis Muro, Guide to the materials in the Archivo Histórico de la Secretaría de la Defensa Nacional (cited hereafter as LMG/AHDN).

jealous of Angeles, causing Villa to reject Angeles' military advice at critical times. The difficulties of exercising power experienced by the men attempting to be administrators within the Convention caused others to leave Villa and Zapata and join Carranza. Even the Conventionist president, Eulalio Gutiérrez, soon realized that he was powerless within the Convention and began to make cautious attempts to realign himself with other leaders, especially with the first chief. Villa's own vitriolic attacks on the Conventionist president, as early as December of 1914, can hardly have helped cement Gutiérrez' loyalty. Gutiérrez clearly feared for his own personal safety within the area controlled by Villista and Zapatista forces.[2]

Meanwhile, Obregón moved to re-form a fighting force for the Constitutionalists. Having made the decision to rejoin Carranza, he threw himself into the fray with his usual energy, starting with a public manifesto filled with his characteristic invective toward declared enemies. On November 17, he issued his call to the Mexican people to rally round Carranza. He accused Villa of being a "monster of crime and treason" and condemned the "unholy trinity of Villa, Angeles, and Maytorena." He then urged the true sons of the country to crush in the "invincible claws of justice the deformed monsters who celebrate the death agony of the country in their own dance macabre."[3]

Obregón then proceeded to direct the evacuation of the capital, hindered only briefly by the defection of Lucio Blanco. Blanco maintained a semblance of subordination to Obregón while making covert attempts to prevent Obregón's leaving the city. Then, after a brief attempt to take military and political command of the capital, he withdrew to Michoacán with the portion of men who remained loyal to him.[4] Those who re-

---

[2]One author has described Villa's attacks on Gutiérrez as "ferocious" and mentions that several other Convention members decided to leave town as quickly as possible (see Robert E. Quirk, *The Mexican Revolution 1914–1915: The Convention of Aguascalientes*, pp. 144–149).

[3]Alvaro Obregón, "Manifesto," DRM-1, p. 396.

[4]Alvaro Obregón, *Ocho mil kilómetros en campaña*, pp. 228–229; Quirk, *The Mexican Revolution*, p. 128.

mained loyal to Obregón and the first chief went to Jalisco.

The weakness of the Constitutionalist position has, perhaps, been overemphasized in most secondary accounts of the Revolution. Actually, although no one leader had as massive a fighting force as Villa's Division of the North nor as solid a base of operations as Zapata's in the south, the loyal Constitutionalists were placed strategically around the country. Carranza, establishing his headquarters with General Cándido Aguilar, his son-in-law, in Veracruz, had a point of access to the sea and also to funds from customs revenues when the U.S. forces pulled out, by happy coincidence, on November 23, the day Obregón was evacuating Mexico City. The Constitutionalists also held Tampico, the port opening on the oil-rich area of the Gulf coast, and were to hold it through months of heroic effort at the strategic rail point of El Ebano.[5]

In addition, the Constitutionalists held important positions in the west. In Jalisco, a defense was forming under the Cananea labor leader, Manuel M. Diéguez, and in Sonora Hill and Calles were still holding out against Maytorena. Furthermore, and extremely important strategically, the Constitutionalists controlled the isthmian railroad, making possible communication between Veracruz on the east and Salina Cruz on the west coast of Mexico, cutting below the Zapata-held areas of Morelos and Guerrero. Therefore, the Constitutionalists were able to travel up and down both coasts and communicate through the southern railroad connection, which also made possible the movement of men and war materiel.

Moreover, the Zapatista forces were unwilling to come east much beyond Puebla and therefore did not threaten the Constitutionalist effort at its heart, Veracruz. This left Obregón free to move troops up close to the center of Mexico on the two railroad lines between Veracruz and Mexico City, the Interoceanic and the Mexicano del Sur. These were considered sufficiently safe in December of 1914 for Carranza himself to come as far into the interior as Apizaco, Tlaxcala, in an attempt

[5]For a first-hand description of this aspect of the Revolution, see Luis F. Bustamante, *La defensa de El Ebano*.

to raise troop morale. The expedition almost ended in disaster, however, when the Conventionists were able to launch a locomotive to crash into Carranza's train. The situation was saved by Carranza's engineer, who slowed down immediately and began backing up in order to soften the impact. All of those traveling with Carranza, including Obregón, leaped out of the car as the train slowed, but the first chief himself remained seated in dignity awaiting the blow. Carranza's only injury was a scratch on the forehead, inflicted by a stuffed eagle jarred from its perch in his train car. The incident caused much amusement, according to one observer, especially to Obregón, whose "jocularity was characteristic."[6]

Carranza and Obregón, however, were still uncertain bedfellows. Carranza, fearing Obregón's military and political power, made him chief of operations against Mexico City but did not make him minister of war. The direction of the overall campaign he reserved to himself, an arrangement Obregón accepted. Although the successes of Obregón's campaign against the center of the country and against Villa would be the most crucial in establishing Constitutionalist hegemony over the country, Obregón remained only first among equals under Carranza, as various other generals were given command over other areas. Carranza was unwilling to give any one of his potentially powerful subordinates a base from which he himself might later be challenged.

Nevertheless, Obregón and others continued to prod the first chief to define his revolutionary goals and to make public statements that would bring support to the Constitutionalist side. In an attempt to bring this pressure more forcefully to bear, Obregón and a number of associates formed a group known as the Confederación Revolucionaria only a few days after the Constitutionalist withdrawal from the Convention of Aguascalientes. During the evacuation of Mexico City in November, 1914, Obregón met with Gerardo Murillo, famous under the pseudonym Dr. Atl, to discuss the future of the armed conflict

---

[6]Juan Barragán, *Historia del Ejército y de la Revolución Constitucionalista*, 2:174.

that was beginning again between the Constitutionalists and Villa. He and Atl decided on the necessity of drawing up a list of principles that would serve as the base for an organizing committee of ten civilians and ten military men, who would work to coordinate the civil and military arms of the Revolution in accordance with those principles. The principles enunciated would be based on the immediate necessities of the country, not on any foreign or any other arbitrarily selected ideology.[7]

The nucleus of the committee was formed on the trains that carried Obregón and his troops to Veracruz. Among the early members was Alberto Pani, who would later collaborate closely with Obregón and Dr. Atl in the attempts to relieve the suffering of the poor in Mexico City in early 1915. Other civilian members were Jesús Urueta, Carranza's minister of foreign relations in Veracruz, Rafael Zubarán Capmany, who as minister of government would conclude the pact with the Casa del Obrero Mundial that Carranza put in jeopardy by his unfriendly attitude, and old Maderista Roque Estrada. Obregón himself insisted on informing Carranza of the formation of the new group, although Urueta and Atl objected, but Obregón pointed out that any secret movement might be misunderstood and would contribute to indiscipline, which would weaken the Constitutionalist cause.[8]

On his arrival in Veracruz, therefore, Atl had a long conference with Carranza to explain to him the principles and projects of the new confederation. Carranza approved it, but it met with considerable opposition from Félix Palavicini and others who surrounded him. Obregón, of course, was absent from Veracruz most of the time, but Atl traveled back and forth regularly. The Revolutionary Confederation, formed by now of a number of cabinet and other government officials, as well as some military men, began to meet to study social questions, publicize them, write articles, and give public speeches and conferences. Urueta, Zubarán Capmany, and Dr. Atl were

---

[7]Gerardo Murillo [pseud. Dr. Atl], "Obregón y el principio de renovación social," in *Obregón, Aspectos de su vida*, pp. 71–73.

[8]Ibid.; Luis Sánchez Pontón, interview, PHO/1/20, p. 21; Murillo, "Obregón," pp. 67–69.

frequent speakers in the series given at the Apolo Theater in Veracruz, keeping constant pressure on the first chief.[9]

Partly in response, Carranza issued a number of decrees from Veracruz, setting out the Constitutionalist social program. In December, he announced his additions to the Plan of Guadalupe, "to satisfy the economic, social, and political necessities of the country." He sketchily indicated the measures he would take to meet these necessities: agrarian laws favoring the formation of small properties; an equitable tax system; legislation to improve the condition of the proletarian classes, defined as farm and urban workers and miners; the reorganization of the army; a divorce law; revision of the civil, penal, and commercial codes; reform of the judicial system; destruction of the monopolies that controlled the natural resources of the country and prevention of the formation of similar monopolies in the future; and, in general, the institution of laws that would provide for the exercise of each citizen's full rights and equality before the law.[10]

Included in this decree was a provision for the establishment of the free municipality, a measure that had already been taken in Sonora by Obregón's associate, Benjamín Hill. No longer would municipal officials be appointed by state officials; instead, they would be locally elected. Hill, acting as military head of the Constitutional forces and interim governor in Sonora, had abolished as well the hated prefectures, intermediate bodies between the state and local governments, and he had given the locally elected councils, the *ayuntamientos*, control over the municipal presidents and the police commissioners.[11] The problem of centralized control over local governments was intimately linked with the question of land as well. During the Porfirian period, much of the alienation of land from individuals and communities had been accomplished through the prefectures. Thus the question of the free municipality had a practical

[9]Francisco Urquizo, *Recuerdo que . . . Visiones aisladas de la Revolución*, 2:45.

[10]"Adiciones al Plan de Guadalupe," DRM-1, pp. 510–511.

[11]Antonio G. Rivera, *La Revolución en Sonora*, pp. 426–427; "Municipio Libre," DRM-1, pp. 512–513.

and immediate importance in relation to the land question. Moreover, it had considerable ideological importance, signaled by Carranza in his own decree, in that it would foster local democracy and responsibility.

By far Carranza's most important social statement was the agrarian decree of January 6, 1915, the day after an Obregón victory over the Zapatistas at Puebla. Carranza promised to return lands, waters, and forest to communities that had lost them and to give lands to those who needed them, whether or not title could be proved. The question of whether the grants would be made to the communities as a whole or divided into small properties for individuals was left open, although Carranza had earlier expressed a preference for small properties. This statement was issued several weeks before Villa and Zapata's Convention put forth its own agrarian program, a fact that was noted acrimoniously in Convention meetings by Antonio Díaz Soto y Gama, Zapata's fiery agrarian theorist.[12]

Still, though Carranza may have envisioned major social reform, he envisioned it under his own control and at his own speed. He feared the masses and was frequently inclined to gut his own reform measures in practice.[13] This proclivity on Carranza's part was to cause constant friction with Obregón, although Obregón subordinated himself militarily and politically to Carranza's wishes for two more years, taking what action he could within this context.

While Carranza and his advisers were elaborating the social goals of the Constitutionalist movement, Obregón was making plans for its military future. He occupied himself during the month of December by making several trips within Constitutionalist-held areas—to get to know the lay of the land, to evaluate his support, to determine what resources he had and what the communications network looked like—and by gen-

[12]"Ley Agraria," DRM-1, pp. 517–521; Luis Fernando Amaya, *La Soberana Convención Revolucionaria 1914–1916*, pp. 216–217.

[13]Arnaldo Córdova, *La ideología de la Revolución Mexicana*, pp. 194, 217–218; Moisés de la Peña, *El pueblo y su tierra: Mito y realidad de la reforma agraria en México*, p. 310; Charles C. Cumberland, *Mexican Revolution: The Constitutionalist Years*, pp. 318–385.

erally preparing for the big push against Villa's forces in the center of Mexico. He traveled along most of the rail lines controlled by the Constitutionalists, including a trip to Salina Cruz on the Pacific coast of Mexico, encouraging the troops and asking for information. He was still thinking of Salina Cruz as a fallback position should his troops be defeated by the Conventionists. By the end of December he was back in Veracruz, preparing for the major attack against the center.

The military news during December had not been good for the Constitutionalists. Felipe Angeles and other Villista officers had been winning victories in the northeast, threatening the oil regions; Maytorena was prevailing, with Villa support, against Calles and Hill in the northwest; and Salvador Alvarado, who had rejoined the first chief in Mexico City during the Convention after having been jailed for a time by Maytorena, was pushed out of Puebla by the Zapatistas on December 15. Still, Villa and Zapata did not press on to expel the Constitutionalists from Veracruz. Villa, fearing attack from the north, had moved out of Mexico City to protect his own territory, Zapatista interest waned after Puebla was taken, and the strategic moment for attack lapsed. It was not to come again.

On December 31, Obregón felt ready to move on Puebla, lost only two weeks before. The time was ripe, as the Zapatistas, who held the town, were already becoming disenchanted with Villa, and Zapata himself had returned to Morelos. By January 5, after hard fighting, Puebla was in Constitutionalist hands.

Meanwhile, Obregón's forces were growing as he moved, as they usually did. One news-service report claimed that 2,000 men had surrendered voluntarily, with arms and ammunition, and many had come over to the Constitutionalist side. Furthermore, 800 Conventionists had been wounded and were being cared for by Obregón's "excellently equipped hospital and sanitary service." The report went on to say that once in possession of Puebla, Obregón had left the rail lines open in the hopes of drawing still more Zapatistas out of Mexico City. They did not accept the challenge.[14]

[14]Pan American News Service Dispatch, January 7, 1915, ASRE-119, L-E-856, Leg. 6.

Obregón's success in Puebla had important political consequences. Eulalio Gutiérrez, faced with a deteriorating political situation in Mexico City, was eager to free himself of Villa's domination, and, as Obregón was on the march toward Mexico City, he was hopeful of coming to terms with him and saving his own political skin. Therefore, he sent a message to Obregón on behalf of himself and of his minister of war, José Isabel Robles, the undersecretary of war, Eugenio Aguirre Benavides—both of whom had helped save Obregón's life when he was threatened by Villa—and Lucio Blanco, now minister of government in the Convention. What he proposed was that Obregón suspend operations on Mexico City while they attempted to run Villa out of the Convention. Obregón, however, arrested the messengers and sent them to Veracruz. Then he wired Gutiérrez that he must prove his loyalty to the Constitutionalist cause by declaring war on Villa and his followers; then and only then would he have Obregón's support.[15]

It is likely that Gutiérrez hoped to separate Obregón from Carranza and thus form a government without either Villa or the first chief, but the time for this partnership had passed when Gutiérrez had named Obregón's old enemy Pancho Villa as chief of military operations for the Convention. Given the ambiguities of Gutiérrez' position, Obregón was in no mood to rescue him from Villa or to reinforce the legitimacy of Gutiérrez' position as president of the Convention.

Meanwhile, he advised Carranza of the exchange of telegrams and Carranza released them to the press, thus exposing Gutiérrez to Villa's ire. Gutiérrez was forced to escape from Mexico City, taking along his title as president of the Convention, a major portion of the Convention treasury, and a number of the cabinet officers. Although the group left in Mexico City maintained its claim to being the "real" Convention, its composition had changed so drastically since Aguascalientes that it was a question whether or not it was the same body. Mean-

---

[15]Gutiérrez to Obregón, January 7, 1915, and Obregón to Gutiérrez, January 12, 1915, both in Obregón, *Ocho mil kilómetros*, pp. 254–255; Arredondo to Wilson, January 19, 1915, USDS 812.00/14277.

while, the Conventionist newspapers hurried to defame the hapless Gutiérrez, lumping him together with Huerta and Carranza to form "the trinity which is penetrated to the core with faithlessness and betrayal."[16] The defections from the Villa- and Zapata-dominated Convention, which Obregón had predicted would take less than two months, had begun on schedule.

The presidency of the Convention in Mexico City passed to Villa's faithful follower, Roque González Garza, who had served him well as leader of the Villistas during the debates in Aguascalientes. Obregón, however, was slowly moving up on the capital. Mexico City newspapers such as La Opinión were strangely silent about the threat to the capital until, on January 27, it was announced that the Convention was moving to Cuernavaca in Zapatista territory.[17] The following day, Obregón's army peacefully occupied the city, entering through the Villa de Guadalupe. Although some resistance was attempted, one Conventionist leader commented that the Zapatistas kept running away. It was a show of as much force and organization as possible: La Opinión estimated 5,000 cavalry, 10,000 infantry, and a substantial amount of artillery, including 200 machine guns and 50 pieces of heavy artillery, mostly mounted on automobiles. As it happened, this was an over-estimate, perhaps designed to please the incoming commander. In any event, it ran a poor second to the triumphal entry of Villa and Zapata two months before. Obregón himself estimated that during his occupation of Mexico City he could count on only about 9,000 men.[18]

The city had been in considerable confusion before the arrival of Obregón's troops, and he did what he could to improve conditions there. To preserve order he closed bars, gam-

---

[16]Los Sucesos (Mexico City), January 18, 1915.

[17]La Opinión (Mexico City), January 27, 1915. One observer, Manuel Garrido Alfaro, who had been in Mexico City for several weeks before it was taken by the Constitutionalists, reported that the press had lied to the inhabitants about the military situation and that even the men in charge of the defense of the city were lulled into inaction until Obregón was already at the Villa de Guadalupe (El Pueblo [Mexico City], February 3, 1915).

[18]Federico Cervantes, interview, PHO/1/9, pp. 37–39; La Opinión (Mexico City), January 29, 1915; Obregón, Ocho mil kilómetros, p. 274.

bling establishments, and "immoral performances" the day after his arrival, and he began to make an effort to provide the city with articles of first necessity such as food and coal, which were scarce and had been soaring in price. He spoke with the Chamber of Commerce on the twenty-ninth of January, offering railroad cars that would bring foodstuffs for sale at low prices to relieve the suffering in the capital. Then, amidst rumors about the state of his health, he went to Veracruz to report to Carranza, leaving Benjamín Hill, who had been called to Mexico City from Sonora, in charge. He was back by the second of February, ready to cope with the problems of the erstwhile capital.[19]

As Obregón concentrated on these difficulties, his associates throughout the country began to put into practice the agrarian decree of January 6. Notable was the activity of General Francisco Coss, who became governor and military commander of Puebla after Obregón had defeated the Zapatistas in the area. In early February, 1915, scarcely a month after Puebla had fallen to Obregón's Constitutionalist forces, Coss called a meeting of the municipal presidents in the state and of representatives of each pueblo to arrange for immediate return of those lands stolen by the *hacendados* and to provide land for those individuals who had none. The Hacienda del Cristo near Puebla was the first scheduled for division. A promise was made that those Zapatistas who turned in their arms to Coss or any other Constitutionalist chief in the area and announced adherence to the Law of January 6 would be given land as well and would enjoy all personal rights and guarantees.[20]

These efforts came at an important time, as the Zapatista-Villista alliance was already falling apart. In fact, Zapata himself had left Puebla before the battle against Obregón, discouraged by reports of Villa's contacts with old Porfiristas, Huertistas, and Felicistas (followers of Díaz' nephew, Félix Díaz) and, even more important, by the murder of Paulino Martínez, Zapata's chief delegate to the Convention, by Villista

[19]See reports in *La Opinión* (Mexico City), December 6, 1914, and January 29 and 31, 1915.
[20]*La Prensa* (Mexico City), February 9 and 16, 1915.

officers in Mexico City.[21] A strong appeal to the Zapatistas in the area of Puebla, along with direct evidence of Constitutionalist good faith, was bound to have a major effect in attracting their support.

The effort in Puebla was not the only land reform program the Constitutionalists were carrying out. In Veracruz, Governor Luis Sánchez Pontón, a member of Confederación Revolucionaria, had made himself accessible to local *campesinos* and intervened in their behalf with the landlords. In Medellín near Veracruz, he carried out one of the first distributions of land under the Law of January 6. In Sonora, Plutarco Elías Calles, though by no means completely in control of the state, issued his own major statement in a pamphlet, *Tierra y libros para todos* ("Land and books for all"). This program emphasized the division of lands, as these formed the "basis of national wealth," but it also emphasized the importance of individual rights, the independence of municipalities, and the importance of public education. Although Sonora was not completely pacified, Calles started a program of land distribution in 1915, even setting up an agrarian bank and encouraging the repair of damaged irrigation works. Calles' activities, in fact, bore a striking resemblance to the Zapatista program, not only in emphasizing the division of lands but in placing limits on the amount of land that could be held by individuals and in establishing rural credit, in defining the role of the government in irrigation and other capital projects, and in asserting the importance of education and agricultural research.[22]

[21]An excellent discussion of Zapata's disillusionment with Villa as an ally may be found in John Womack, Jr., *Zapata and the Mexican Revolution*, pp. 221–223.

[22]*El Pueblo* (Veracruz), February 9, 1915; Sánchez Pontón, interview, PHO/1/20, p. 21; Manuel González Ramírez, *La revolución social de México*, 3:214; Plutarco Elías Calles, "Tierra y libros para todos! Programa de Gobierno," reprinted in *La cuestión de la tierra*, ed. J. D. Ramírez Garrido et al., pp. 143–153; Gobernador de Sonora to Pacheco, January 10, 1915, and anonymous to Luis L. León, January 30, 1915, both in PHS/59; Plutarco Elías Calles, "Programa de gobierno," August 4, 1915, and Calles decree establishing Comisión Local Agraria, September 1, 1915, both in PHS/60; Calles decree of expropriation, January 27, 1916, PHS/61; Comisión Local Agraria de Sonora, July 3, 1919, PHS/70. For Zapatista program, see Womack, *Zapata*, appendix C, pp. 405–411.

Meanwhile, Obregón was faced with enormous problems in the capital. Not yet won over, the Zapatistas lingered in the suburbs to the south of the city, harassing the populace and damaging the pumping station at Xochimilco so that the city was left almost without water. The problems of scarcity grew worse when Carranza ordered that the Villista paper money that had been circulating be declared worthless in favor of Carrancista currency. Despite Obregón's wish that all bills continue to be used at least for the time being to ease the suffering of the inhabitants of the city, Carranza insisted that the Villista currency be declared worthless. Carranza wired Obregón on February 4 not to let Villista money circulate under any circumstances and instructed Obregón to leave the city and its problems and move out if it became impossible to control. On February 5, a decree signed by Obregón circulated through the city, suppressing by Carranza's order the circulation of Villista currency and announcing the establishment by his headquarters of an "office of aid to the needy classes," which would be funded by the first chief. The ensuing confusion caused many merchants to close their doors.[23] Carranza's explanation that the circulation of the enormous quantities of paper money that Villa had issued would destroy Mexican credit abroad underlined Carranza's lack of understanding of the condition of the poor in Mexico's cities during the Revolution. Indeed, Carranza seemed almost eager to punish the capital.

Obregón, on the contrary, hoped to aid the cities' laboring classes, whose support he wished to enlist in the fight against the Conventionists. His efforts in this direction had begun during the fight against Huerta. However, his major concerns during this period were almost entirely military, and he left decisions about social actions to those revolutionary governors he left in his wake. Manuel Diéguez in Jalisco issued a decree on September 2, 1914, providing for vacation days of rest from work. The Constitutionalist interest in labor reform was by no means confined to the Army of the Northwest. The same month

23Carranza to Obregón, February 4, 1915, in *La Prensa* (Mexico City), February 10, 1915; Circular from Jefatura, Ejército de Operaciones, February 5, 1915, MPPP.

Eulalio Gutiérrez in San Luis Potosí issued a more sweeping decree in labor's behalf, and similar actions in favor of the working class were taken in various parts of the Republic.[24]

However, when he arrived in Mexico City in August, 1914, and was for a few weeks military commander of the city and thus more concerned with administrative than with strictly military matters, one of his first acts was to permit the Casa del Obrero Mundial ("House of World Workers"), closed by Huerta, to reopen. Moreover, he infuriated Catholic opinion when he gave the Casa the Church of Santa Brígida and the Colegio Josefino next door to use as a headquarters.

After the evacuation of Mexico City in November, 1914, Obregón made efforts to maintain these relationships. As Obregón made his way back toward Mexico City fighting principally against the Zapatistas, he began to give *veladas* in the areas he was covering—that is, evenings of musical entertainment and speeches about the social goals of the Revolution. Dr. Atl, who was closely associated with the labor movement, was now traveling with him regularly, although Atl made frequent trips to Veracruz to check the political situation and to maintain contacts with labor leaders in the port. When Obregón retook Puebla, for example, the program included a speech by Dr. Atl, an anticlerical speech by a law student from Nuevo León, and a performance by the "notable violinist" Nicasio Jurado, accompanied by Obregón's own military band. The program was well received, leading one observer to conclude that Puebla, noted as a center of religious piety and conservative political spirit, was "not as reactionary as they claim." Atl was convinced that he could persuade the "workers, students, and middle class" to join the Constitutionalist Army, and, as it happened, his confidence was justified.[25]

When Obregón's forces moved into Mexico City in late January, 1915, Atl immediately began to work with the labor

[24]Córdova, *La ideología*, p. 209; Cumberland, *Mexican Revolution*, pp. 255–256.

[25]Aarón Sáenz, interview, in Píndaro Urióstegui Miranda, *Testimonios del proceso revolucionario de México*, p. 373; Atl to Carranza, January 18, 1915, quoted in Cumberland, *Mexican Revolution*, p. 257.

groups there. On February 2, in the name of the Confederación Revolucionaria, he gave a speech in the Arbeu Theater, attacking the reaction—religion, the military, and businessmen—and urging the unification of the Constitutionalist movement with international socialism. He cited a number of socialist leaders as having been especially encouraging to the Mexican Revolution, among them Clemenceau and Juares of France and the Catalán leader Ribas. Among the enemies of the Revolution, on the other hand, he denounced the financial conspiracies between banks, bourgeoisie, and foreign governments in London, Paris, and New York.[26] Having identified labor's allies as Constitutionalist allies and having attacked labor's enemies, he immediately gained the attention of the leaders of the organized movement.

Aided in his appeal by Obregón's attempts to provide food and other provisions for the poor of the city and later by his attacks on the merchants, bankers, clergy, and foreigners, Atl shrewdly routed much of the aid, both in money and in kind, through the Casa del Obrero Mundial. The first problem was getting the workers to accept Constitutionalist aid in the first place, but on February 7 the Confederación de Sindicatos Obreros del D.F., meeting at the Casa, decided affirmatively and established a Junta de Socorros ("mutual aid society"). The following day three thousand unemployed workers, mostly from the textile plants, which had closed down while unable to get cotton from the Laguna region controlled by Villa, received five pesos apiece, courtesy of the Casa, Dr. Atl, and the Constitutionalist government.[27]

On the ninth of February, Atl was ready to ask Casa members with mechanical skills to lend their assistance in the Constitutionalist factories making military articles. A discussion followed during which many members discussed their own skills and aptitudes. Dr. Atl, for his part, indicated what the salaries for individuals with these skills would be. When it

26Gerardo Murillo [pseud. Dr. Atl], *La importancia mundial de la Revolución Mexicana*, pp. 4, 17, 20–23.

27*El Pueblo* (Veracruz), February 9, 1915; *La Prensa* (Mexico City), February 8, 1915.

became clear that the workers would have to move to Veracruz, their enthusiasm became somewhat muted. Once the subject of cooperation with the Constitutionalists was broached, however, the idea of full military participation in the Constitutionalist movement was soon to follow. Within two days, the Casa had definitely decided to join the Constitutionalist effort. After an acrimonious meeting of sixty-seven Casa leaders, which had lasted all night on February 10, the decision was made to close the Casa so that all could fight against Villismo and Zapatismo, which, according to those voting in favor, contained the enemies of the workers: the clergy, the bourgeoisie, and the militarists. The effort would be total—female workers would form nursing groups to accompany the labor battalions, with the ever-present Dr. Atl to supply bandages and drugs.[28]

Once the decision to aid the Constitutionalists had been taken, the Casa also joined Dr. Atl's propaganda battle, trying to persuade other workers that the Zapatistas and Villistas were enemies. On February 14, 1915, *La Prensa* carried a report that more than thirty workers of the Sindicato de Obreros Tejidores ("weavers' union") of Tizapán had been killed by the Zapatistas. Some of them were unable to flee when they heard that the attack was coming, but the Zapatistas had slaughtered all whom they caught, including defenseless women, according to the reports. Comments by various labor leaders were included, pointing out that this attack was evidence that the Villistas and Zapatistas were reactionaries.[29]

Whether or not the report was true, it is instructive that such a large number of urban laborers chose to join the Constitutionalists at this time just after the experience of the Villista-Zapatista occupation of the city. The Villistas and Zapatistas, however well they might understand the aspirations of the people of the countryside, did not understand the aspirations of urban labor and did not know how to contend with urban problems in general. Only later did the Zapatistas begin to under-

[28]*La Prensa* (Mexico City), February 12 and 14, 1915; *El Pueblo* (Veracruz), February 13 and 14, 1915.
[29]*La Prensa* (Mexico City), February 14, 1915.

stand the importance of an alliance with labor, which was already obvious to Obregón.

Meanwhile, Obregón was beginning to receive representatives of the labor movement himself. Apart from the Casa, the employees of La Compañía de Tranvías Eléctricos de México (streetcar company) went directly to Obregón to offer him their services in the military effort. The Casa, meanwhile, had formed a revolutionary committee, which met with Obregón at his residence. The committee resolved to publish a bulletin that would describe labor efforts in the Constitutionalist cause.[30]

The bandwagon was already rolling. By February 17, the streetcar employees officially adhered to the Constitutionalists at a meeting at the Casa, and by the evening of February 19, many other groups, including the carpenters, painters, tailors, harness and hardware makers, teamsters, and masons, resolved to join. The workers in the textile factories and in the National Armory as well as the general union Sindicato de Obreros del D.F. had already declared their adherence. The employees of the armory and of the national arsenal were to form an artillery battalion, for which their special knowledge would equip them. The assembled group adopted a red and black flag with the motto *Solidaridad Humana* ("human solidarity").[31]

Dr. Atl continued to give speeches and help with recruitment, as the Casa itself was not strong enough to mount a significant campaign unaided. He took an increasingly anti-clerical tone as he warned workers that their own wives and mothers, in their own homes, might be badly influenced by the clergy. He urged workers to educate their families in the "principles of liberty and social well-being." He also warned that the clergy were seeking an alliance with Villa and Zapata, hoping to regain their power, and might be successful with Zapata.[32]

Another theme of his lectures was the proper role for workers within the politics of the country. By February 16,

[30]Ibid., February 15, 1915.
[31]Ibid., February 19, 1915.
[32]*El Pueblo* (Veracruz), February 16, 1915.

it was estimated that he had given more than forty speeches in Mexico City alone. Moreover, he was functioning as liaison between the workers and the Constitutionalist leadership in resolving specific grievances. For example, when workers at the national arsenal complained that the director cut their pay double time when they were late, Atl promised to contact Ignacio Pesqueira, the acting minister of war, to see that the situation was resolved.[33]

Meanwhile, Obregón was becoming more and more impatient with the inaction he perceived in the middle and upper classes of the city. He particularly became irritated with the middle men (or monopolists, as he was inclined to refer to them), who he felt were refusing to sell their goods to the public because they thought that the Constitutionalist forces were too weak to prevent the return of Villa and Zapata to the city.[34]

Obregón therefore determined to take direct action to oblige the clergy, the middlemen, and the monied and propertied classes to help in easing the situation of the poor. His first action of this nature was to impose a "contribution" of a half-million pesos on the clergy, which was to be paid to Pani's Revolutionary Junta for Aid to the Poor. When the vicar-general of the archdiocese, Antonio de Jesús Paredes, indicated that the church was unable to pay and in any case would not give such a sum to Obregón's relief organization, preferring to keep any charitable works within the parish structure of the church itself, Obregón responded by imprisoning Paredes and 167 other priests. This action outraged the foreign community, especially since many of the clergy imprisoned were from other countries, but contributed greatly to Obregón's image as a leader and revolutionary.[35]

His second action was to impose a 10 percent tax in kind on all businessmen dealing in merchandise of first necessity, in an attempt to provide for the needy from the stores of goods already in the city but unavailable for sale because of the un-

[33]*La Prensa* (Mexico City), February 16, 17, and 21, 1915.
[34]Alberto J. Pani, *Apuntes autobiográficos*, 1:227–229.
[35]Obregón, *Ocho mil kilómetros*, p. 272.

willingness of the businessmen to accept Constitutionalist currency. Articles of first necessity were carefully defined as corn, various kinds of peas and beans, lentils, chile, coffee, sugar, lard, salt, coal, wood, oil, and candles. Unfortunately, although some smaller merchants complied with this order, the majority of the larger business houses refused to cooperate or simply hid their stores of these items. In practice, the decree was impossible to enforce.[36]

Obregón therefore proceeded to a third and even more all-encompassing decree, fixing a tax that would be levied on capital, real estate, professional practices and lucrative employments, patent rights, and other property, such as cars and carriages. Obregón had managed to threaten the entire upper-middle and upper classes at once—bankers, professional men, owners of all kinds of capitalistic enterprises, and even those wealthy enough to own carriages. This decree caused the business community to rise up in a fury and led to protests from many of the foreign legations, as it applied to foreign as well as domestic enterprises. A meeting was held at the Hidalgo Theater by the perturbed capitalists, who decided to refuse to pay the levy. Obregón was particularly offended when foreign protests to Carranza resulted in Carranza's exempting foreign business from the decree.[37] This action by Carranza put yet another doubt in Obre-

36Ibid. For reaction in the city, see Camacho to Maytorena, March 3, 1915, PHS/59.

37Obregón, *Ocho mil kilómetros*, pp. 274–278; Pani, *Apuntes*, 2:228–229. The statement "Declaraciones del Gral. A. Obregón hechas en México sobre el subsidio a los extranjeros," February 25, 1915, ASRE-125, L-E-1573 (1915–1920), indicates Obregón's strong feelings against foreign exploitation of Mexico and his opinion that foreigners should be forced to contribute to the country. Under pressure from Carranza and the foreign community, he softened his harsh words, saying that men should be judged by their morality, not their nationality or their capital. He did, however, condemn those who were trying to avoid the opportunity to do good, i.e., pay the subsidy he had demanded (*El Pueblo* [Veracruz], February 27, 1915). For foreign pressure and response, see Silliman to Urueta, February 27, 1915, and Subsecretaria del Despacho to Silliman, February 27, 1915, both in ASRE-125. Silliman's note even claimed that the food shortage had been created artificially in order to force the starving working classes into the army, that the military was actually shipping out food from Mexico City, and that Obregón had refused help from foreigners on the grounds that Mexicans did not need charity. These claims

gón's mind about the nature of Carranza's revolutionary ideals and his support for his own commanders.

Obregón had no doubts, however, about the proper attitude to take toward the Mexican businessmen who had refused to pay. He attended their next meeting in the Hidalgo Theater and put those who still refused to cooperate in jail. Obregón viewed action against them on behalf of the poor as action against the privileged class, or, as he was inclined to denominate them, the "wicked" or "accursed" class.[38] Although some may question the sincerity of his rhetoric, there can be little doubt that while in Mexico City in February and March of 1915 he viewed this group as the enemy.

Obregón's actions to force the well-to-do of the city, especially the merchants, clergy, and foreigners, to help the poor were increasing the feeling of solidarity the workers felt with the Constitutionalist cause.[39] Obregón's general headquarters even ordered that all members of the Casa be authorized to carry arms in the city. The effort was spreading to other labor organizations and to other parts of the country as well. By the beginning of March, the railway workers had announced the formation of the military corps *Palanca Social*, and in Orizaba the textile workers, encouraged by Casa recruiters, had requested help in forming a battalion, which became the *Batallón Regional Río Blanco*, named for the area of one of the earliest and bloodiest industrial strikes during the Porfiriato.[40]

Moreover, the workers were beginning to see Obregón as their leader, rather than Carranza. Carranza had been hostile to Casa leaders when they had gone to Veracruz to offer their support, while in Mexico City the workers were already treated

---

were precisely the opposite of what was actually happening. Silliman was in Veracruz at the time, not in Mexico City, and Obregón's pact with the members of the Casa del Obrero Mundial had been concluded almost two weeks earlier.

[38]Cardoso de Oliveira to Bryan, March 4, 1915, USDS 812.00/14500; Obregón, *Ocho mil kilómetros*, p. 270.

[39]See comments in the *New York Times*, February 13, 1915.

[40]*La Prensa* (Mexico City), February 24 and March 1, 1915; Urquizo, *Recuerdo que*, 2:32–34.

as companions in arms by Obregón.[41] On the evening of March 2, 1915, four thousand workers marched through the streets of Mexico City, cheering the Constitutionalist Army and the social revolution. They went to Obregón's hotel, the St. Francis, but as he was not there his aide, Captain Cienfuegos, spoke to the crowd about the Revolution and its social goals. In answer, one of the workers said that Obregón was right when he said that the people of Mexico had not yet defended themselves and their rights, but that they intended to remedy that now. One of Obregón's closest associates, Major Jesús M. Garza, thanked the crowd in Obregón's name and eulogized their patriotism. One of the leaders of the Casa later commented that in 1915 Obregón was like "the motor of a fighting party shaped by the basic goals floating in the revolutionary flags."[42]

Obregón, further exasperated by the lack of cooperation of the church and the monied classes of Mexico City, warned on March 2 that in the event of riot by the "hungry multitude" he would pull his troops out of Mexico City to avoid firing on the crowd. The foreign community, especially, took this statement as a clear threat, and the diplomatic representatives still in Mexico City began to protest Obregón's belligerent attitude. Obregón's odium toward foreigners was not improved when, on March 7, the Brazilian ambassador, acting for the U.S. Department of State, delivered to him a note, protesting that his statements were encouraging the population of Mexico City to riot and putting "innocent foreigners" in danger. It referred to the "incredible demands" that had been put upon the city and went on to accuse Obregón of purposefully starving the city by preventing it from being supplied with food. As Obregón had offered use of the railroads to the business community precisely for this purpose, and, this attempt to supply the city failing due to lack of action by the Chamber of Commerce, had sent out emissaries of his own to buy food in the country-

[41]For Carranza's attitude, see Luis Araiza, *Historia del movimiento obrero mexicano*, 3:69, and Rosendo Salazar and José G. Escobedo, *Las pugnas de la gleba*, 1:97.
[42]*La Prensa* (Mexico City), March 3, 1915; Rosendo Salazar, *La Casa del Obrero Mundial*, p. 85.

side and to ship it into Mexico City, this accusation infuriated him. However, he declined to reply directly, properly sending the protest along to the first chief and following it up with his own angry explanation of what had in fact happened during the Constitutionalist occupation of Mexico City. The entire incident contributed greatly to his bitterness towards the wealthy of the city, both foreigners and Mexican nationals, whom he felt had created the very situation of which they were complaining through their "unmeasured avarice."[43]

By this time, the city itself had become a liability for the Constitutionalists, and its governing was taking up valuable time and resources that could be better spent fighting the Villistas in the north. As a railway line was available for use that by-passed the city to the northeast and furnished a line of communications from Veracruz into the center of the country, Obregón gladly evacuated the city. His stay there, however, had given him time to prepare for his fight against Villa. He had contributed to his own reputation as a defender of the poor and of the interests of Mexico against foreigners, adding to the nationalistic fervor that was to become characteristic of the Revolution. He had gained a number of recruits from the poorer classes, notably the Red Battalions from the Casa del Obrero Mundial, who migrated in a group with their families to Veracruz. He had provided an opportunity for the families of other Constitutionalists to go to Veracruz as well, putting them out of the range of possible Conventionist retributions. Government offices and even munitions factories, which had been left behind in the earlier evacuation, had been transferred to the port city. Lastly, he had been approached by a number of uncommitted or nominally Conventionist leaders who wished to come over to his side and whose help he ultimately decided to accept. Notable among these were Alfredo Elizondo and especially Joaquín Amaro of Michoacán. Amaro was to rise to prominence during the battles against Villa and would be the

[43]La Prensa (Mexico City), March 2, 1915; Obregón, Ocho mil kiló-metros, pp. 280–285. Carranza's comments are available in El Pueblo (Vera-cruz), March 11, 1915.

man who, following Obregón's direction, organized the Constitutionalist Army into the more professional and far less political institution it was to become after the Revolution.[44]

Furthermore, Obregón had now come to the attention of
the world outside. The *New York Times*, discussing the Mexican situation editorially, concluded on February 27 that it was
"fair to predict that he is planning to play a larger part in the
Mexican game."[45]

Thus, in a few short months, Obregón had gone a long
way toward recouping his losses at Aguascalientes and toward
building a political base of his own. He had established his
interest and good intentions toward peasants who wanted land
and workers who wanted guarantees and a better standard of
living, and he had already begun to take specific measures in
these areas. These efforts were beginning to bring him support
in the military struggle against Villa. Further, he had developed
lines of political support among Constitutionalist leaders, both
military and intellectual, which would help him deal with Carranza. As an added advantage, he was developing an image,
both national and international, ⸍as a rational and reasonable
revolutionary leader.

[44]Juan Barragán in Urióstegui, *Testimonios*, p. 240; Vicente Estrada
Cajigal, interview, PHO/4/12, 1st transcription, pp. 12–13. The final arrangements for the incorporation of Amaro and Elizondo into the Constitutionalist
forces were completed in Tula, Hidalgo (*El Pueblo* [Veracruz], March 17,
1915).

[45]*New York Times*, February 27, 1915.

CHAPTER 8

Obregón versus Villa:
Confrontation in the Bajío

Obregón's popular image was built first and foremost on his military accomplishments, which, in the period 1912–1915, were formidable. He had established himself as an audacious and intelligent leader from the time of his earliest actions against the Orozquistas, and his ability as a military strategist developed through these years to its highest point at the time of the showdown with Villa and the Conventionists in the Bajío after the abandonment of the capital. After the victories against Villa between May and December of 1915, he did not again lead his troops in major battles until the challenges that arose during his presidency. The striking fact about his military prowess was that he himself was self-taught, basing his military strategy on his own observations, judgment, and psychological insight rather than on textbooks of military lore.

Therefore, the specific strategies he employed differed considerably in different circumstances, in different geographical surroundings, and against different opponents. Basically, however, the tenets he observed were fourfold. The first was to know perfectly the land on which the battle was to be fought. He was helped in this task by his own extraordinary memory for detail, and whenever possible he himself would make a careful reconnaissance of the area. Further, he studied his opponents as individuals and worked to counter their strengths and to use their weaknesses against them. This knowledge of his opponents, both as military men and as personalities, was to be of particular benefit in his battles against Villa.

Thirdly, he conducted good intelligence operations, both clandestine and otherwise, and always maintained a substantial espionage system. In addition, he would welcome visitors to his camp and quiz them extensively about enemy numbers, conditions, and morale.[1] Needless to say, information thus gathered, along with his understanding of opposing military leaders, would permit careful planning for battle and would make possible fairly accurate prediction of enemy moves and countermoves. He would then brief his troops on possible contingencies. Lastly, he consciously waged and won the propaganda battle, thus attracting more recruits to his own side as well as influencing foreign, especially U.S., opinion in his own favor.

One companion in arms decribes several additional characteristics of Obregón's military style. First of all, he had an exact knowledge of his own resources. Aided again by his extraordinary memory, he was able to remember precisely what men and materiel he had to use and the terrain and other circumstances that would affect his use of them. He maintained flexibility in action and had a special ability to meet changing situations, characteristics he carried into his political activities as well. He always ensured that he had logistic support adequate to the job at hand and that the lines of communication were clear and efficient, a kind of planning of which Villa seemed incapable and which would put him at a disadvantage with Obregón. Obregón pursued a policy of dislocation of the enemy to provide maximum demoralization; he was a master of surprise and dramatic bluff. He insisted on and arranged for constant contact between his units so that he would know what was going on and what resources he had to meet military challenges.[2]

Further, he would bypass objectives he judged to be secondary and focus instead on more important goals, as he did when he left the Sonoran port of Guaymas in the hands of the federals in order to move more quickly on Mexico City. This

---

[1] See Juan de Dios Bojórquez, *Obregón: Apuntes biográficos*, p. 33, on Obregón's intelligence system and prebattle analyses.

[2] Francisco L. Urquizo, "Obregón, militar," in Alvaro Obregón, *Ocho mil kilómetros en campaña*, pp. xxiv–xxv.

ability to set priorities based on importance and on potential cost would serve him well in the political as well as the military sphere.

These characteristics, developing from the time of Obregón's earliest battles against Orozco, were most apparent in the series of engagements he would fight with Villa in April and May of 1915. These struggles took place in the Bajío, the broad central plain north of Mexico City.

More than just a battle between contending military forces, it was a showdown between the two military leaders, Obregón and Villa, and the course of the battles there reflected their personalities as well as their military tactics. Both men looked on the encounter as a personal showdown, and both were eager for it. Obregón, understanding Villa well, was able to use this understanding to outmaneuver his former ally and near assassin.

The military situation in March of 1915 urgently required action in the center of the country to draw off Villista pressure on various points in the north. With Calles virtually isolated in Sonora and with heavy pressure on El Ebano, gateway to the oil regions of the northeast, both Carranza and Obregón recognized the necessity of a diversion for Villa's forces.

Logistically, Villa had an advantage, being able to transport men and materiel quickly over the extensive railway network in the central portion of the country. Obregón and Carranza were to use this advantage against him, knowing that he would rise to the challenge of a fight with Obregón by bringing all available troops to one point, in the hope of defeating Obregón with one decisive blow. Obregón, on the other hand, was handicapped as he moved into the center of the country, as he had only one available rail line between his forces and Veracruz and was thus vulnerable along the length of it. Therefore, he worked his way into the center of the country slowly, keeping his forces as close together as possible to avoid being cut off.

Moreover, the Constitutionalists were probably at a disadvantage in terms of available forces. Obregón estimated his own troop strength before the first battle of Celaya at a total of 11,000 men, of whom 6,000 were cavalry and the other

5,000 infantry.[3] Villa, on the other hand, had more men available—according to estimates, up to three times as many as Obregón. Probably only about 12,000 were committed originally for the first battle of Celaya, as Villa had expected an easy victory and had not brought in the bulk of his forces. Before the battles were over, however, the Villistas probably numbered between 32,000 and 35,000.[4]

Obregón had prepared for the encounter as carefully as he could, but he was uncertain as to where and under what conditions he would meet the Villista troops. Villa himself had set up his headquarters temporarily at Irapuato, the rail junction where the lines from Jalisco in the west and Villa territory in the north intersect on the way to Mexico City. Villa was thus in a good position to move either way, depending on the situation—either west toward Diéguez or east toward Obregón. It was at Irapuato that Obregón had effectively cut Villa off from the south when he was driving on Mexico City during the fight against Huerta, and the strategic importance of this point had not escaped Villa. What did escape Villa was that Obregón was setting him up, with his challenge drawing him off from other important areas of the country in order to satisfy a point of honor.

It did occur to Villa's advisers, however. Felipe Angeles had warned Villa at the end of March that it would be courting disaster to meet Obregón so far from the main Villista base in Chihuahua. Angeles encouraged him to draw Obregón slowly into Villa territory, meanwhile gathering forces and ammunition, at that time in short supply. Villa would not listen. He

---

[3]Obregón, *Ocho mil kilómetros*, p. 319.

[4]Villa to Associated Press, April 6, 1914, in ibid., p. 319. Villa announced that he was sending 12,000 men to Celaya to fight Obregón and that he himself would proceed to Jalisco to fight Diéguez with 20,000 troops. This telegram was a ruse to confuse Obregón about Villa's actual plans and troop strength. In Martín Luis Guzmán, *Memorias de Pancho Villa*, the estimate of the number of Villa's troops at the time of the first battle is only 8,000, and Obregón's 12,000 (p. 909). This estimate seems very low for the Villistas. Charles C. Cumberland, *Mexican Revolution: The Constitutionalist Years*, estimates that Obregón had 7,000 men actually available, Villa 20,000 (p. 200). Villa continued to bring in more troops during the course of the two battles.

was eager to go and "pegarle al perfumado," as he put it, "strike down the perfumed one," and he badly underestimated the problems involved.[5] Villa had made the mistake of not respecting his adversary, a mistake Obregón himself never made about Villa despite his personal contempt for him.

The tactic Obregón employed over and over again with Villa, and which was always successful, was that of drawing him by one means or another onto Obregón's own ground. Villa, unable to wait patiently for the enemy to come to him, inevitably brought the battle to his opponent. Obregón, knowing that he would, was almost always able to choose the places for the battles and to deploy his troops in the most advantageous positions possible.

Obregón was by no means above baiting Villa to achieve the results he wanted. His success is shown by the message Villa sent to Maytorena, his ally in Sonora, on the eve of the first battle of Celaya. Obregón, according to him, had been boasting about his future success and had baptized two of his battalions "the Battalion of Death" and "the Battalion of the Black Hand." Villa, rising to the bait, reported that Obregón had even had the audacity to dedicate the battle to some of his friends. Villa's intelligence reported that Obregón had 12,000 to 15,000 men (an exaggeration), but Villa promised Maytorena that he would fight him with energy and that he himself dedicated the battle to the sons of Sonora, as they would suffer more than anyone else if Obregón could bring his plans to invade that state to fruition.[6] It was obvious from the message that Villa's honor had become involved and that he would do anything possible to show up Obregón for the posturing, pompous fool he believed him to be. Obregón was willing to let him think so for the time being.

Obregón had arrived in Celaya on April 4, 1915, and had

[5]Federico Cervantes, *Felipe Angeles en la Revolución Mexicana*, p. 210. Villa was more concerned with a possible threat to the rear of his position from "reactionary" elements gathering in Texas (Villa to Llorente, March 24, 1915, ELA).

[6]Maytorena for Villa to Secretario del Estado, Hermosillo, April 5, 1915, PHS/60.

heard that Villa was mobilizing his troops for an attack on Obregón's vanguard almost immediately. On April 5 Obregón sent out a column, under Fortunato Maycotte and Cesáreo Castro, along the rail line to see what the Villistas would do, while he himself checked over the topography around Celaya itself. The next day he received news that Maycotte's column had been surrounded in Guaje station, about eighteen miles north of Celaya, and needed reinforcements. Obregón personally accompanied the reinforcements, which proceeded by train up the rail line. As they approached Guaje, Obregón ordered the engineer to pull the whistle so as to divert the fire of the Villistas and thus give Maycotte's men time to escape. This ploy worked, and Maycotte and his men joined the reinforcements in fighting as they slowly retreated toward Celaya.

Obregón ordered the train to go just fast enough so that the Villistas could almost catch them, but not quite, and in this way he pulled the Villistas along with them to the edge of Celaya where the rest of his forces were concentrated. After bitter fighting for two days, the Villistas almost broke through one part of Obregón's line, which was being abandoned by Obregón's men as they ran out of ammunition and were forced to find new supplies. On hearing this news, Obregón went immediately to the weak spot in the line with his ten-year-old bugler, Jesús Martínez, and ordered him to play the "Diana," the signal to advance. The Villistas, disconcerted and fearing that Obregón was leading them into a trap, as he had originally led them into Celaya, hesitated long enough for the line to be reinforced and Obregón's men resupplied with ammunition. By the middle of the day on the seventh, Obregón felt that the Villa forces were sufficiently exhausted to be susceptible to cavalry charges, and he ordered Castro, Maycotte, and others to attack the Villista troops on both flanks. Terrified, the Villistas began to fall back, and the battle turned into a rout. The Constitutionalist cavalry pursued them for fifteen kilometers, until darkness fell. Villa was suffering his first major defeat.[7]

[7] The official reports of the battle are in Alvaro Obregón, "Partes oficiales de las batallas de Celaya, 6, 7, 13, 14, 15 de abril de 1915," and are reprinted in Obregón, *Ocho mil kilómetros*, pp. 299–305.

Villa was stung by the disaster but unable to comprehend just what had happened. He blamed the defeat on a lack of ammunition, rather than on any military strategy on Obregón's part. Villa was as conscious of public opinion as Obregón, and he was concerned, with good reason, about the effect his defeat would have in Mexico and in the United States. Villa therefore resolved to pull up all possible men and resources to throw into a second battle against Obregón in Celaya, drawing even more men off from other important points around the country.

Meanwhile, Carranza and the Constitutionalists in Veracruz were enjoying the sweet smell of success. They had followed the battle closely, publishing Obregón's telegrams in their semi-official newspaper, *El Pueblo*. Obregón informed them on April 7 that, after thirty hours of desperate combat, the Constitutionalists had taken the offensive at 1:10 P.M. and were beginning to take Villista arms and prisoners, noted in that order. Obregón at that moment was preparing trains, which he would accompany, to advance through the center to support the cavalry charges on each flank. It was at this point that Obregón made the famous comment that "Fortunately, Villa is directing the battle personally."[8] This comment was not a reflection on Villa's courage, which Obregón did not doubt, or on his intelligence, but on his predictability.

At 3:30, Obregón reported that the Villistas were in full retreat. By April 8, Villa had retired well to the north, taking with him a hundred priests from Celaya. Villa was claiming that he had retreated because of a lack of ammunition, of which he supposedly had plenty in Irapuato, and because the continued battle would have meant destroying the city, especially the churches, and would have caused the deaths of many civilians. His withdrawal was, he said, designed to bring the battle into open land where the innocent would not suffer. Obregón acidly pointed out that Villa's artillery fire during the battle itself

[8]Two communications from Obregón to Carranza, both dated April 7, 1915, in *El Pueblo* (Veracruz), April 8, 1915.

had repeatedly fallen on the churches and the center of the city.[9]

Carranza replied to Obregón's telegrams with delight. On April 8 he wired: "With great pleasure I have received the report of the heroism of the ten-year-old bugler during yesterday's battle. Call him to you, congratulate him in my name, and confirm his elevation in rank to corporal. Along with my congratulations to the heroic child, the General in Chief of the Army of the Northwest receives them as well, as during the action to which I refer, the one was as heroic as the other."[10]

The propaganda battle between the two forces continued in the wake of the military encounter. Villa, unwilling to admit his defeat, deliberately misled George Carothers, the U.S. observer traveling with him on President Wilson's behalf, into thinking that the engagement had been at worst a draw between the two forces. Carothers had stayed behind in Irapuato during the battle. In fact, Villa's feeding of erroneous information to Carothers during this whole period was to cause both to lose credibility with Woodrow Wilson and with the Department of State in Washington.[11] The U.S. consul in Aguascalientes was also in the dark as to the actual results of the battle as late as April 12. However, he had had an intimation of the disaster on April 8, when Villa had wired his backup forces in Aguascalientes to prepare accommodations for several thousand wounded soldiers. Bryan, irritated by the lack of sound information from Villa's side of the line, wired Carothers to quit prognosticating about the future and instead to report on battles already fought.[12]

[9]Obregón to Carranza, April 8, 1915, in *El Pueblo* (Veracruz), April 10, 1915.

[10]Carranza to Obregón, April 8, 1915, in *El Pueblo* (Veracruz), April 10, 1915.

[11]For an evaluation of this episode, see Larry D. Hill, *Emissaries to a Revolution: Woodrow Wilson's Agents in Mexico*, pp. 326–328.

[12]Schmutz to Secretary of State, April 12, 1914, USDS 812.00/14895; Schmutz to Secretary of State, April 8, 1915, USDS 812.00/14862; Bryan to Carothers, April 14, 1915, USDS 812.00/14895.

On the other hand, the battle had been far less decisive than the Constitutionalists, from the safety of Veracruz, were proclaiming, as Villa's quick mounting of yet another fierce attack on Celaya was to show.

Villa's military attack was preceded by yet another grand-stand play to public opinion. Continuing to emphasize that his retreat had been ordered out of consideration for the populace of Celaya, he called for Obregón to come out of Celaya to fight him on open ground. Villa took the precaution of sending this communication to the consuls of France, Germany, England, and the United States in Celaya, who sent along a rather timid communication of their own urging Obregón to permit all non-combatants in the city to evacuate to a place where they would be safe from the artillery of the Division of the North.[13]

Obregón refused to be lured from Celaya by Villa's challenge, and he made a testy reply to the consuls, saying that it was unnecessary for foreigners to outline his duty to him. He added that Villa was only trying to obscure the extent of his earlier defeat, that he doubted that the assassin (Villa) of Benton and Bauch was really very concerned with foreign lives or any others, that Villa himself would choose the battlefield, since he was now in retreat, and finally—another piece of bait for Villa—that he doubted that Villa would dare to return to attack an army that had just defeated him so badly. Obregón wanted Villa to attack him at Celaya, before cooler heads such as Felipe Angeles' could prevail, as he now felt he could defeat him definitively. The Constitutionalist News Office immediately published this exchange of messages, disseminating it from Vera-cruz in the hope of giving it the widest possible propaganda value.[14]

In the meantime, Obregón's forces were growing substan-tially. On April 12, the Empleados de Comercio, a group of white-collar workers who had joined the Constitutionalists, arrived from Orizaba, followed shortly by two of the Red Battalions, the Third and the Fourth, which were formed from

---

[13]Obregón, *Ocho mil kilómetros*, p. 307.
[14]Ibid.; *El Pueblo* (Veracruz), April 13, 1915.

the recruits from the Casa del Obrero Mundial, now armed and placed under the command of the Cananea labor leader, Juan José Ríos. The First Division of the East, along with the forces of Generals Porfirio González and Jesús Novoa, had also incorporated themselves into Obregón's forces. Further, Obregón could now count on the forces of Joaquín Amaro, the "rayados de Celaya," so called because they were dressed in the striped uniforms of the convicts in the prison San Juan de Ulúa, the only uniform Carranza had available at the time. Obregón's forces had thus grown from a rather doubtful 11,000 at the time of the first battle to around 15,000—8,000 cavalry and 7,000 infantry, of whom 3,000 were raw recruits.[15]

Amaro was a particularly important addition to Obregón's forces. He had originally opted for the Conventionists but had decided in the wake of their administrative if not yet military collapse to join the Constitutionalists, after having received arms and ammunition from Villa. Obregón had had his doubts about accepting him originally but had finally decided that he would be a valuable ally. Amaro was rumored to be of Indian blood, probably Yaqui, and a semisavage, as he gave no quarter in battle and ruthlessly killed all prisoners, but in fact he had been an accountant in Zacatecas before the Revolution. He was an excellent general, however, of puritanical habits (he neither smoked nor drank), and he required his troops to read about military strategy and especially about the use of cavalry.[16] Amaro was to prove so valuable that he would later be secretary of war during Calles' presidency.

Villa was preparing for the battle as well, gathering as many men for the second assault as he could, but he was beginning to run out of supplies and money. He continued to urge his forces to press the attack on El Ebano, in order to obtain the oil fields of the Tampico area, which would have afforded

[15]*El Pueblo* (Veracruz), April 13, 1915; Obregón, *Ocho mil kilómetros*, p. 327; Vicente Estrada Cajigal, interview, PHO/4/12, p. 12; Obregón, *Ocho mil kilómetros*, p. 327.
[16]Estrada Cajigal, interview, PHO/4/12, p. 18; Nicolás Fernández Carrillo, interview in Píndaro Urióstegui Miranda, *Testimonios del proceso revolucionario de México*, p. 113.

him a new source of income. However, they were unable to defeat the Constitutionalist defenders. Meanwhile, he was engaged in diplomatic maneuvers, trying to keep foreign countries, and especially the United States, on his side.[17] While Villa was engaged in all these endeavors, Obregón was carefully planning for the battle. Knowing Villa's only strategy was to attack, again and again, he was planning to suck him into yet another untenable position.

Obregón set up his forces in a ring around Celaya, in order to permit Villa to surround the city completely, thus requiring Villa to disperse his forces along a front of almost twenty kilometers. Meanwhile, he sent 7,000 cavalry under Cesáreo Castro well to the rear where Villa couldn't see them and arranged a system of heliographs and flags that would inform Castro when to advance. His plan was to permit Villa to wear himself out along the long front encircling Celaya, and when he was sufficiently weakened Castro would come, seemingly out of nowhere, to attack the Villistas' left flank with his cavalry to the north of the town. Simultaneously, the front line of Obregón's forces defending the city would perform a flanking movement on the south, thus permitting the cavalry units under Amaro, Elizondo, and others, who had remained in the city, to burst out and attack the Villa forces on the right flank.[18]

The battle began on April 13, and by the evening of April 14 Obregón judged that the Villista forces were sufficiently weakened to prepare for the cavalry charge in the morning. Villa, as expected, had thrown his men against Obregón's fortified position over and over again, without being able to break through into the city, and they were demoralized and running out of ammunition. On the morning of April 15, the cavalry forces within the city began to break out south of the siege line, following the advancing infantry, and Castro's fresh caval-

[17]For a complete discussion of Villa's position, see Guzmán, *Memorias*, pp. 929–942.

[18]Obregón, "Partes de Celaya," pp. 17–22; Francisco J. Grajales, "Interpretación de las campañas militares de General Obregón," in Obregón, *Ocho mil kilómetros*, pp. cx–cxvii.

ry came charging to the north. Villa's men, faced with Obregón's cavalry to their left and right, were terrified and broke ranks, retreating in disorder and devastation toward Irapuato, where those who could entrained for the north.[19] The plan had worked perfectly.

Militarily, Villa was not beaten yet, as the month-long battle around León, Guanajuato, was to show. However, he was hurt badly in more subtle ways. Obregón had destroyed the myth of his invincibility, and many military leaders began changing sides in the hope of joining the ultimate winner. Many of Villa's troops either deserted or changed sides as well. Although Obregón shot more than one hundred Villista officers after the battle, some of them reported to be personal enemies, his amnesty policies toward troops were very liberal. Usually, he would accept any troops who wanted to join him into his armies, provided that they brought their weapons with them. Otherwise, after requiring that they turn in their weapons, he would permit them to return to their homes.[20] Obviously he would have been unable to provide for the large number of prisoners taken, and his well-known amnesty policies were an incentive to the other side to surrender.

Almost as important, Villa was losing his credibility both inside and outside Mexico. Suppliers of war materiel, particularly ammunition, began to charge higher prices and demand cash on the barrelhead for the purchases. Lázaro de la Garza, one of Villa's principal fiscal agents, wrote to Villa that, as a result of his retreat from Celaya and of the comments in the U.S. press that the defeat had been caused by a lack of ammunition, the price of ammunition had risen steeply to $72.00 (U.S.) per

[19]Gilberto Navas Presa, interview, PHO/1/26, pp. 36–37; Victor Anda, interview, PHO/1/46, 1st transcription, p. 45; Aarón Sáenz, in Urióstegui, *Testimonios*, pp. 376–378; Obregón, "Partes de Celaya," pp. 23–28.

[20]Fernando Torreblanca, interview, July 24, 1974; Obregón to Carranza, April 15, 1915, in Juan Barragán, *Historia del Ejército y de la Revolución Constitucionalista*, 2:298. See the appeal from the prisoners in the Penitenciaría del Estado, Monterrey, October 17, 1915, AC. Knowing that Obregón had offered widespread amnesty to those surrendering to his forces, they had surrendered to another Constitutionalist group and had wound up in jail. Also see Ricardo Pozas, *Juan: The Chamula*, p. 42.

thousand. Although there were still supplies available for immediate delivery, the price was not negotiable. In view of Villa's desperate need for the commodity, de la Garza recommended buying 5 million of the available 15 million rounds and then waiting for the price to drop.[21]

Unfortunately for Villa, his money was also running out. Although he was still able to export cotton and *ixtle*, a native rope-making fiber, his supplies of cattle to sell for ready cash were dwindling, and he had been unable to take the oil regions, which he so greatly coveted.[22] Villa's credit within Mexico was beginning to slip as well. His own currency was beginning to lose value rapidly.

Moreover, the Constitutionalists now knew how fragile the coalition between Zapata and Villa had been. Although Obregón's supply lines into the center of the country were constantly vulnerable to Zapatista attack, no concerted attempt was made to cut them. As Wilson's special agent to Carranza commented at the time, Obregón was extremely vulnerable if defeated because his retreat could have been cut off by the Zapatistas. He went on to say, "It is a wonder that they have not also cut the line as they are known to have a considerable force at Otumba," near the rail line Obregón was using to bypass Mexico City.[23]

The war news had brought jubilation to Veracruz. Carranza, exaggerating, no doubt, stated that the "reaction" was now defeated. He reported that the multitude in Veracruz was acclaiming the victory and that a spontaneous celebration had sprung up. Various orators were making speeches from an automobile, among them representatives of the people of the town and countryside, others from the Casa del Obrero Mundial, and others from the Partido Nacional Democrático (P.N.C.). For his part, the U.S. special agent Silliman was inclined to believe that the reports of victory were real, as "a general celebration is on here with the bells pealing."[24]

[21]De la Garza to Villa, April 21, 1915, DLGA-I-K-35.
[22]De la Garza to Villa, April 13, 1915, DLGA-I-K-28.
[23]Silliman to Secretary of State, April 15, 1915, USDS 812.00/14860.
[24]*El Pueblo* (Veracruz), April 16, 1915; Silliman to Secretary of State, April 15, 1915, USDS 812.00/14857.

The Constitutionalists moved quickly to exploit this new victory in propaganda terms. On April 19, the director of the Mexican consular service wired to the Constitutionalist consuls around the world that Obregón's forces had that day inflicted a tremendous rout to the "reactionary army" personally commanded by General Villa. The Villista losses were reported at 30 cannons, 5,000 Mausers with ammunition, and 14,000 men. The telegram concluded: "Villa with rest of his men escaped north after this new and complete disaster. Publish it."[25]

The *New York Times* hesitated for several days before printing news of the Constitutionalist victory, as they were getting news of the battle from the State Department, which in turn was awaiting Carothers' report. Finally on April 20, Carothers wired the real news: Villa had been routed. The *New York Times* reported this fact the same day; Villa had lost the battle and was trying to regroup at Aguascalientes.[26]

Obregón's strategy after the battle of Celaya changed considerably. After pursuing the enemy rapidly for several days and taking Irapuato virtually without resistance on April 22, he slowed down his advance to the north. Throughout most of May and early June, Villista and Constitutionalist troops faced each other in the vicinity of León, Guanajuato. In spite of propaganda to the contrary, both armies had been badly hurt by the battle of Celaya, and it had cost Villa a major effort to pull his forces back together to offer resistance to Obregón's advance. Obregón, on the other hand, was getting farther and farther from his supply base in Veracruz. Still, to Villa's distress, the Zapatistas made no real effort to interrupt Obregón's supply lines. Obregón was adopting the strategy that Felipe Angeles had suggested to Villa: he was permitting Villa to wear himself out slowly in a prolonged battle that would ultimately prove inconclusive and was waiting for a moment at which Villa was weakened to move.[27]

[25]For example, see Director, Consulmex, Veracruz, to Consulmex, Paris, France, April 19, 1915, ASRE-119, L-E-730, Leg. 2.

[26]Carothers to Secretary of State, April 20, 1915, USDS 812.00/14897; *New York Times*, April 20, 1915.

[27]Obregón, *Ocho mil kilómetros*, p. 364.

Angeles recognized this strategy and encouraged Villa to move to Torreón or Chihuahua, closer to Villa's base and more suitable for Villa's sort of aggressive pitched battle, but Villa's pride was engaged and he was still determined to resist at León. Even after Angeles had looked over the flat terrain at León and had again emphasized its unsuitability to Villa's sort of warfare, Villa continued to insist that it would be the site of his resistance to the advancing Constitutionalists.[28]

The battle dragged on through May, until Obregón felt that his forces were in a sufficiently strong position to take the offensive again. It was while he was on his way to a meeting with his officers to coordinate this offensive that he was hit by an enemy artillery shell that blew off his right arm. Obregón, convinced that he was dying, grabbed his pistol in his left hand and fired into his left temple, but the attempted suicide failed as there was no shell in the chamber. His aide, Lieutenant Colonel Jesús M. Garza, prevented him from firing again and then sent Aarón Sáenz to look for a doctor for a *compañero*. Despite efforts to keep Obregón's wound a secret, Villistas found out almost immediately, and that evening the Constitutionalist troops heard the Villistas, from the other side of the line, shouting "Come get Obregón's arm, Carrancistas," along with a hail of bullets and insults.[29]

Obregón later enjoyed telling macabre anecdotes about the loss of his arm. To Edward Larocque Tinker, who asked if he had indeed been close to death, he replied that he must have been, for he fainted and awoke to find his staff "dividing my money and drawing lots for my watch." Obregón's own story about the recovery of the lost arm, now housed in his monument in Mexico City, was that a member of his staff walked through the battleground holding a gold coin and calling, "Alvaro, Alvaro, where are you?" When the severed arm

[28]Cervantes, *Felipe Angeles*, p. 210.
[29]Sáenz, in Urióstegui, *Testimonios*, pp. 380–383; Gustavo Salinas, interview, PHO/1/11, p. 32.

jumped up and grabbed the gold coin, he knew that he had found the right one.[30]

In spite of the levity with which Obregón looked back upon the event, the situation on June 3, 1915, was very grave. Obregón's wound was serious, although no vital organs were affected. Had it not been for quick medical action to stanch the flow of blood, he could easily have died. If Villa's forces were beginning to weaken and were running out of ammunition, so were Obregón's. None of their opponents ever doubted that the Villistas, once they had a hope of victory, could be formidable opponents. As Obregón was carried behind the lines to safety and further medical attention, direction of the troops passed to his trusted friend General Benjamín Hill. It was, however, a question whether or not Obregón's troops would follow Hill with the same confidence they had given to Obregón. Furthermore, in the situation, Obregón's generals were uncertain about what to do: whether the offensive should continue, or whether the battle should be temporarily delayed. Moreover, Obregón was not the only casualty resulting from the new offensive; losses had been heavy, and the Constitutionalist leader from Jalisco, Amado Aguirre, had been among those wounded.[31]

At a meeting between Generals Murguía, Castro, Diéguez, who had come from Jalisco to join Obregón, and Hill, it was decided that the attack must be pressed to preserve the momentum in Obregón's favor and to prevent the news of Obregón's wound from encouraging Villa's troops and demoralizing their own. Various versions of these discussions exist, but it seems probable that General Murguía was the one responsible for the decision to take rapid action against the enemy and that his

[30]Edward Larocque Tinker, *New Yorker Unlimited: The Memoirs of Edward Larocque Tinker*, p. 144; Fernando Torreblanca, interview, November 15, 1972.

[31]Amado Aguirre, "Report of the Battle of Trinidad," Archivo del Ejército del Noroeste, in Archivo de Amado Aguirre, Mexico City.

direction and planning were most important in securing victory. On June 5, the attack was resumed, the vanguard taken by Yaquis who crept up to the Villista trenches at daybreak. The Villistas, unsuspecting and terrified, were on the run again.[32]

On June 5, 1915, León fell into Constitutionalist hands. Obregón himself, although he had not directed the battle, wired Carranza that the battle was the "most important triumph of our armies against the traitors Villa and Angeles."[33]

In a military sense, this assessment was probably correct. It had been an important psychological victory as well, because it proved that the Constitutionalist armies could prevail even without Obregón's direction, whereas Villa himself was the only one who could hold the Division of the North together. The Constitutionalist effort, centrally directed and organized, would prove too much for the disorganized and diffuse Villista effort, which was based on the charismatic leadership of one man.

Obregón was also a charismatic leader, but his subordination of himself to the direction of the first chief and his cooperation in a coordinated military effort had put the success of the Constitutionalists beyond the vulnerability of one individual. The Conventionist effort was one based on support of individual leaders, loosely coordinated at best and sometimes openly hostile to each other, who were unwilling or unable to support one another strategically. Zapata's failures to cut Obregón's supply lines in central Mexico had contributed seriously to Villa's failure in the north. The Constitutionalist effort, co-

---

[32]See, for example, Salinas interview, PHO/1/11, pp. 34–35; Sáenz, in Urióstegui, *Testimonios*, pp. 383–385; Hill to Obregón, July 2, 1915, in Obregón, *Ocho mil kilómetros*, pp. 374–375; Obregón to Carranza, June 7, 1915, in Barragán, *Historia del Ejército*, 2:349–352. William B. Davis, the U.S. consular officer in Guadalajara, reported that by the end of June Constitutionalist recruiting was better than ever, which he attributed to the lack of paid work in any field except soldiering (William B. Davis, *Experiences and Observations of an American Consular Officer during the Recent Mexican Revolutions*, pp. 155–156). I would suggest that by this time news of the Constitutionalist victories had spread and that individuals were trying to enlist on the winning side.

[33]Obregón to Carranza, June 5, 1915, in Barragán, *Historia del Ejército*, p. 346.

ordinated through the first chief in Veracruz, permitted mutual support and supportive strategic action between the various military chiefs, thus leading to victory.

The battles in the Bajío had shown the difference between Obregón and Villa as men and as military leaders. As one Villista who knew them both observed, Villa was "the greatest warrior in the world"; Obregón, "the greatest Mexican general."[34] The distinction is an important one. Villa won when he did, not because of strategy or knowledge of his opponent's weaknesses; he won because of his audacity and his prodigality with the resources he had at his disposal, resources ranging from ammunition to human lives. Obregón, on the contrary, carefully took the measure of his opponent and used his resources when and where they would do the most good. In the Bajío, when men and war materiel were in relatively short supply for both sides, a war of attrition would bring victory to the one who used his resources more wisely, in this case Obregón.

Had Villa followed Angeles' advice, withdrawn to a more secure area, and forced Obregón to take the offensive under unfavorable terms, the outcome of the battles might have been different; but it was not in Villa's nature to fight such a battle. As Martín Luis Guzmán perceptively imagined Villa's thoughts,

If, for lack of resources, I do not go out to fight Obregón, but retreat before his forces, protecting myself by assuming what is called the defensive, seeking shelter . . . the prestige of my troops will shrink away in the eyes of my enemy and my name will suffer. For when, since our first attack and the taking of Torreón in September of 1913, have we permitted the enemy to tire himself out looking for us in our territory? When have I not gone out to fight, taking away his towns, breaking him with my thrust, tearing him apart? Which of my troops would stay with me if coming upon Obregón we did not throw ourselves upon him and defeat him?[35]

Obregón, understanding well Villa's psychological makeup, was able to exploit Villa's tendency to throw himself into battle against the enemy and to lure him, time after time, into dis-

---

[34]Roberto Fierro Villalobos, interview, PHO/1/42, p. 46.
[35]Guzmán, *Memorias*, p. 910.

advantageous situations. Villa, faced with reverses in battle, would answer by throwing in more men and ammunition until no more were available. Obregón, on the other hand, would contact various parts of his line through his careful system of communications, review his circumstances in view of what he discovered and of what he remembered of the terrain in his earlier reconnaissance, and then plan his strategy accordingly. Villa simply continued to press the battle with all resources at hand. Obregón in battle was cagey and opportunistic; Villa was always predictable.

Both were charismatic leaders of men, but that was not the key to their victory or defeat. Both were courageous and audacious, but Obregón saved his audacity for the moment at which it would be most effective. Both were continually close to the front during the height of the battle, checking and rechecking the situation and encouraging their men. Neither broke on the battlefield, setting an example for their men, and both fraternized extensively with their troops during the lulls between military actions, thus inspiring a high degree of personal loyalty. Villa, however, depended greatly on the myth of his invincibility, and when it was shown that he could be defeated much of his support melted away. Obregón's organization was much more businesslike: the potential difficulties of the battle were explained before the action started, and potential changes in strategies in the event of reverses were discussed. Villa, haranguing his men before a battle, would never admit that reverses were possible, and when they came his men were terrified, surprised, and demoralized.

Thus, when Villa began to be defeated by Obregón, his ability to regroup was severely handicapped. The morale of his troops plummeted, desertions were rampant, and the Constitutionalists were able to keep him on the run. Further, his defeat caused him major difficulties in the United States, slowing the flow of credit and thus supplies as his ultimate defeat seemed more likely, and eroding the tacit support that he had received from the U.S. government.

Obregón, on the other hand, was able to carry his image as a winner into the political arena, where he would eventually challenge Carranza for the leadership of the Constitutionalist movement. The defeat of Villa would make him the preeminent military hero of the Revolution and would immeasurably strengthen his hand in the political battle to come.

CHAPTER 9

Obregón and Carranza:
The Political Struggle

While Obregón was carrying forward the military struggle against Pancho Villa, his relationship with his ostensible ally, Carranza, was far from comfortable. In fact, a subtle but serious political battle was going on between them from Obregón's return from the Aguascalientes Convention until May, 1917, when he resigned from Carranza's cabinet. Until then, they needed each other, and both feared an open break. However, Obregón continued to work on a secure power base of his own, despite considerable problems with his health. He also pursued his policy of developing strong ties with labor and the agrarian movement, he began to move toward the professionalization of the army, and he oversaw mopping up operations against Villa. During this time, he continued to gather supporters, both in the highest political ranks and among working people in the city and the countryside.

These supporters were mobilized from the top by the Confederación Revolucionaria, which Obregón and others had begun on the trains that originally carried them to Veracruz in December, 1914, as they fled from the Villistas. One of the principal points the Confederation pushed was the question of land reform, and it was at least partly under pressure from this organization that Carranza issued his Agrarian Law of January 6, 1915. The Agrarian Law, of course, was necessary to counterbalance the popular appeal of the Villa-Zapata Convention, and, though it promised the land reform that Obregón and others strongly urged, Carranza was dubious about enforcing it. Although land distribution by revolutionary forces began almost immediately and had been going on in some areas even before January 6, Carranza finally ordered it stopped and cancelled further conferences by the Confederation.[1]

The Confederation continued to grow, albeit in an informal and haphazard fashion, and its composition came to include students, lawyers, artists, workers, *campesinos*, and even women—of all social classes, Atl once noted. As a matter of fact, Obregón, a handsome man, attracted women to his cause and welcomed them as workers in his behalf. Frequently during the gala evenings that followed his military victories one or more of the speakers would be female, and women played a notable role in his later presidential campaign.

In any case, the Revolutionary Confederation was establishing a wide-ranging popular base, and Confederation newspapers were started in Guadalajara, Tampico, and Orizaba. Juan de Dios Bojórquez, later to be a radical delegate to the Constitutional Convention, founded one called *El Sector*, which he published aboard a military train. Atl began publishing another, usually originating from Orizaba, called *Vanguardia*. New groups formed wherever Obregón's troops went. His enemies in Veracruz began to comment that at the end of the military campaign, Obregón would have an army of civilians even more powerful than his army of soldiers.[2] Certainly the Confederation was contributing enormously to Obregón's popular support, while at the same time recruiting a number of young, usually middle-class, intellectuals, despite the opposition of some of Carranza's civilian advisers.[3]

[1]Gerardo Murillo [pseud. Dr. Atl], "Obregón y el principio de renovación social," in *Obregón: Aspectos de su vida*, p. 73; Luis Sánchez Pontón, interview, PHS/1/20, p. 21.

[2]Murillo, "Obregón," pp. 76–77; Félix Palavicini, *Mi vida revolucionaria*, p. 259.

[3]Juan C. Zertuche, an early member of the Confederación Revolucionaria, formed a corps of students called the Cuerpo Especial Reforma, which fought at the first battle of Celaya and later performed garrison duty under the labor leader General Juan José Ríos in Colima on Mexico's West Coast, an area important to Obregón (Juan de Dios Bojórquez, *Hombres y aspectos de México*, pp. 90–92; Juan Gualberto Amaya, *Síntesis social de la Revolución Mexicana*, pp. 69–70).

The importance of the Revolutionary Confederation, and especially the influence of its newspapers, began to worry Carranza, and precipitated a cabinet crisis in June of 1915, simultaneous with Obregón's wound and subsequent Constitutionalist military victories at León. Constitutionalist official publications, including the newspaper *El Pueblo*, had been under the control of Rafael Zubarán Capmany, Carranza's secretary of government and member of the Confederation. Carranza called his devoted follower Félix Palavicini into his office and directed him to take over the management of the newspapers "of the Revolution."[4] These would include *El Pueblo*, *El Demócrata*, and a number of other newspapers and magazines, especially in the U.S. border region. Most important, Dr. Atl's *Vanguardia* would be affected.

Carranza sent Palavicini himself to report the change to Secretary of Government Zubarán, who refused to turn the newspapers over until he had spoken with Carranza. As Palavicini later pointed out, Carranza's decision indicated complete withdrawal of confidence from Zubarán and inevitably led to his resignation. A period of turmoil followed, during which Palavicini in fact took over as editor of *El Pueblo*, saw members of his staff arrested by the Ministry of Justice, and began to spar publicly with Dr. Atl's *Vanguardia*, still appearing in Orizaba. Eventually four Constitutionalist cabinet members submitted their resignations: Zubarán, Manuel Escudero y Verdugo, Luis Cabrera, and Jesús Urueta, another member of the Confederation. Cabrera, a strong Carrancista, later withdrew his resignation. Meanwhile, Confederation membership in Carranza's cabinet had been gutted. Obregón wired his concern to the first chief. Carranza simply indicated that the problems had been with Palavicini, not with him, and that the departure of these men indicated no real change in policy.[5]

Carranza had been moving in other ways to limit Obregón's power and the power of the military generally. Obregón was as concerned about the dangers of military factionalism as Carranza was; indeed, he was in the front line of the battle against

[4]Palavicini, *Mi vida*, pp. 255–256.
[5]Ibid., pp. 258, 264–287.

Villa, which had developed out of just this factionalism at Aguascalientes. His concern about the dangers of military factionalism had led him to wire Carranza from Puebla after the first major victory on the road back to Mexico City. He began:

Deeply preoccupied by the disgraces that have afflicted our country since the early days of our Republic, I have become convinced that the principal cause of all of them has been the unbridled ambitions of an odious militarism, which, in recent times, has been manifested strikingly in a series of coups, assassinations, and betrayals. The rest of the world sees our country unredeemed from brutally ambitious men who do not measure the consequences in order to obtain whatever public post is most in reach of their military rank.

He went on to name as examples the Orozco rebellion, the Huerta coup, and the Villa "betrayal." Even between loyal Constitutionalist leaders, frictions had developed in the various states as each man tried to capture the government of that state for himself. With this background in mind, Obregón moved to suggest that active members of the military be prohibited from holding public office. To become eligible for elective office, they should resign completely from the military six months before they entered the political arena. Obregón credited these ideas to the civilian Sonoran leaders Adolfo de la Huerta and Roberto Pesqueira.[6] Carranza did not respond.

Nevertheless, Obregón did not approve of the division of military from civil government in the period before the military struggle had ended. On April 22, 1915, Carranza wired Obregón that he thought the time had come to divide the position of military commander in the Constitutionalist-held territories from the position of governor. He therefore informed Obregón that this division of responsibility would be observed in the future. It should be noted that he took this action only a few days after the victory at Celaya, when the military situation was still precarious. Obregón wired back his opinion that such a division would cause great difficulties between the two individuals named in any specific case, "given the character of our

6Obregón to Carranza, January 19, 1915, DRM-16, pp. 20–21.

men." Carranza replied that it was dangerous for governors with local political power to have military forces at their disposal and that the first chief would have to keep a close eye on them to be sure that they did not "take actions against the public interest." Therefore, he felt that the best way to achieve such control would be for the military forces in the states to report directly to him, thus providing a check on the actions of the governors.[7]

That this procedure would limit political action by military leaders, among them Obregón himself, was implicit in the exchange. Given the slightly improved military situation, Carranza was already trying to pull the reins of control back to the central Constitutionalist government and, of course, to himself. Carranza did not change his mind, although in fact he was never really able to control the state governors, and in many cases, such as Sonora and Sinaloa, both jobs continued to be held by one man for some time.

A further problem between Obregón and Carranza came in regard to their attitudes toward the old elite. Obregón was suspicious of Carranza's too benevolent attitude toward property owners, former Federal officers who had fought under Huerta, and former members of congress who had served during the Huerta administration. He expressed his concerns to Carranza in a series of memoranda beginning in May of 1915 and extending through December. The former members of Huerta's congress were of particular concern, as several of them had become advisers to Carranza and were, in general, opposed to the Confederation members. Carranza either did not answer Obregón's messages on these subjects or answered them negatively.[8] He was only postponing, however, a split between Confederation members, who would become more and more strongly associated with Obregón as their leader, and his own

[7]Carranza to Obregón, April 22, 1915, Obregón to Carranza, April 23, 1915, and Carranza to Obregón, May 15, 1915, all in LMG/AHDN, XI/481.5/316, f. 127.

[8]Carranza to Obregón, May 15, 1915, Obregón to Carranza, September 11, 1915, Carranza to Obregón, September 29, 1915, Obregón to Carranza, December 6, 1915, all in DRM-16, pp. 140–141, 226–228, 240–241, 270–271.

personal followers. This split would become evident at the time of the Constitutional Convention in late 1916 and early 1917.

Meanwhile, the United States, in the wake of Obregón's victories against Villa, was becoming more favorable to the Carranza government. Ironically, Carranza was gaining the security to move to restrict his principal military leader. Indeed, he was attempting to reduce the power of the military in general, and thus of the Sonoran group, who were significant within the military hierarchy. U.S. de facto recognition came on October 19, 1915, and on October 28 Carranza wired Obregón, Pablo González, and other military leaders to suspend their recruitment of forces, despite the fact that Villa was still marauding in Sonora and Obregón was about to begin a campaign to drive him from that state.[9]

Carranza's attempt to reduce the power of the military continued in the early months of 1916. On January 1, 1916, he announced through his supporter Mario Méndez, director general of the national telegraph system, that the use of telegraph services by the armed forces, heretofore almost completely unrestricted, would be severely limited. The criteria for use were not clearly stated, but it seemed obvious that those individuals favored by the Carranza government would be allowed to use free telegraph services, whereas those out of favor would not. On January 20, in Querétaro, Carranza moved still further to limit the freedom of movement by the military when he imposed restrictions on the use of the railroads.[10]

Obregón's position was rapidly becoming more difficult, and rumors about the possibility of his revolting against the first chief were rife. In a still more ironic twist of fate, it was Villa himself, through his attacks on the U.S. border, who made it possible for Obregón to recoup his political position by forc-

[9]Carranza to Pesqueira, October 28, 1915, *Revista del Ejército y Marina: Organo del Departamento de Estado Mayor de la Guerra y Marina* (November, 1915): 19. For Obregón's campaign, see Lansing to Secretary of War, November 5, 1915, Funston to Adjutant General, November 6, 16, and 25, 1915, all in AGO/VR, Box 7647.

[10]Circular #62, Dirección General de Telégrafos Nacionales, and Carranza Decree, January 20, 1916, both in *Revista del Ejército y Marina* (February, 1916): 187, 185.

ing Carranza once again to call on him in a time of crisis.

On March 9, 1916, Villa attacked Columbus, New Mexico, bringing into the picture the possibility of U.S. intervention in Mexico. Carranza, who had been touring the country, returned immediately to Querétaro, where he called on Obregón to join him, and on March 13, 1916, Carranza swore him in as secretary of war. Both Carranza and Obregón signed a statement to the effect that they would join in a "faithful and patriotic attempt to restore constitutional order in the Republic."[11] Obregón's job was not only to defeat Villa, but also to bring other recalcitrant local military leaders into the government. Further, Carranza needed him as window dressing to prove to the United States that he was moving energetically to control the country and to stop the Villista threat on the border.

Obregón was the most famous of his military leaders and by now the one most generally regarded by the United States as able to control Villa; indeed, he was probably the only general Carranza had who could control Villa. His appointment was also a good move from the point of view of internal public opinion. If anyone were able to pacify the country—and there were many threats in other areas in addition to the Villista problem—it would be Obregón. His appointment would give the Mexican people an impression of unity and power in the Carranza government. Carranza was not strong enough to discard his best general, although without Villa he might well have tried.

Further, Carranza was faced with the possibility of war with Mexico's neighbor to the north. In the wake of Villa's attack on Columbus, the United States had sent an expeditionary force under John J. Pershing into Mexico to pursue Villa. The chances of the U.S. Army's actually being able to catch Villa in the midst of a hostile population were slim, as General Pershing admitted in an undated letter to Hugh L. Scott: "I hope that your office and the War Department in general have

[11]Confirmation document from Carranza to Obregón, March 13, 1916, ASRE-125.

Generals Benjamín Hill, Manuel M. Diéguez, and Obregón (*left to right*) .on the battlefield at Trinidad, shortly before Obregón was wounded, May or June, 1915. *Fondo de Cultura Economica*

Three of Obregón's principal aides in the northern campaign against Villa, shown here during the Battle of León, May, 1915. *Left to right*: Aarón Sáenz, Francisco Serrano, and Josue Sáenz. *Library, Universidad de Sonora*

Colonel Amado Aguirre (*fourth from left*) in the line of fire at Trinidad during the Battle of León, May, 1915. *Library, Universidad de Sonora*

Obregón shortly after his wound at Trinidad during the Battle of León, June, 1915. *Casasola, INAH*

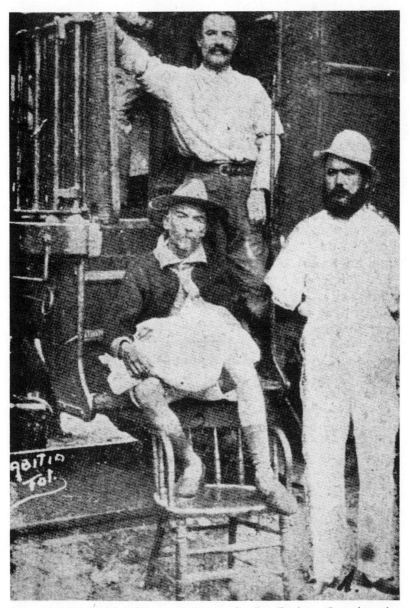

General Manuel M. Diéguez (*left, seated*), Dr. Enrique Osornio, who
had probably saved Obregón's life after the loss of his arm, and Obregón
in Lagos de Moreno, Jalisco, after that town was attacked by Villista
forces, July, 1915. *Casasola, INAH*

Generals Francisco Serrano (*on horse*) and Obregón (*on track*) and
Captain Valdez, in a stop on the way to Valle de Santiago, Guanajuato,
in July, 1915. *Fondo de Cultura Economica*

Constitutionalist leaders at a fiesta given by the governor of Querétaro
upon Obregón's return from the successful northern campaign against
Villa, January, 1916. *Left to right*: First Chief Venustiano Carranza,
General Pablo González, and Obregón (*standing*). *Casasola, INAH*

Obregón and his bride, the former María Tapia, arriving in Querétaro on their honeymoon, mid-1916. *Casasola, INAH*

Andrés García

Alvaro Obre

Left: Obregón with General Frederick Funston, commander of the Southern Department of the U.S. Army, during negotiations for the removal of the Pershing expedition, 1916. *Arizona Historical Society*.
Right: Andrés García (*left*) and Obregón on the border during negotiations for removal of the Pershing expedition, 1916. *Arizona Historical Society*

Minister of War Obregón, decorating soldiers wounded in the Revolution, late 1916 or early 1917. *Casasola, INAH*

Obregón, while minister of war, in a reunion with the young bugler, Jesús Martínez, whose signal to advance had frightened the Villistas at the Battle of Celaya, late 1916 or early 1917. *Casasola, INAH*

Minister of War Obregón speaking at the opening of the military academy in San Jacinto, October, 1916. *Casasola, INAH*

Left: Obregón (*center*) arriving in Mexico after his conferences with Generals Hugh Scott and Frederick Funston, May, 1916. *Casasola, INAH*. *Right*: Lázaro Cárdenas, who joined the Revolution at age 15, supported Obregón, and later became governor of Michoacán and, in the 1930's, President of Mexico.

Obregón (*center*) disguised as a railwayman, escaping from Mexico City with the help of Margarito Ramírez, April, 1920. *Casasola, INAH*

not allowed yourselves to become optimistic over the capture of this brigand, Villa. You know from your own experience that it is going to be a very difficult matter to run him down. It is a source of much regret that we could not have crossed the line immediately instead of waiting for a convention and an understanding between the two governments."[12]

In fact, there had been no real agreement between Mexico and the United States, and the Carranza government and most of the population of Mexico, including even those areas which had suffered from Villa's depredations, were bitterly opposed to the presence of U.S. troops on Mexican soil. The possibility of war between the two countries seemed strong. This risk was fanned by an incident in mid-April at Parral, Chihuahua, when U.S. troops were attacked by Mexican civilians. The regular Mexican army prevented the citizens from pursuing the troops, but one American was reported killed and several Mexicans were wounded. Carranza wired his representative in Washington to inform the U.S. secretary of state that Obregón had sent orders to cease the fighting, but that "such is the excitement of the people that I am not sure that the fighting can be stopped." He further urged that the U.S. troops be withdrawn at once, to prevent "even more serious results. . . ."[13]

Within the week, U.S. commanders began to express deep concern to Washington about the hostile attitude of the Mexican people and of the government and to report Mexican army troop movements from Sonora toward the U.S. lines of communication in Chihuahua. Pershing's recommendation was to capture both the city and the state of Chihuahua, including all the railroads therein, a step that almost certainly would have led to war.[14]

Despite Carranza's hostility toward the United States,

[12]Pershing to Scott, in Hugh Lenox Scott Papers, Library of Congress, Washington, D.C. (cited hereafter as HLS). Though undated, the letter is filed with other letters to Scott dated April of 1916.

[13]Aguilar to Arredondo, April 12, 1916, Carranza to Arredondo, April 12, 1916, both in U.S. Department of State, *Papers Relating to the Foreign Relations of the United States, 1916* (cited hereafter as PRFR), pp. 513–514.

[14]Pershing to Funston, April 17, 1916, included in Funston to Adjutant General, April 17, 1916, PRFR, pp. 521–522.

Mexico was in no condition to fight a war with another country. He therefore sent Obregón as minister of war to negotiate for a settlement of the differences between the two countries. However, Carranza's idea of negotiation was to present his terms—namely, the immediate withdrawal of U.S. troops from Mexico—and to force the United States to accept them, an unrealistic idea at best. It seems probable that Carranza knew that the United States would not withdraw as long as the possibility of serious depredations along the border existed.

In choosing Obregón to negotiate, he first of all was using the individual then regarded both in Mexico and in the United States as most capable of dealing with Villa. Thus, he was sending the most effective negotiator possible. In the event that Obregón failed to achieve the withdrawal, Carranza could then tag Obregón with the failure. On the other hand, should Obregón negotiate an agreement for something less than complete withdrawal, Carranza could burn him by accusing him of giving in to the North Americans and thus damage a man who had become a serious threat to his own power position. In fact, observers in Mexico were commenting constantly about a breach between Obregón and Carranza and even predicting that Obregón would overthrow Carranza in a coup d'etat and then throw Pershing and his troops back across the border.[15] Sending Obregón as a negotiator was, therefore, a way for Carranza to keep him tied to his own government, while retaining the possibility of repudiating any agreement Obregón might make.

Strangely enough, it seems to have been Obregón himself who first suggested negotiations to the U.S. authorities, although the official initiative came from the U.S. side. Probably Obregón, as secretary of war, was even more acutely aware than Carranza of the disadvantages Mexico would face in an international war. Further, Obregón must have realized that U.S. approval would be a great advantage to any Mexican leader, and this incident gave him an opportunity to deal direct-

---

[15]Constant to Scott, April 30, 1916, HLS. The best secondary source on the Scott-Obregón talks is Clarence Clendenen, *The United States and Pancho Villa*, pp. 270–285.

ly with North Americans from a position in which he could be influential. Indeed, the negotiator chosen by the American president was General Hugh L. Scott, army chief of staff, an acquaintance of Pancho Villa and a man with long experience in the American West and as a mediator along the border. Arrangements for the conference itself were made by Carranza through his representative in Washington, but as Obregón started north the rumors that he and Carranza had had a major disagreement, that Carranza was "very jealous of Obregón," and that Carranza would not respect the results of the conferences were circulating widely.[16]

The talks were approached both cautiously and nervously by the United States. First of all, no one was quite sure where on the border the talks would take place, and a good deal of correspondence was sent to Scott, first telling him to remain in San Antonio at the headquarters of the Southern Department, then telling him to proceed to one or another point on the border. Finally, he was instructed to find out, if possible, where Obregón would arrive and to make his way there. The Mexico City papers, meanwhile, simply said that Obregón was touring the northern states with his wife.[17] Some U.S. representatives in Mexico were concerned that Scott's former good relationship with Villa might prejudice General Obregón against him, a concern that was communicated to Scott by Secretary of War Newton D. Baker. As Obregón moved north, interviewing the local *jefes políticos* ("political bosses") along the way, U.S. observers became further concerned that Obregón's real object was rebellion against Carranza. Thus Scott was urged to take "especial precautions for . . . personal safety."[18]

Nevertheless, on April 26, Scott was given his negotiating instructions. In short, he was to offer full cooperation with the

---

[16]Scott to Bliss, April 27, 1916, Bliss to Scott, April 27, 1916, García to Beltran, April 27, 1916, and Scott to Secretary of War, April 22, 1916, all in HLS.

[17]McCain to Scott, April 25, 1916, and McCain to Scott, April 26, 1916, both in HLS; *El Pueblo* (Mexico City), April 27, 1916.

[18]Baker to Scott, April 26, 1916, and McCain to Scott, April 28, 1916, both in HLS.

Mexican military and to assure that U.S. troops would be withdrawn as soon as Villa was captured. He was to point out that the United States would be happy for the Mexicans to apprehend him themselves, as "the government of the United States has no pride involved in who makes the capture, and its only interest is that it should be done expeditiously so that American troops can be withdrawn and the peace of its borders assured." Should Obregón seem cooperative, Scott's attitude should meet this spirit "fully and generously." However, if Obregón should insist on the withdrawal of the troops, Scott should back off and suggest that further negotiations be worked out through the departments of foreign affairs of the two countries.[19] As Obregón was authorized only to negotiate for the immediate withdrawal of all U.S. forces, the conference seemed doomed from the start.

Despite the confusion about place and time, both Obregón and Scott made it to the meeting place by April 28, Obregón in Juárez and Scott across the border in El Paso. That evening, Scott and General Frederick Funston, commander of the Southern Department, called on Obregón, who returned their visit in El Paso the next morning. He insisted that their official negotiations continue in Juárez, a request that was "acceded to at once." Though the conference was amicable, the mutually exclusive nature of the instructions of the two sides made discussion virtually impossible. As Scott and Funston reported: "He made no threats. We evidently came to discuss one question, Obregón another."[20] Both sides then retired to await further instructions from their governments.

Despite the amicability, there was vivid concern that the United States and Mexico were headed toward war. The communications between Funston and Scott and Washington emphasized this concern, the two commanders being urged to "safeguard your own persons. . . ." Scott and Funston believed that a peremptory demand by the Mexicans for the removal of American forces had been avoided only because of the diplo-

[19]McCain to Scott, April 26, 1916, HLS.
[20]Scott and Funston to Secretary of War and Secretary of State, April 29, 1916, HLS.

matic termination of their meeting with Obregón, and they urged that immediate steps be taken to reinforce the border to "repel invasion at many border points and cause Mexicans to feel that the United States is able and willing to repel attacks. . . ." One of the major problems, they pointed out, was that the Mexicans were certain that the United States was unprepared for war and that a major show of strength might act as a deterrent. They noted the departures of Generals Calles and Gutiérrez from the conference area, "probably to prepare for an overt act if we do not withdraw." Further, they believed that Carranza's influence over Obregón was negligible, citing the rumors of a major break and the fact that Carranza's name had not been mentioned once during the negotiations. Secretary of War Newton Baker wired tensely from Washington: "On no account give excuse for attack. If attacked, take all necessary steps to make answer decisive and speedy."[21]

Obregón did not officially meet with Scott and Funston until late in the evening on May 2. The meeting was arranged by A. J. McQuatters, who, as president of the Alvarado Mining Company of Parral, Chihuahua, had previously employed Scott's son. The meeting was arranged for midnight, in the hope that it could be held away from the glare of publicity and from the pressures of various hangers-on and would-be advisers. However, when the two arrived at McQuatters' room, they discovered that word had leaked out and that a swarm of reporters was waiting for them. The meeting proceeded, nevertheless, and was described by Scott and Funston as "a continuous struggle of twelve hours duration which was not equalled by any similar struggle with the wildest and most exasperated Indian heretofore encountered." The struggle was "unusually amicable," however, the strain being caused not by bad temper but by the mutually exclusive negotiating stances assumed by the two governments to which they were subject.[22]

[21]McCain to Scott, April 30, 1916, Baker to Scott, May 1, 1916, and Scott and Funston to Secretary of War, May 1, 1916, all in HLS.

[22]Obregón to McQuatters, May 2, 1916, McQuatters to Scott, May 2, 1916, McQuatters to Obregón, May 2, 1916, and Scott and Funston to Secretary of War, May 3, 1916, all in HLS.

The agreement reached was favorable to both sides. The United States had already conceded that the major danger from the Villista band had ceased, and the North Americans were willing to move the troops back to a position closer to the border. In the May 2 agreement, in several paragraphs dictated by Obregón, the United States agreed that, since the group of bandits that had attacked Columbus, New Mexico, had been dispersed, and because the Constitutionalist government had agreed to continue the "vigorous pursuit" of such bandits or "lawless elements" as might remain and would reinforce the effort with additional troops, the government of the United States had decided to gradually withdraw its forces from Mexico, starting immediately.[23]

Thus, although there was no assurance that all troops would be out immediately, the Mexicans obtained a commitment to withdraw, and as a quid pro quo the North Americans were assured that the Constitutionalists would continue to pursue any Villista forces that might remain, a task the Constitutionalists would have had to complete in any case. Both sides left feeling relatively reassured, Scott remarking that "the agreement is not altogether satisfactory, but if circumstances are considered it will be recognized that it has not been easy to avert a war with Mexico which all believed was imminent."[24] The U.S. desire to avoid war on its southern border while Europe was plunging itself into a major struggle in which the United States might have to take part no doubt greatly influenced the position of her negotiators. Meanwhile, Obregón had emerged with a significant victory, which reflected the faith of the U.S. negotiators that his army could deal with what was left of Villa. Thus Carranza had permitted Obregón to emerge even more strongly as a national hero.

Carranza was therefore faced with repudiating the agreement or letting a tremendous political edge pass to Obregón. He remained silent for several days and then pressed his attack.

[23]Memorandum of Conference between General Alvaro Obregón and Major General Hugh L. Scott, first draft and final draft, and Obregón draft, notes for memorandum, May 2, 1916, all in HLS.
[24]Scott and Funston to Secretary of War, May 3, 1916, HLS.

In order to appear tougher on the Americans than his war minister, he objected to the clause in the agreement that stated that the withdrawal of the American forces might be delayed should the Mexican army be unable to prevent incursions across the border. According to Carranza, this clause would permit the United States to stay in Mexico indefinitely, and he therefore insisted upon its removal. Obregón was forced to return to the American negotiators to ask for such a change. Scott and Funston, of course, refused, pointing out to him that he had already signed the agreement and that the clause had seemed reasonable to him then. Obregón replied that it simply showed that Carranza "had more sense than he had."[25] In fact, the situation was dangerous, and Carranza was playing around with the international situation in an attempt to gain an advantage over a domestic foe he was coming to fear and hate. Obregón, however, was not yet ready to break openly with Carranza, although he was willing to continue to negotiate with Scott and Funston to obtain at least an understanding among themselves.

Another, more disturbing possibility is raised by Carranza's own involvement in some of the raiding along the Texas border. Recent scholarship has indicated Carranza's cynical involvement in the so-called Plan of San Diego, in which a group of Mexicans and Mexican-Americans came marauding into Texas with the intention of recapturing the area, creating a new Republic of Texas, and then gradually liberating the areas of Oklahoma, New Mexico, Arizona, Colorado, and California. The raids had begun in 1915 and had continued intermittently into 1916. It seems that Carranza, through his principal general in northeastern Mexico, Pablo González, had been encouraging the continuation of these raids to put pressure on the United States to recognize his regime. Even after recognition, however, Carranza had maintained contact with the leaders of the Plan. As Scott and Obregón were meeting at the border, he seems to have been

---

[25]*El Nacional* (Mexico City), May 8, 1916; Scott and Funston to Secretary of War, May 8, 1916, Obregón to Scott, May 9, 1916, both in PRFR, pp. 543, 547.

working with those leaders and with González for yet another round of raids, to begin after the talks failed.[26]

This would suggest that Carranza knew that the talks would fail, never intended to approve any agreement between Scott and Obregón, and very possibly hoped that the general who had caused him so much concern for his own political position and who had almost lost his life in the fight against Villa might finally be eliminated in a struggle on the northern border with the North Americans. At the very least, he could hope to discredit him in the eyes of other Mexicans and of the North Americans. At the same time, he could unite Mexican factions, which might otherwise question his leadership, in a fight against the unwelcome Yankees. However, he failed to discredit Obregón either to the Mexicans or to the North Americans. Although Obregón and Scott could make no agreements binding on either government, they continued to negotiate an understanding between themselves that would help to solve the problem of raids along the border. O. P. Brown, an unofficial emissary between Obregón and Scott, reported to Scott on May 8 that Obregón had suggested that U.S. troops withdraw and take up posts on the U.S. side from Presidio on the east to the Colorado River in Arizona on the west and that Mexican troops be placed opposite to protect the U.S. position. He reported Obregón as having said that "men did not usually take a cannon to kill birds with and that people did not usually take artillery and infantry to hunt outlaws and that it looked suspicious to them as if it meant permanent occupation or a means to scare their people. . . ." Obregón also objected to the North Americans' holding up delivery of munitions to the Mexican government. Both he and his companions continued to insist that any final decision on an official agreement would rest with Carranza.[27]

[26]McCain to Funston, May 23, 1916, USDS 812.00/18245 and 812.00/18248. For a complete discussion of the Plan of San Diego and Carranza's involvement, see Charles Harris and Louis R. Sadler, "The Plan of San Diego and the Mexican–United States War Crisis of 1916: A Re-Examination," *Hispanic American Historical Review* 58 (August, 1978): 381–408.
[27]O. P. Brown Memoranda, May 8 and 9, 1916, HLS.

Scott and Obregón met again on May 9 to produce a memorandum of their talks. Scott would declare that since the Villista band had been dispersed, the North American troops would begin to evacuate Mexico. Obregón would declare that Mexican troops would be moved into a position to guard the border. On May 10, the memorandum was drawn up, providing for the points mentioned above and including permission for the U.S. troops to use the Mexico Northwestern Railroad from Juárez to Casas Grandes, both for provisioning their forces and for the purposes of withdrawal. The agreement does not appear to have been signed, but it stood as an understanding between the two men.[28]

Scott expressed his feelings about the agreement in a letter to a friend several days after leaving El Paso. Although he felt that he had had a "very tough time of it at El Paso" and though no written agreement had been reached, he indicated that the situation was better than at any time since the Columbus raid. Obregón had sent ten thousand of his best troops into the major areas of bandit infestation, the "imminence of war has passed for the time being, and we are in better accord now than we have been for a long time. The troops will stay in Mexico as a guaranty [*sic*] that our border will be safeguarded."[29]

Although relations between the United States and Mexico continued to be tense for some time, Obregón was no longer directly involved in these problems. Open warfare never broke out, and the United States finally began troop withdrawals in January, 1917, during the Mexican Constitutional Convention at Querétaro. During the balance of Obregón's tenure as secretary of war, he was more concerned with administration than with chasing down the remaining dissident elements. He was content to leave most of the actual fighting to subordinates, while he directed the overall campaign. He first appointed General Jacinto Treviño, who had successfully defended Tampico, to continue the campaign against Villa, and when Treviño

[28]Obregón and Scott, draft memorandum, May 9, 1916, and Obregón and Scott, unsigned memorandum, May 10, 1916, both in HLS.

[29]Scott to Charles, May 16, 1916, HLS.

appeared to be unable to handle the job he assigned General Francisco Murguía, who had led the attack at León, to take over. Villa, for his part, was still unable to mount a major effort, but he was capable of an occasional dramatic raid. He attacked Chihuahua City in September and again in November of 1916, but each time government forces were able to drive him out again.[30] By 1917, the Villista threat was again on the wane. Unfortunately, Obregón had gained himself a new enemy. Treviño, furious at having been relieved, threatened in the presence of friends to kill Obregón or be killed himself, and feeling between Treviño's and Murguía's men was very tense for awhile. One observer predicted that this incident would precipitate the long-expected break between Obregón and Carranza.[31] It did not.

Obregón was indeed tired of his duties as secretary of war, and his many differences, both personal and ideological, with the first chief were becoming more and more obvious. Nevertheless, he resolved to stay until the Constitutional Convention in progress in December, 1916, and January, 1917, was over, the Constitution promulgated, and the new government installed.

Meanwhile, with the major military threat contained, he was moving to modernize and professionalize the army and get it out of politics. He himself had given up none of his personal ambitions, but he considered a politicized army under the control of various regional chiefs to be the major danger that would threaten centralized control of the country and lead to further bloodshed. This effort was consistent with his own wish to come to power as a civilian, able to count on a controllable, professional army instead of a collection of powerful regional *caudillos* with forces of their own.

In his relatively short tenure as secretary of war, he was able to make major strides in professionalization and administration of the army, although he was unable at that time truly

---

[30]A collection of several hundred telegrams to and from Obregón during the 1916 campaign against Villa may be found in PHS/61.

[31]Carothers to Secretary of State, December 19, 1916, USDS 812.00/20099.

to curb regional power. The major campaign of depoliticization of regional forces and institutionalization of central control would come during his presidency and during Calles' term of office, and as secretary of war he was only able to make a beginning. A number of industries, especially those related to the production of munitions, were subsumed under army control during the period, and in the purchase and operation of these industries, Carranza relied heavily on Obregón's organizing skills. Obregón set up a unified purchasing office for these establishments and arranged for central warehousing facilities. He encouraged experimentation and modernization in these industries and began to set up a central system of administration to coordinate their activities.[32]

His interest in administration extended to the direction of the army in general. During his tenure he ordered a census of the number of men under arms in each area and within a few days also ordered a survey of the officers in the revolutionary army, with special attention to the source of their commissions—the first chief or some other military or governmental leader. He obviously intended to regularize the chain of command. Shortly thereafter he organized the health services of the armed forces, including military hospitals, clinics, and aid stations, under twelve regional centers directly dependent on the War Department, although he provided that those units actually in battle would temporarily retain control over their own medical groups.[33] His own war wound had made him vividly aware of the need for the improvement of these services.

[32]Carranza to Obregón, December 17, 1916, AC; Proveeduría General del Ejército to Obregón, May 1, 1916, attached "Reglamento," unsigned and undated, AGES, Tomo 3090; *Revista del Ejército y Marina* (January, 1916): 77. Even the *Revista* itself took on a more professional appearance and moved from battle reports and stories to articles on such technical subjects as the proper use of artillery, military tactics, and strategy. An interesting suggestion for the reorganization of the military may be found in Francisco L. Urquizo, *Organización del Ejército Constitucionalista*. Urquizo was serving as one of Obregón's aides at the time of his book's publication.

[33]Circular, Ignacio Enríquez, Subsecretario de Guerra, in *El Universal* (Mexico City), December 8, 1916; Circular, Secretaría de Guerra, in *El Universal* (Mexico City), December 10, 1916; *El Universal* (Mexico City), November 15, 1916.

158   Alvaro Obregón

The training of medical doctors for help in the revolutionary forces was also of concern to Obregón. In the early days of the Revolution, the revolutionary army had had almost no medical services, but Obregón had gradually organized a nursing service for his own troops, with hospitals and clinics behind the lines. As secretary of war, he ordered the reorganization of the Escuela de Medicina Militar under the director of the Department of Military Health, the surgeon Enrique Osornio. It was associated directly with the main Hospital Militar, and the development of new and better techniques of dealing with war wounds was encouraged. The school was a good one and began to give the army a regular group of trained physicians, rather than the rejects who had heretofore joined the army when unable to attract clients on their own.[34]

Pursuing his interest in the increasing technical and technological capabilities of the armed forces, he fostered the new Department of Aviation under Alberto Salinas. In late 1916 and early 1917, the department imported twelve motors and began construction of airplanes themselves in a workshop in San Lázaro. The engineers and aviators employed there experimented with new designs better suited to Mexico's high altitudes than those employed in European models. Obregón later encouraged the development of a school of aviation under Rafael Ponce de León.[35]

For the purpose of creating a trained military, he began special classes for his officers even before the Villista threat was completely under control. By the end of 1916, special workshops were being conducted in command and rules of maneuver, documentation and military law, mathematics and military surveying, fortification and transport services, portable weapons and cavalry maneuvers. He also established the Aca-

[34]Bernardo Gastélum, interview, PHO/4/43; Francisco L. Urquizo, "Obregón, militar," in Alvaro Obregón, *Ocho mil kilómetros en campaña,* p. xxix; "El Hospital Militar de Instrucción y la Escuela Médico Militar," *Revista de Revistas* (January 23, 1927): 62–63.

[35]*El Universal* (Mexico City), December 8, 1916; *Excelsior* (Mexico City), September 27, 1916; Roberto Fierro Villalobos, interview, PHO/1/42, p. 87.

demia del Estado Mayor on October 8, 1916, which would admit students on the basis of merit and pay their expenses during the term of schooling.[36]

He had first been suspicious of the idea of a special school to train officers when it was suggested to him by an aide, Francisco Urquizo, and had commented that he himself had not needed any such training to become a general. Later, however, he saw the importance of such an institution in creating the type of military mentality he wanted, one dedicated to the goals of the Revolution and subordinate to the rule of law and the executive arm of government. He came to see, as well, the need for training in military strategy and new techniques. In his speech of October 22, 1916, inaugurating the new academy, he stated the mission of the new army:

People are pacified with laws, and laws are defended with rifles. When the Constitutionalist Revolution finishes the task of condensing into laws and decrees the institutions for which it has fought and the ideals for which the people have shed their blood, peace will be a fact in the entire extension of the national territory. . . .

But these laws and decrees, which must have a social base that favors the exploited and oppressed working classes, will necessarily injure the private interests which grew up in the shade of immoral governments. . . .

When these laws and these decrees are put into effect, there will be those who attempt to violate them against all principles of morality and right. And then, against these attacks and intrigues, we will be prepared to defend our institutions with our arms in hand. . . .[37]

In other words, the army was to be the guarantor of revolutionary institutions from possible counterrevolution, not a political actor itself.

He also began to put into practice his ideas for taking the military out of politics. Before the elections of 1917, he cir-

[36]*El Universal* (Mexico City), November 5, 1916; Obregón to Gobernador de Sonora, August 5, 1916, and Convocatoria, July 29, 1916, both in AGES, Tomo 3809.

[37]Urquizo, "Obregón, militar," pp. xxvii–xxix; Alvaro Obregón, "Discurso sobre las nuevas leyes," December 22, 1916, in Narciso Bassols Batalla, *El pensamiento político de Alvaro Obregón*, p. 119.

culated an order, which was not always observed, enjoining those military officers with command of troops from campaigning for political office in their own behalf until they had received a complete discharge from the army. Moreover, in the meetings of the Partido Liberal Constitucionalista, he supported resolutions to the effect that no military man should be permitted to run for office without first completely separating himself from the military, although for obvious reasons he was not in favor of entirely barring former military leaders from political positions.[38] Although military *caudillos* continued to exercise an important function in Mexican politics for a number of years thereafter, these were important first steps to achieve the subordination of the military to the central government.

Meanwhile, Obregón used his position as secretary of war to influence activities in other areas. Realizing the importance of immediate land reform in rewarding his followers during the fights against Huerta and Villa and in cementing their loyalty to him, he aided the Sonoran land reform which was going on under his associate, Governor Plutarco Elías Calles. When Calles established the Comisión Local Agraria in Sonora, he called on Juan de Dios Bojórquez, a young agronomist who had been closely associated with Obregón and who was publishing one of the newspapers of the Confederación Revolucionaria. Bojórquez had also served as secretary to Lino Morales, the Yaqui chief who commanded the 20th Sonoran Battalion under Obregón. Determining from Bojórquez that what was needed to begin the division of land was engineers, surveying instruments, and drawing materials, Calles sent him to the capital to get them. He was accompanied by another agronomist, Jesús M. Garza, one of Obregón's most trusted aides and formerly a member of his military staff. The money was furnished by Obregón, whom they consulted in Querétaro. Later he gave the young reformers uniforms and even transportation, allowing them to use the gunboat *Guerrero* to get up and down the Sonoran coast. Many of the members of the Sonoran commission were brought to the capital during Obregón's presidency

[38]*Gladiador* (Mexico City), December 19, 15, and 18, 1916.

and were instrumental in the first substantial national program of land distribution after the Revolution.[39]

Moreover, Obregón continued to champion organized labor, such as it was, just as Carranza and his government were cracking down on it. Carranza, recognizing the importance of the Red Battalions both as an arm of Obregón's military capability and as an aid to organized labor during a period of unrest, dissolved them on January 13, 1916. They returned to Mexico City and centered their activities around the House of Tiles in Mexico City, headquarters of the Casa del Obrero Mundial, which had been given them by Jesús Acuña. Acuña, the new minister of government, had associated himself with Obregón and the more progressive faction of the Constitutionalists. Labor unrest, manifested in protest demonstrations, led Pablo González, Carranza's favorite general, to close down the House of Tiles, and at the same time the government ordered the closure of regional Casas in a number of states. Problems continued through the spring, and during a general strike on May 22, Benjamín Hill, military commander of the Federal District and close associate of fellow Sonoran Obregón, arranged for negotiations between the Casa, employers, and the government. The crisis was then temporarily resolved.

Carranza, however, continued to put pressure on organized labor, and another general strike was called for July 31–August 2. At this time, a number of members of the First Strike Committee of the Casa were arrested, and it was reported to be Obregón's influence that saved a number of them, who were being tried in military courts, from the death sentence. One labor leader has recorded that Obregón met with leaders of the Casa the day after the arrests and suggested that if they would temporarily suspend their activities during the trial of their imprisoned comrades he would use his influence to get them off.[40] The men were brought to trial, acquitted and re-

[39] Juan de Dios Bojórquez, *Forjadores de la Revolución Mexicana*, pp. 125–129; idem, *Los agríos de Sonora en los albores de 1916*, pp. 3, 6–10, 13.

[40] Luis Araiza, *Historia del movimiento obrero mexicano*, 3:175; Rosendo Salazar and José G. Escobedo, *Las pugnas de la gleba*, p. 153. Carranza's hostility is further described in Rosendo Salazar, *Líderes y sindicatos*, p. 70.

leased, then rearrested and released again. When threatened by a third trial, many left Mexico City, but others were arrested and kept in prison for months. One, Ernesto Velasco, was sentenced to death but saved and eventually released through the intervention of Obregón.[41] Thus, Obregón's image as labor's protector against a reactionary Carranza was reinforced.

Still, Obregón remained unwilling to break openly with Carranza. Despite the open attempts by Carranza to damage him politically and perhaps even militarily and despite the clear policy differences between them, Obregón stayed inside the government during the formation and promulgation of the Mexican Constitution of 1917.

[41]Marjorie Ruth Clark, *Organized Labor in Mexico*, p. 43; Araiza, *Historia del movimiento*, 3:170. An excellent secondary treatment of the period is John M. Hart, *Anarchism and the Mexican Working Class, 1860-1931*, pp. 140-155.

CHAPTER 10

The Constitutional Congress of 1917:
Beginnings of Revolutionary Institutionalization

Between 1912 and 1916, then, Obregón's military victories, his international negotiations, and his position as secretary of war were bringing him increasing recognition and power. He had skipped, in four short years, from a minimal local power base in Huatabampo to national prominence without ever controlling his own region. Further, he had acquired a charismatic aura that identified him with the goals and ideals of the Revolution itself. This charisma, which both enhanced his actual power and was in turn enhanced by it, frightened Carranza and led to his repeated attempts to isolate Obregón and to neutralize him politically. By 1916, this effort was already problematic, given Obregón's widespread and rapidly developing popular appeal.

Charisma has been defined as "a certain quality of an individual by virtue of which he is set apart from ordinary men and treated as endowed with supernatural, superhuman, or at least specifically exceptional qualities." Military heroism is one of the classic ways of attaining such a superhuman aura.[1] Obregón was the military hero of the Revolution, with victories to his credit against the Orozquistas, the Huertistas, and finally and most importantly, against Villa and his followers. As the myth of invincibility passed from Villa to Obregón after Celaya, Obregón's charismatic appeal increased along with the real benefits he, as a winner, could offer potential followers.

[1] Max Weber, *On Charisma and Institution Building*, ed. S. N. Eisenstadt, pp. 48, 25.

Of course, Obregón's sometimes miraculous escapes from death had added to his image of virtual indestructibility. Despite a number of close encounters, he went unharmed in battle for three years. Several assassination attempts failed, on one occasion, described in chapter 4, because he simply talked himself out of it. He had faced and survived physical danger by going himself to meet Villa in Chihuahua and by returning close to Villa's lines during the Convention of Aguascalientes. Most extraordinarily, he had suffered a severe wound and survived, becoming a partial martyr to the Revolution. Even his severed arm became a symbol of the Revolution and remains one to this day.

Obregón was thus widely known in Mexico, and his fame had spread even to the United States. The nature of his military campaigns, as they moved down from Sonora and later up from Veracruz, had brought him into contact with thousands of people, frequently as their own leader or as the successful leader of the enemy. In any case, his presence had a profound impact. Newspapers, both in Mexico and abroad, publicized his triumphs even though news of them might be suppressed for a few days by Villa, who well understood their potential effect on his own position, or somewhat underplayed by Carranza, who feared Obregón's growing reputation and appeal. Word of mouth spread news rapidly from the towns that had newspapers out into the countryside. Within Mexico, he was a famous man.

Throughout, however, he maintained an open and relaxed personal style, accessible and warm to friends and potential allies, even though they might be of humble birth or of limited importance. People of widely varying stations in life were admitted to his presence and frequently actually sought out, listened to, and remembered. There are many testimonies to his warmth and interest, to his ability to remember by name innumerable people with whom he came in contact.[2] This excep-

[2]On his characteristics as a friend, an interesting testimony is to be found in the interview with Johnny Clark, PHO/5/8. Clark, several years younger than Obregón, remembers his visiting in the Clark home during his childhood and speaks with warmth about Obregón's greeting him with an embrace, paying attention to him though he was just a youngster, and helping

tional warmth and memory for individuals provided a balance to the heroic image he was acquiring, making him seem very human, a real friend. Thus he had enormous personal appeal: in addition to his natural charm, those he approached felt that they had the friendship and regard of the hero himself.

In this way, personal qualities were added to his leadership ability and luck to reinforce the image of his exceptionality. Recognition and personal devotion to his cause arose out of enthusiasm for the Revolution and enthusiasm for his victories in its service. During the fight against Huerta, Obregón's cheerful jauntiness and accessibility contrasted sharply with the image of Huerta, who with his drinking, his slyness, his physical comportment, and especially his reputation as the murderer of Madero, was an almost perfect villian in the popular mind. The population saw Obregón as the victor over Huerta, and there was wide dissemination of photographs of Obregón signing the Treaty of Teoloyucan, in which Huerta's representatives surrendered Mexico City to the Constitutionalists. Films made at the time of Huerta's presidency show Huerta walking about in a manner that can best be described as skulking. Later, films of Obregón show him first signing the Treaty of Teoloyucan on the hood of a car and then him and his aides exuberantly playing catch with ripe ears of corn in a nearby field.[3]

Moreover, his image contrasted sharply with those of Villa, who was seen as an authentic revolutionary by many but who was also regarded as dangerous and arbitrary, and Carranza, who seemed aloof and distant, seldom venturing out of Veracruz during the struggle against Villa and Zapata. Obregón, on the contrary, seemed both safe and present. Though he was unable to resolve the problems between factions at Aguascalientes, he was beginning to acquire the image of a peacemaker. More and more, he was seen as the man who could

him when he needed it. Another source on the warmth of his personality is the Daniel Cosío Villegas interview, COHC.

[3]The reader is referred to the films taken by Jesús Abitia during the Revolution.

bring peace out of violence, as the people tired of war.[4]

Obregón was thus emerging as the figure who could move the enthusiasms of the Revolution into the stage of institutionalization. He was achieving what S. N. Eisenstadt has called "charismatic legitimation," a claim to power based on both deeds and the intense and personal response of the populace to his personality, his charisma. His power and his charisma would continue to build on one another. Carranza, in a situation of rapid and intense social change, stood always, and perhaps too much, for a legitimacy associated with the past, with the Constitution of 1857. Rather than proposing a new era, he seemed to the people to represent changes in, rather than replacement of, the old order. Obregón, while loyal at least in deed to Carranza throughout this period, furnished a contrast. He was able to convince the populace that he was the most notable among the new men who stood for victory over this old order, providing hope for both peace and change, a focus for control and elimination of the violence along with potential future rewards in both economic and social terms.[5]

But as Max Weber has pointed out, and as Obregón recognized, charismatic authority would be transitory, and either would be traditionalized and rationalized or would disappear. Thus Obregón understood the importance of new institutions, organizations, and discipline, and his tendency to provide these was evident as early as his organization of the Army of the Northwest into a real, professional army dependent on regular pay rather than loot for its existence.[6] It would also be evident in the way he organized his own political coalition, as he combined the building of new political institutions with the develop-

---

[4]On the feelings of the people toward the violence and social and economic dislocations of the Revolution, see for example Alberto Ruíz González, interview, PHO/5/7.

[5]S. N. Eisenstadt, Introduction to Weber, On Charisma, pp. xviii–xix. See Weber (p. 49) on the psychological aspects of the recognition of charismatic authority "arising out of enthusiasm, or of despair and hope."

[6]Weber, On Charisma, p. 54. See pay scales in AAA-EN. See also Hector Aguilar Camín, "The Relevant Tradition: Sonoran Leaders in the Revolution," in Caudillo and Peasant in the Mexican Revolution, ed. D. A. Brading, pp. 94, 108–109.

ment of links with the groups that would come to support him in the political arena: the former members of the revolutionary army, labor and agrarian groups that had fought in the Revolution or had been organized in its wake, new political parties, and the group of close supporters in the northwest, who had at last prevailed over the Maytorenistas in the area.

The first major conjunction of his charismatic leadership and his drive to institutionalize would be in the Constitutional Congress of 1917, where his name and image would be closely associated with the more radical group of delegates, who became known as the Jacobins and who prevailed on the major points of the Constitution. And the Constitution of 1917 would become at once the primary underpinning of Mexican institutionalization and a major symbol of revolutionary triumph, associated directly with the ideals that had emerged from the Revolution and with the figure of Obregón himself. These ideals—agrarian reform, more equitable distribution of economic benefits throughout the society, anticlericalism, economic nationalism, and guarantees for labor—would thus become associated in the mind of the populace with Obregón, although this association was not always entirely accurate.

Nevertheless, if Obregón's victories against Huerta and then against Villa had established his position as the military hero of the Revolution, the Constitutional Congress of Querétaro would establish him firmly in the minds of the populace as the defender and champion of its social goals. Even before the congress, Obregón, bearing the physical evidence of an arm lost in battle, had acquired a national image that rivaled Carranza's own. His overt public support of the radical delegates at the congress would further establish the legitimacy of his claim to the presidential succession after Carranza's term of office.

The convention itself quickly became divided into two major factions: the radicals or Jacobins, who became associated with the figure of Obregón, and the renovators, who were supporters of Carranza. The antagonism between Carranza and Obregón was well known, and rumors that Obregón would revolt continued throughout the proceedings. Indeed, Obregón was eager to disassociate himself from the Carranza administration for the political reasons mentioned above. He also had personal reasons: he was in poor health, both emotionally and physically, and he had just married María Tapia, the daughter of a wealthy but nonpolitical Sonoran.[7]

Carranza was eager for Obregón to stay in office through the Constitutional Congress to provide a show of unity and to help keep the peace in the country. Obregón was, after all, an able and efficient administrator and an effective commander. At the same time, even if he had not wanted to, Carranza was forced to leave Obregón in a position of power from which he could aid and encourage the more radical delegates.[8]

Although Obregón took almost no part in the actual formation of the articles themselves, his personal and military support of the radical group was clearly understood. He himself maintained a high public profile during the convention, making frequent visits to Querétaro. The radical delegates could not be properly called Obregonistas, as they were not necessarily supporters of his; he, however, was a supporter of theirs.[9] To a large extent, they were the military leaders who had fought personally for their revolutionary ideals, surrounded by an eager group of young deputies who desired drastic measures to destroy the past. The most radical, moreover, came from the Gulf coast and the Pacific northwest, which was Obregón's territory.[10]

[7]Fernando Torreblanca, interview, November 15, 1972; Juan Barragán, interview, in Pindaro Urióstegui Miranda, *Testimonios del proceso revolucionario de México*, p. 256. On Obregón's health, see Special Report, November 26, 1916, 8536–149, and Report, Montano Interview, November 30, 1916, 8536–149, both in U.S. Military Intelligence Division, National Archives, Washington, D.C. (cited hereafter as MID/RG), Record Group 165.

[8]Barragán, interview, in Urióstegui, *Testimonios*, p. 256; Andrés Molina Enríquez, *Esbozo de la historia de los primeros diez años de la revolución agraria en México*, 5:173–174.

[9]Molina Enríquez, *Esbozo de la historia*, pp. 173–176; Torreblanca, interview, November 15, 1972; Ignacio Ramos Praslow, interview, November 16, 1972.

[10]Pastor Rouaix, *Génesis de los Artículos 27 y 123 de la Constitución Política de 1917*, p. 229; Daniel Cosío Villegas, interview, COHC; Luis Sánchez Pontón, interview, PHO/1/20, p. 25. For the provenance of the delegates, see map in Peter H. Smith, "La política dentro de la Revolución: El Congreso Constituyente de 1916–1917," *Historia Mexicana* 22 (January–March, 1973): 395.

The control of the army was a major factor in Obregón's ability to offset Carranza's political prestige and power as Carranza attempted to influence the delegates. Carranza had sent his own draft of projected revisions of the Constitution of 1857 to the convention, but a majority of the delegates found it insufficiently radical. His draft contained no provision for the definition or protection of the rights of labor, did not discuss the question of subsoil rights (a critical issue in view of the heavy foreign involvement in mining and petroleum), and, beyond providing for *ejidal* ("community-held") lands to be worked in common until divided by law, did not deal with the agrarian question. All of these omissions troubled the delegates and would be dealt with during the Constituyente, as the Constitutional Congress was called.[11]

Not only did the draft itself have shortcomings, a political split between a group of Carranza's closest supporters and the rest of the delegates soon developed. The roots of this split lay in the history of the fight against Huerta. A nucleus of Carranza's supporters, who came to be called renovators, had been members of the Madero congress who remained in Mexico City when Huerta took over. Although they had done little to aid Huerta, forcing a crisis in his government and eventually leaving Mexico City to join Carranza, they had nevertheless voted for Madero's resignation, ostensibly to save his life, and had for a time accepted payment as legislators from the Huerta government. They were, moreover, among Carranza's closest advisers, having been old friends since the Madero era. One of them, Luis Manuel Rojas, was to be president of the Constituyente. Rojas and yet another renovator, José Natividad Macías, were responsible for most of the actual drafting of the Carranza proposal. Félix Palavicini, editor of official Constitutionalist publications, was the most vocal and abrasive of the renovators and was hated by the radicals.[12]

Palavicini had been a bitter enemy of Obregón since before the battles of Celaya, and it was he who had endangered the

[11]E. V. Niemeyer, *Revolution at Querétaro: The Mexican Constitutional Convention of 1916–1917*, pp. 32–58.

[12]Ibid., pp. 45–46.

Constitutionalist effort against Villa by causing a mass resignation of the Carranza cabinet in June of 1915.[13] He had repeatedly demonstrated his personal hostility to Obregón, being jealous of Obregón's prestige as a military man as well as of his quick and ready wit and his ability to dominate social and political gatherings.

According to Palavicini, Obregón had on one occasion in Veracruz been telling jokes and stories to cheer up the "somewhat solemn atmosphere" and had turned his wit heavy-handedly on Palavicini himself. Looking at Palavicini, he had commented that there was one profession, journalism, that was easier than any other. When asked why, he replied, "All you have to do is write about everything without knowing about anything, and then just sign your name." Palavicini was stung and replied that the easiest profession was actually that of hero, as a hero could send his troops out to fight and, when the battle was won, could appear from miles behind the lines and take credit for the victory.[14] As Obregón was known for staying close to the lines and checking constantly on the troops, in contrast to Carranza, this sally fell rather flat and had the principal effect of irritating Obregón. Palavicini, however, proud of his witticism, recounted the anecdote in his memoirs.

Palavicini alienated not only Obregón but most of the other delegates to the Constituyente as well. He asked one individual, a metallurgical engineer, if he knew arithmetic, and in the course of one harangue, accused another of being successively a "flea," a "pumpkin," and an "inept child." Nevertheless, Carranza wanted him in attendance. In an early incident of the Constituyente, Palavicini's right to be seated was denied by the major credentials committee, but he was finally allowed in by the delegates. This skirmish showed that neither Obregón nor Carranza could completely dominate the congress; it would

---

[13]His own report of the incident is self-indicting (see Félix Palavicini, *Mi vida revolucionaria*, pp. 255–290). It may be said in his defense that he may merely have been playing Carranza's hand.

[14]Ibid., pp. 249–250.

act as an independent body in both political and ideological matters.[15]

Meanwhile, Obregón was keeping himself much in the public eye. The newspapers were full of his activities as secretary of war. Throughout December and January he was constantly in the news, encouraging the establishment of military schools under his trusted aide Jesús M. Garza, who used this excuse to tour the country widely; appearing at the reburial of one of his lieutenant colonels who had died in the assault on Culiacán, Sinaloa, one of Obregón's earliest major victories in the fight against Huerta; and, perhaps most important of all, appearing constantly in public with the only military figure who could have provided a counterbalance to Obregón's power: Pablo González.[16]

In fact, in the early part of January, an enormous party was held at González' home in honor of Obregón, González himself, and Obregón's old friend, Benjamín Hill. It was given by the members of the three men's combined military staffs. A comment in the Mexico City press illuminates the purpose of the gathering: "In general, it can be said that last night's party was yet another proof of the harmony and unity that exist among the members of the Armed Forces." However, their support for Carranza and Constitutional government was demonstrated by the three military leaders when they presided at a commemorative ceremony for the first chief's dead brother, Jesús Carranza.[17]

---

[15]Charles C. Cumberland, *Mexican Revolution: The Constitutionalist Years*, pp. 337, 342; Mexico, *Diario de los debates del Congreso Constituyente*, 1:154. The *Diario*, which has been used for most major studies of the Constituyente, must be used carefully as a source, since the moderate Carrancistas controlled the stenographic and printed versions of the sessions and were accused of changing the texts of the speeches (Juan de Dios Bojórquez [pseud. Djed Bórquez], *Crónica del Constituyente*, p. 553).

[16]*El Pueblo* (Mexico City), December 16 and 19, 1916.

[17]Ibid., January 6, 7, and 15, 1917. González himself was eager to make no enemies and regularly communicated with Carranza to declare his loyalty (for example, see González to Carranza, December 4, 1916, AC). Obregón's letters, in contrast, were cool and directed in general to winding up his affairs

A direct if less than official link between Obregón and the Constituyente was through the Partido Liberal Constitucionalista (P.L.C.). The P.L.C., as the party was known, had been formed in early 1916 by civilian and military leaders, notably Obregón, González, Hill, Eduardo Hay, and Cándido Aguilar, for the stated purpose of putting into practice the principles for which the Revolution had been fought. However, the party was only beginning to take on a life of its own in December of 1916. Although many candidates in the elections for delegates to the Constitutional Congress had called themselves members of the Partido Liberal, this had in fact been more of a label to identify themselves with the Revolution than a membership in a functioning political organization.[18]

The first real meeting of what was to become the Partido Liberal Constitucionalista was held just as the Constitutional Congress at Querétaro was beginning, and it took place at the magnificent residence General Pablo González had acquired in Mexico City. Among those attending were Obregón, Aguilar, Hay, General Cesáreo Castro who had fought with Obregón at Celaya and was now governor and military commander of Puebla, and General Alejo González, along with many other civil and military leaders, described by Palavicini's paper El Universal as "the most outstanding members of the Constitutionalist Party." The reasons González gave for the meeting were twofold: on the one hand to unify revolutionary policy and on the other to nominate Venustiano Carranza for president for the period of Constitutional government that would follow the Constituyente. Carranza was duly nominated, although González claimed from exile a number of years later that Obregón and Dr. Atl had spoken strongly against Carranza's nomination. Nevertheless, Carranza became the candidate, and El Universal was quick to indicate its support.[19]

---

as secretary of war and getting possession of his papers (see Obregón to Carranza, December 9, 1916, AC).

[18]El Universal (Mexico City), October 24, 1916; Pablo González, "Postrimerías del periódo pre-constitucional," La Prensa (San Antonio), May 10, 1921.

[19]Ibid.; El Universal (Mexico City), October 24, 1916; Basilio Rojas, Un gran rebelde: Manuel García Vigil, p. 229; Amado Aguirre, Mis memorias

Meanwhile, the party had chosen a name. Several suggestions had been made, among them Constitucionalismo Electoral and Constitucionalista. Obregón's suggestion was characteristically broad and inclusive, indicating his interest in attracting the widest possible support. He recommended the Partido Liberal Constitucionalista, in order to emphasize the ideological stance—liberal—and the commitment to legality—constitutional. This title was also advantageous, as he pointed out, because it conserved the name that had brought them to power. Thus the link between the Revolution and the P.L.C. would be made explicit, and, as Obregón hoped, the party would seem to be speaking for the Revolution itself.[20] Moreover, the term *Liberal* would evoke the pre-Porfirian revolutionary epoch of Benito Juárez, indicating historical antecedents for the party in the struggles of that great leader. It may be that Obregón also wished to establish a link with that immediate precursor movement of his own revolutionary epoch, the Partido Liberal Mexicano.

The P.L.C. moved very quickly to begin its campaign. Aguilar suggested at the second meeting that a newspaper or newsletter be started, and Obregón, González, and Jesús Urueta supported this idea. However, when it was suggested that Félix Palavicini be invited to join the party, Obregón attacked the idea bitterly, leading Palavicini to protest publicly to Eduardo Hay that in the first place he had not asked to become a member and in the second the charges made against him were not true. Nevertheless, for the time being Palavicini's paper, *El Universal*, published reports of the P.L.C. meetings as well as their press releases and bulletins.[21]

In fact, these meetings were becoming arenas for attack on the renovators, Palavicini, Luis Manuel Rojas, and others who were leading the moderate effort in the Constitutional Convention. The principles of the party hammered out in these meetings were very much the same as those that emerged from

de campaña: Apuntes para la historia, p. 302.

[20]*El Universal* (Mexico City), October 25, 1916; *Boletín del Partido Liberal Constitucionalista*, November 7, 1916, PHS/65.

[21]*El Universal* (Mexico City), October 26, 28, and 31, 1916.

the sessions of the Constituyente: effective suffrage, no reelection, agrarian reform, protection of the rights of labor and provision for the social welfare, rapid and effective administration of justice, separation of powers, municipal autonomy, and respect for state sovereignty.[22] In fact, the identification of the party with the Constituyente was so close that instead of formulating a specific platform for the congressional campaign that would follow, the new head of the party, Juan Sánchez Azcona, declared that they would simply work for the implementation of those "Constitutional reforms decreed by the Constitutional Congress."[23]

Two major concerns of both the Constituyente and the P.L.C. were agrarian reform and provision for the rights and welfare of labor. As many as one thousand persons attended the P.L.C. sessions running simultaneously with the congress.[24] Obregón himself attended regularly. Many of the Constitutional delegates such as the Sonorans Monzón and Juan de Dios Bojórquez, and Rafael Martínez de Escobar, one of the men who had led the fight to reject Palavicini's credentials, attended the P.L.C. sessions to inform the party of the thinking and progress of the congress. Another important individual who also attended the sessions of the P.L.C. was Andrés Molina Enríquez, who, along with Pastor Rouaix, would be responsible for Article 27 of the Constitution, the one dealing with agrarian reform and subsoil rights. Molina Enríquez was reported to have revisited Obregón regularly at the Secretariat of War during this period, and, as he was perhaps the most noted agrarian theorist associated with the Constitutionalists, it seems fair to assume that this was the topic under discussion.[25]

It was the religious question, however, that was to occasion the first major ideological debate of the congress and that furnished an example of the way Obregón's influence operated in practice. The question erupted during the debate on Article 3, which dealt with the role of the Catholic church in education.

[22]Emilio Portes Gil, *Autobiografía de la Revolución Mexicana*, p. 231.
[23]*El Pueblo* (Mexico City), February 1, 1917.
[24]Portes Gil, *Autobiografía*, p. 231; idem, interview, March 10, 1972.
[25]Portes Gil, *Autobiografía*, pp. 232–233.

The moderates on the question wanted public education, to be provided for by the government and to be free from religious influence, but they also supported the right of the church or anyone else to set up private schools.

The radicals supported an alternate proposal that would prevent any religious body from establishing or directing primary schools and further would bar any member of a religious order from teaching in any primary school. Led by Francisco J. Múgica, chairman of the committee on the constitution, the radicals seemed to be winning the battle, but the process was bitter. Toward the end of the session, one delegate rose and warned that adoption of the radical measure would threaten the possibility of recognition by the United States. Concerned, several of the delegates—including Amado Aguirre, a delegate from Jalisco who was a trusted friend of Obregón's, Esteban Baca Calderón, who had led the strike at Cananea in 1906, and Jesús Romero Flores—went to visit Obregón, who was staying in Querétaro. When Aguirre told him what had happened, Obregón urged his visitors to draw up the constitution to serve the needs of the people and pointed out that, if the United States did not immediately recognize the Carranza government and the new constitution, they would get around to it sooner or later. When the delegates emphasized the importance of recognition, given the fact that Villa was still marauding in the north, Obregón added that if the fight against Villa began again he would defeat him again.[26] Romero Flores recalled, "When we left the hotel we were sure of what we had to do, and the next day we voted for Article 3."[27] The radicals had won, and

[26] Jesús Romero Flores, interview, April 12, 1973.

[27] Jesús Romero Flores, interview in Urióstegui, *Testimonios*, p. 293. It was also reported to the Constituyente by Rojas himself that Obregón had sent a letter to the Jaliscenses and other western delegates urging them to be intransigent on this article (Mexico, *Diario de los debates del Congreso Constituyente*, 1:438). The existence of the letter seems likely, as Obregón had written the Jaliscense delegate Amado Aguirre in November, declaring his faith in the radical delegates in their fight against the "reactionary elements which will always be the major obstacle to the achievement of our revolutionary principles" (Obregón to Aguirre, November 23, 1916, in Aguirre, *Mis memorias de campaña*, p. 286).

though Obregón had had no part in the formulation of the article his support was important in its passage.

It was during the days of the debate on this article that Obregón himself was attacked most fiercely by the renovators, especially the president of the Constituyente, Rojas. He accused Obregón by name, along with Manuel Aguirre Berlanga, who had left the convention to take over as Carranza's secretary of government, of intriguing against the first chief and the Revolution. Others, including the Sonoran Monzón, rose to defend Obregón, and one delegate stated to applause that Obregón, "a great military leader and a great patriot as well," did not have to descend to cabinet politics or any other kind of secret intrigues. Rojas' further attacks on Obregón were greeted with hisses, as was his observation that the Constituyente was now divided into two opposing groups. At least in the minds of the participants, however, two groups had emerged, with the moderates associated clearly with Carranza and the Jacobins with Obregón.[28] A U.S. diplomatic observer, reporting the exchanges to his government, noted the bitter attacks on the military element in general and Obregón in particular and went on to say that rumors of Obregón's resignation were heard everywhere.[29] Obregón would not resign until the convention was well over, however.

Nevertheless, the strains between Carranza and Obregón were growing constantly more acute, with Carranza fearing the possibility of Obregón's open rebellion.[30] As the attacks on the secretary of war spread during December to the floor of the Constituyente, Obregón was finally moved to retaliate publicly. In a letter to the assembled delegates, read on the twenty-second

[28]Mexico, *Diario de los debates del Congreso Constituyente*, 1:437–439. See discussion of factional struggle in Smith, "La política," pp. 363–382.

[29]Parker to Secretary of State, December 15, 1916, USDS 812.00/20080.

[30]Molina Enríquez, *Esbozo de la Historia*, 5:174. Rumors of such a possibility circulated widely and were included in U.S. military intelligence reports (see Report, Montano interview, November 30, 1916, 8536–149, and Weekly Border Report, January 20, 1917, 8536–156, both in MID/RG 165). Even after the congress ended, Obregón had to deny officially that he was intending to revolt (see Knabenshue to Department Intelligence Officer, March 30, 1917, 8536–211, MID/RG 165).

of December, he protested that the group directed by Rojas, Macías, and Palavicini had been making unfounded charges that he along with the former secretary of government and others had been trying to eliminate them from the convention. Obregón emphatically denied this charge, but equally emphatically and publicly questioned their patriotism, given the fact that they had collaborated with Huerta. As for the supposed orders Carranza had given the renovators to remain behind and work to subvert the Huerta government from within, he doubted that they had actually been issued at the time Carranza claimed, and he added further that in any case this situation had made the renovators traitors either to Huerta or to the Constitutionalist cause and therefore "conveniently usable as instruments of treason." He ended by encouraging the delegates to let their duty prevail, stating, "let men be mutilated and die for principles, but do not let principles die or be mutilated for men."[31]

Although Carranza replied to the letter, reiterating that it was he who had told the renovators to remain in Mexico City, the impact on the delegates and on public opinion had already been made by Obregón's openly defiant statement. The break with Carranza was at last imminent.

The next major issue to arise was the question of the rights of labor. In the Carranza draft, the articles pertaining to labor were scattered and relatively weak. Nowhere was there a consistent and concise statement about what the position of labor was within the Revolution. However, the discussion of the section on individual rights, Article 5, led to a demand for such a comprehensive code. Debate on Article 5 began on December 26, and Obregón was conveniently in Querétaro, along with Pablo González, for the purpose of conferring with the first chief. The two had arrived on December 25, and then on December 26 they had a two-hour conference with Carranza. Afterwards, Obregón left immediately for Mexico City.[32]

Meanwhile, in the convention, Article 5 was reported out of committee with few major changes from the Carranza draft.

[31]Mexico, *Diario de los debates del Congreso Constituyente*, 1:595–596.
[32]*El Pueblo* (Mexico City), December 26 and 27, 1916.

Its importance, however, was immediately evident when four-teen delegates registered to speak about it. Debate went on for three heated days, one of the speakers being the Sonoran Monzón, who pointed out that the committee's so-called radi-calism was mild compared to the Sonoran government's (under the governorship of Obregón's associate Calles), which had already provided for freedom to work, decent pay, the eight-hour day, and protection for the rights of working women and children, as well as a weekly day of rest such as prevailed in the southwestern United States.[33] He therefore urged that these rights and benefits be extended to all the workers of Mexico.

The surprise, however, was yet to come. On the evening of December 28, José Natividad Macías, the renovator who had been repeatedly attacked as a reactionary, rose to present in Carranza's name an extraordinarily advanced labor code. It was carefully drafted and included almost all of the provisions that had been suggested in the three days of debate except for profit-sharing, which had been proposed by Deputy Gracidas, a mem-ber of the linotyper's union and a former employee of Félix Palavicini. It was, in fact, this labor code which, after it had been carefully studied and revised by a committee composed of both renovators and radicals, was to become Article 123 of the constitution.[34]

It is hard to understand why Carranza chose to present this labor code three days after debate had begun. Possibly, recognizing that the radicals were in control of the congress and himself under pressure from Obregón for a strong labor article, Carranza had decided to make his own proposal and thus

[33]Niemeyer, *Revolution*, pp. 112–113; Ravola to Gompers, October 17, 1916, 8536–131, MID/RG 165.

[34]For Gracidas' attitude during the discussion of Article 123, see Rosendo Salazar, *Carta del Trabajo de la Revolución Mexicana*, p. 110. According to Luis Araiza, Article 123 developed out of a study by the Casa del Obrero Mundial that Obregón had requested, and his ideas were carried to the assembly by Francisco J. Múgica, whom Araiza describes as Obregón's rep-resentative (Luis Araiza, interview, July 30, 1974). Although Obregón may well have consulted the Casa as to what they wanted in the labor code, it was the Macías draft that furnished the basis for Article 123, and, from the balance of evidence, Múgica seems to have been operating quite independently during the Constitutional Convention.

steal the credit from the leftists.[35] However, Macías had been studying the basis for labor legislation since the last days of 1914 when the Constitutionalists so badly needed labor support, and he had traveled widely in the United States, studying labor conditions there.[36] Certainly Carranza and his group had been considering labor legislation for some time, whether or not they wanted it in the constitution and whether or not they intended to enforce it. It may be that Carranza, his own natural fear of the masses deepened by the labor troubles of 1916, had decided against the presentation of a labor code but then had been forced to resurrect the idea under pressure from Obregón and the constitutional assembly.

The last major article to come up for consideration was Article 27, and again Obregón made trips to Querétaro at strategic moments. The Carranza draft had included only a brief mention of the return of common lands to the villages, and that restitution was to be only temporary until the land could be divided into small properties. When the draft was issued, Pastor Rouaix passed on a copy to one of the members of the National Agrarian Commission, Andrés Molina Enríquez, who also frequently attended meetings of the P.L.C. and was a friend of Obregón. Molina Enríquez, disturbed by the incomplete nature of the article, called an emergency meeting of the Agrarian Commission, which agreed that the article was insufficient. Molina Enríquez then left for Querétaro, where he met with Pastor Rouaix, who as secretary of development was known to be close to the first chief, and implored him to ask Carranza for an expanded article, which would treat the questions of land reform, property rights, and subsoil rights in "an integral manner." According to Molina Enríquez, Carranza refused "peremptorily."[37]

Unwilling to give up so easily, Molina Enríquez returned to Rouaix and emphasized the importance of the problem. Rouaix therefore asked him to prepare his own draft of a

[35]This is essentially the thesis presented in Niemeyer, *Revolution*, p. 116. See also Molina Enríquez, *Esbozo de la historia*, 5:175.

[36]Niemeyer, *Revolution*, pp. 113–114.

[37]Molina Enríquez, *Esbozo de la historia*, 5:171–172.

potential Article 27. Unfortunately, when Molina Enríquez presented the article to an informal meeting of interested delegates, it was too theoretical to be used. Therefore, an ad hoc committee under Rouaix was formed to put together an article that would be suitable for inclusion in the constitution. Molina Enríquez remained to help out with the revisions.[38]

The committee met daily between January 14 and January 24, and on the afternoon of January 25 it turned the new draft over to the Committee for the Constitution. Obregón, handily, was in Querétaro, where the Sonoran delegates, known to be radical, gave a banquet in his honor.[39] The Sonoran delegate Monzón was a member of precisely that Committee for the Constitution which would be considering the draft.

The new article needed little help, however. On the afternoon of January 29, it was presented to the Constituyente, and on January 30 it was passed unanimously by the 150 delegates in attendance.

Article 27 was to prove the most important article in the Constitution of 1917. It made a substantial change in the entire concept of private property: all lands and waters reverted to the nation, which then had the right to transmit title to private persons, thus constituting private property.[40] It subordinated the property rights of the individual to the needs of the society; the right to land became a social right. It went beyond the concept of eminent domain to declare that the nation could, in behalf of the public interest, impose whatever restrictions on private ownership seemed necessary. The nation could divide natural resources in order to insure an equitable distribution of the public wealth, which meant that the *latifundios* ("large estates") could be divided.[41] Other elements, such as water,

[38]Niemeyer, *Revolution*, p. 137; Rouaix, *Génesis*, pp. 147–148; Julian Adame Alatorre (interview, PHO/1/32, p. 49) maintains that Adame himself helped Rouaix draft Article 27, then turned it over to Molina Enríquez for review.

[39]*El Pueblo* (Mexico City), January 25, 1917.

[40]The discussion of Article 27 is based on the translation in Niemeyer, *Revolution*, pp. 250–259.

[41]Alberto Trueba Urbina, *La primera constitución político-social del mundo*, pp. 52, 57.

could likewise be apportioned by the federal government, a very important consideration for much of Mexico and for Sonora in particular, as the land was useless without water for irrigation.

Moreover, the nation was declared the owner of all sub-soil rights, a direct blow at the extensive foreign interests in mining and petroleum. Again, the mining interests in Sonora and the oil interests on the Gulf coast were significant. Concessions to exploit such resources could be extended to foreigners only if they agreed to subject themselves to Mexican law and to renounce any claim to help from their own governments. Commercial stock companies, either foreign or Mexican, were forbidden to "acquire, hold, or administer" any rural properties. Sonora in particular had suffered from abuses by large land companies such as the Compañía Constructora Richardson, which had owned a major portion of the land in the valley of the Río Yaqui, the best land in the state. Another limitation on the holding of property extended to the church: all real property held by any religious association would revert to the nation, and the federal government would determine which of the places of public worship could continue to be used for that purpose. Again, this provision struck a chord with the anti-clerical Sonorans; Calles, as Sonoran governor, had already expelled all clergy from his state.[42]

On January 31, the delegates signed the completed constitution. It was a remarkable document, more radical than any other constitution in the world at that time. In general, social rights were emphasized over individual rights, and although occasionally the articles were either too general to be understood or too specific to be carried out immediately in practice, the document stood at least as a statement of goals for the Mexican nation. It had been written by the delegates, acting independently in spite of pressures from the first chief, under the guarantee provided by Obregón's control of the armed forces. To a remarkable degree, it realized in legal form the goals and aspirations for which the revolutionaries had said they were

[42]Calles to Moreno, March, 1916, and Moreno to Calles, March 21, 1916, both in PHS/66.

fighting from the beginning of the struggle against Díaz. Rather than a document based on any foreign doctrines, it was a response to actual conditions within the country itself. As Amado Aguirre stated, it satisfied "to the fullest extent the greatest aspirations and necessities of the population understood by the revolutionaries, who saw them face to face. . . ."[43]

In the public mind, Obregón received a great deal of the credit for the content of the constitution, certainly more than he deserved, although unquestionably the delegates had felt freer to add their ideas to Carranza's draft because of Obregón's support. In fact, it was the strong supporters of Carranza, the renovators, who had called attention to Obregón's radical role over and over again. To a degree their very opposition led the radicals to use Obregón as a rallying point and kept him in the public eye as the champion of a popularly oriented constitution.

The radicals continued to attack the renovators even on January 31, the day of the signing of the constitution itself. They issued a "Manifesto to the Nation" indicting the renovators for a number of sins, including interfering with the radical delegates' telegrams, trying to influence delegates by ignoring the bylaws and by changing the order of speakers, and attempting to cause a break between Obregón and Carranza. Ninety-four delegates signed, more than half the usual number of delegates in attendance. This manifesto was even more surprising in view of the fact that Obregón, Pablo González, and almost all of the major military and civilian leaders of revolutionary Mexico were in Querétaro to attend a banquet given by the first chief to show revolutionary solidarity in support of the constitution.[44]

Despite the political cracks in the revolutionary ranks, the euphoria among the delegates was high. Juan de Dios Bojórquez, the young Sonoran delegate, recalled that he had spent the evening in the company of those young officers who formed the military staffs of Sonoran generals Obregón, Hill, and Diéguez

[43]Quoted in Niemeyer, *Revolution*, p. 226.
[44]Bojórquez, *Crónica*, pp. 553–562, 667–668; *El Pueblo* (Mexico City), February 2, 1917.

in Hill's special railway car. In the middle of the night Bojórquez and twenty or thirty young officers walked out into the
streets of Querétaro, marching in time and singing "La Marseil-
laise." These delegates felt that they had established a basis for
a real social revolution in their country.[45]

However, many problems remained. The political bitterness
building between Obregón and Carranza would continue to
fester and would delay the institutionalization of the principles
of the Revolution until the bloody resolution in 1920. Further,
Carranza himself was not convinced of the prudence of many of
the provisions and would simply ignore them during his tenure
as president. The delegates had drawn up a document that provided for an active, interventionist socioeconomic state, while
limiting its political power, particularly that of the president,
in favor of local control.

Carranza, as president, went precisely against the wishes of
the framers of the constitution: the central government did not
intervene heavily to change socioeconomic patterns, but in fact
frequently attempted to slow down efforts made in this direction by the governors of the various states. However, Carranza
tried to pull more and more political control to himself, using
the army and communications networks to do so, thus alienating
many revolutionaries and the masses themselves. Obregón, who
in the public eye had become the counterpoise to Carranza's
power and the defender of the freedom of the delegates, was
therefore the obvious candidate to become the champion of
the masses who would unseat Carranza as president in 1920. For
this very reason, as a successor he would be anathema to Carranza himself.

---

[45]Bojórquez, *Crónica*, p. 674. See the testimony on the delegates'
attitudes in Niemeyer, *Revolution*, pp. 225–234.

CHAPTER 11

The Obregón-Carranza Break:
Respite from Power

Despite major differences, both political and personal, between Obregón and Carranza, Obregón stayed as secretary of war through the preconstitutional period until Carranza assumed the presidency in May, 1917. As Carranza consistently worked to undermine any independent power base of his principal general, the question that emerges most strongly is why he stayed. Certainly the possibility of a break with Carranza occurred to Obregón, and as early as October, 1916, United States agents on the border were reporting that Obregonistas in the area were expecting a move against Carranza. At least, Obregón was expected to run against the first chief for the presidency, and it seems likely that his original interest in the establishment of the P.L.C. was to be its candidate for that office.[1]

Certainly, Obregón was trying to consolidate his own political support. One of his aides, Jesús M. Garza, approached dissident leader Esteban Cantú in Baja California in October to discuss a possible alliance. Garza maintained that these overtures were intended more to milk Cantú for information than as a real offer of alliance, but it is difficult to tell just what Obregón had in mind. As Garza himself commented, "Mi general es muy águila, como tu sabes," that is, "The general is very cagey, as you know."[2]

---

[1] Special Report, October 30, 1916, 8536–133, and Montano, interview, November 30, 1916, 8536–149, both in MID/RG 165.
[2] Ibid.

Obregón also tried to establish his direct control over Sonora in October, removing Calles from the military command of the state and replacing him with a former member of his staff, his undersecretary of war, Francisco Serrano. He also circulated an order that all military men who wished to seek public office in the coming elections must give up their commands. At the same time, he arranged for Sonoran governor Adolfo de la Huerta to go to Mexico City, where de la Huerta expected to be given a cabinet appointment. Meanwhile, Obregón's brother José was planning to run against Calles to succeed de la Huerta as governor. However, Calles and de la Huerta were able to protect themselves. De la Huerta returned to Sonora for the time being, and though Serrano remained as military commander, Calles used the military hierarchy to organize his gubernatorial campaign. The military band was even placed at his service. Calles' popularity forced Obregón to come to terms with him and not interfere in the election, which Calles won handily. Thus it was clear that Obregón would have to foster his political alliance with Calles if he wished to maintain a political base in Sonora.[3]

However, Obregón had ceased his political maneuvering against Carranza by January of 1917, and he resigned as secretary of war to return to Sonora in May. The major reason he did not challenge the first chief at this time, either politically or militarily, seems to have been his health. Certainly, he was suffering both physically and emotionally. A nun who had lived in the Obregón household in Mexico City reported that he had been in a "most critical condition" in September, not sleeping "two nights in the same bed, having a haunting fear of assassination."[4] Of course, such a fear was not entirely unwarranted, given his own experiences and the survival record of other Mexican revolutionary leaders.

A U.S. border agent the following January confirmed his poor health, reporting that "undermined by disease and the

---

[3]Special Reports, November 21, 1916, 8536–140, and January 20, 1917, 8536–156, both in MID/RG 165.
[4]Special Report, November 26, 1916, 8536–145, MID/RG 165.

nervous tension of the past five years, he has been breaking down and only by superhuman efforts has he been able to remain at his post and guide the destinies of the republic with such influence as he has attained." An aide added that "during his periods of acute illness and mental depression, he is willing to listen to the importunities of his family and friends, and usually agrees to forego all thought of the presidency. . . ."[5] His family does seem to have been a major factor in his decision to retire from the political arena at this time; their concern was well known.

A further reason was Obregón's strong identification with the Constitutionalist cause. An open break between himself and Carranza might well have been seen by portions of the population as treasonable or at least unethical. In addition, such a political breach might well have led to further war, either before or after the Constitutional Congress. Finally, Obregón and his supporters were convinced of Carranza's incompetence and unwillingness to carry out the principles of the Constitution of 1917. As one observer described his position, "he had been a faithful follower of Carranza to the present time, should remain so, and let Carranza find a way out of the trouble or fall from power by the weight of his own incompetency. . . ." He continued astutely that Obregón would "wait until the people actually call on him to save the country from the final ruin of Carranza's rule. One idea in Obregón's mind is to launch his candidacy to succeed Carranza at the close of the latter's elective term, should he succeed in remaining that long at the head of the Mexican Government."[6]

Thus, Obregón would return to Sonora to recover his health, to mend his fences politically in that state, and to begin to consolidate political support for his candidacy against Carranza in the 1920 presidential elections.

Although he abstained from overt participation in politics during the two years between his retirement as secretary of

---

[5]Weekly Border Report, January 20, 1916, 8536–156, MID/RG 165; Montano, interview, November 30, 1916, 8536–149, MID/RG 165.
[6]Montano, interview, November 30, 1916.

war in May, 1917, and the announcement of his presidential candidacy in June, 1919, a number of forces were combining to form a powerful political base. First of all, he had friends and allies from his days in the revolutionary army. He had support from the labor and agrarian movements, whose champion he had seemed to become during the Constitutional Congress. He was able to work with emerging political parties, particularly the Partido Liberal Constitucionalista (P.L.C.), and many of the new politicians, former members of either the revolutionary army or the Constituyente or both, felt a personal loyalty to Obregón forged during the crises of those times. Moreover, he was able to obtain the support of most regional leaders in the Mexican northwest. All of these groups were organized through a small group of very close associates whom he gathered around him in Sonora.

Carranza was also preparing for the campaign almost from the time of his resignation. Carranza moved increasingly toward personal control of all of the machinery of government, placing his own supporters not only in strategic military commands but also in key spots such as directorships of communications and railway services. Actual and potential Obregonistas were sent out of the country to consulates around the world; even Adolfo de la Huerta was lured away from Sonora temporarily by the offer of a consular office in New York.[7] Elections, after reaching a high point of freedom and peacefulness before the Constituyente in 1917, began to be typified by fraud and repression.[8] The social reforms of the new constitution were ignored for the most part, at least at the national level. P.L.C. pressure in the congress for reforms was regarded by Carranza as Obregón-inspired and thus suspect.[9]

Obregón, meanwhile, kept his internal political activities relatively quiet, focusing on business and on the international

[7]Bernardino Mena Brito, *Ocho diálogos con Carranza*, p. 69.

[8]For a general discussion based on materials from the Archivo Histórico de la Defensa Nacional, see Charles C. Cumberland, *Mexican Revolution: The Constitutionalist Years*, pp. 362–375.

[9]Anonymous memorandum to Carranza, September 4, 1917, LMG/AHDN, XI/481.5/100, ff. 2310–2311.

scene. He was working during this period to make himself acceptable to the United States as a potential Mexican president, and in late 1917 he toured extensively in the country to the north. The Carranza government had had only de facto recognition from the United States; de jure recognition had been withheld. Moreover, Villa off and on raided near the border, and the problems of the Pershing expedition still embittered relationships. Obregón was eager to regularize diplomatic recognition from the United States and to attract U.S. capital to help rebuild the country. He himself had seen the differences in pay and working conditions on both sides of the border, and he was eager for Mexicans to enjoy the same advantages that U.S. workers did. However, he recognized that raising the standard of living would necessitate an increase in productivity, which would in turn require great capital expenditures. If Mexico did not have the money, it would have to come from somewhere else.

Further, the United States was one of the largest markets for garbanzos—particularly New York, which had large Spanish and Puerto Rican populations—and in immediate terms he wanted to check out the possibility of sales there. Finally, he was still in poor health, as he had been ever since he was wounded at León, and he wished to consult doctors at the Mayo Clinic. Although he does not seem to have ever actually gotten to the clinic, the state of his health was a real consideration. In any case he had a close friend who was also a physician with him on the trip.[10]

Regardless of his motives, Obregón was received with considerable pomp in the United States. On crossing the border into Nogales, Arizona, he was greeted by the U.S. commanding officer of that border city and by the Mexican consul. He received a salute of four flourishes, which was designated for a secretary of war, and the 35th U.S. Infantry rendered "appro-

[10]U.S. Consul, Mazatlán, to Department of State, August 1, 1917, USDS 812.00/21200; Bernardo Gastélum, interview, PHO/4/43. The reports of Obregón's ill health during this period and throughout his presidency are legion, although he was never inactive for more than a few days at a time. The rumor was that he had epilepsy, but it seems more likely that he was suffering from a nervous disorder resulting from the massive trauma of his wound at León.

priate music." One battalion of infantry and two troops of cavalry escorted him from the border to the railroad station. Apparently the effusiveness of his official reception was misconstrued by the residents of Nogales, both North American and Mexican, and various rumors as to the reasons for it circulated through the town, the most bizarre being that Obregón was coming to take command of U.S. troops, which he would lead against the Germans. Carranza and Calles were both reported to be displeased by the friendliness of his reception.[11]

Obregón went first to the West Coast, then on to the East via St. Louis, Chicago, and New York, where he consulted both doctors and businessmen, and finally to Washington. Though the Department of Justice had ordered surveillance on him while he was in the United States, this surveillance was cancelled when the attempts to shadow him proved ineffective and checks of his mail, telephone calls, and telegrams turned up nothing useful.[12] The main concern seemed to be whether Obregón might or might not be pro-German, and when it became apparent that he was not in contact with German agents the Department of Justice lost interest.[13] Obregón went on to meet with President Woodrow Wilson, who received him cordially. They seemed to be mutually impressed with one another. In general, Obregón's trip seems to have combined health, business, and politics successfully.[14]

[11]War Department Weekly Report on Border Conditions, September 22, 1917, USDS 812.00/21312; War Department Weekly Report on Border Conditions, September 29, 1917, USDS 812.00/21336.

[12]A. B. Bielaski to Department of Justice, Bureau of Investigations, File of Agents' Reports, October 17, 1917, USDS 812.00/21445.

[13]Interest was so great that note was even made of Mrs. Obregón's reaction to the war news. When she was brought to the point of tears by word of the Italian reverses against the Germans, it was reported to Washington that there was no doubt of her anti-German sentiments (War Department Weekly Report of Border Conditions, November 3, 1917, USDS 812.00/21485).

[14]¿Quién es Obregón?, p. 63. Wilson and his close associate, Colonel I. M. House, had agreed as early as September, 1915, that Obregón was responsible for Carranza's military successes against Villa, that he might be the answer to the problem of Mexican pacification, and that he might be the "man of the hour in Mexico" (Charles Seymour, *The Intimate Papers of Colonel House*, 1:223–224; the quote is from House's diary, September 23, 1915, included in Seymour's narrative, p. 224).

He further improved his image in the United States when, in early 1918, he sent a circular to members of the Society of Producers of Garbanzo urging them to observe the U.S. Enemy Trading Act and to abstain from business relationships with Germans. Later he sold most of the 1918 garbanzo crop to the U.S. Food Administration under Herbert Hoover for use in Europe. Although attacked for this action by some individuals in Sonora, the deal both made money and made him friends in the U.S. administration.[15]

Meanwhile, Obregón, who well understood the usefulness of the press, was giving interviews expressing his loyalty to the new Constitutional government of Mexico and his intention to support it peacefully. If he contemplated any kind of armed rebellion, there does not seem to be any evidence to this effect. As in the Sinaloan case, he instructed his friends and political allies to avoid confrontations with the Carranza administration, and he himself constantly denied any intention of leading any armed opposition against Carranza.[16] It was no secret, however, that he intended to be president when Carranza's term was over. As he assessed the situation in 1917 and early 1918, he would not have to use force. He thought that Carranza, faced with his overwhelming popularity and support in the country, would finally acknowledge him as his successor.

He was wrong, of course, and Carranza was moving to checkmate both Obregón and the P.L.C. Although the P.L.C. had supported him as their candidate for the presidency in 1917 after an exchange of lengthy professions of loyalty, Carranza quickly realized that the P.L.C. might challenge his own power. He was particularly concerned that they might win a majority in the new congress. When the party began to try to

[15]Simpich to Department of State, January 11, 1918, USDS 812.00/21690; War Department Weekly Report of Border Conditions, May 4, 1918, USDS 812.00/21977. Many U.S. citizens who had been residents in Mexico during the Revolution still resented Obregón for his pressures on them during the occupation of Mexico City and attempted to smear him in the United States. See, for example, William Buckley Papers, University of Texas at Austin, Folder 213.

[16]Obregón to Sáenz, August 7, 1917, in Roberto Quiros Martínez, *Alvaro Obregón: Su vida y su obra*, p. 97.

establish a national network with affiliates in every state, Carranza told the state governors not to furnish any information that would be helpful in establishing state political alliances.[17]

However, the P.L.C., partly through the radical delegates in the Constituyente and partly through the extensive connections of its own members, most of whom had been active in either the civil or military arena, were successful in attracting widespread support. After the elections for the 27th Congress in 1917, the P.L.C. formed a block of about 80 percent of the members of the two houses. From this vantage point they gave Carranza constant difficulties. In mid-1917, despite the P.L.C.'s earlier support in electing him president, Carranza suppressed the party newspaper, *Gladiador*, and by 1918 the radical Dr. Atl, one of the first to attend P.L.C. meetings in 1916, had been run into exile in the United States, where he continued to work for Obregón's future presidential candidacy.[18]

Obregón, despite his retirement as secretary of war in 1917 and his return to Sonora, came to be more and more favored as a potential presidential candidate, though he himself was rarely in Mexico City. However, his friends were prominent in the P.L.C. and in the congress: Acuña, Urueta, Eduardo Hay, Luis Sánchez Pontón, and Aarón Sáenz all served as president of the lower house during the sessions of the 27th Congress.[19] Acuña, Urueta, and Sánchez Pontón had all been members of Confederación Revolucionaria, Hay the first president of the P.L.C., and Sáenz chief of Obregón's military staff for some time. When the Zapatistas wished to approach Obregón in search of a possible alliance in 1918, the channel they chose was through Aarón Sáenz and the P.L.C. Another major connection with the P.L.C. was through his old friend Benjamín

---

[17]Cumberland, *Mexican Revolution*, pp. 361–362.

[18]Emilio Portes Gil, *Autobiografía de la Revolución Mexicana*, pp. 238–239; Luis Sánchez Pontón, interview, PHO/1/20, pp. 32–33; Cumberland, *Mexican Revolution*, p. 361; Villarina to Carranza, May 31, 1918, DRM-18, pp. 39–42.

[19]Mexico, *Diario de los debates de la Cámara de Diputados*, Vol. I, 1, Tomo I, #9, p. 1; Vol. I, 2, Tomo I, #46, p. 1; Vol. II, 1, Tomo II, #1, p. 1, and #29, p. 1; and Vol. II, 3, Tomo II, #76, p. 1.

192   Alvaro Obregón

Hill, who had moved to Mexico City. The P.L.C. offices were actually in Hill's residence in Mexico City, and some authorities claim that Hill himself was the one who had originally inspired the creation of the party. In any case, he was a major factor in holding it together.[20]

Therefore, by 1918, though Obregón was officially out of politics, support for his candidacy was growing among politicians inside the congress and out of it. Atl was working for the P.L.C. outside the country in his behalf, although Atl favored Obregón's political reconciliation with Salvador Alvarado, now radical governor of Yucatán—an unlikely possibility. Within the congress, Obregón supporters—such as Emilio Portes Gil, Eduardo Hay, José Siurob, Juan de Dios Bojórquez, and others who had been involved with him in his military campaigns and who had looked to him for support during the Constitutional Congress and in the early days of the P.L.C.—began to work openly and actively in his behalf.[21]

Carranza, on the other hand, began to regard both the congress and Obregón himself as enemies. Rather than recognizing Obregón's extensive support and acknowledging him as his successor, he became more and more opposed to the possibility of Obregón as president. During the years 1919 and 1920, his intransigence increased.[22]

At the same time, Carranza's circle of advisers had shrunk markedly, and according to observers he paid little attention to the ones that he had. Despite Luis Cabrera's efforts to reconcile the congress and President Carranza, Carranza continued to regard the congress as too independent and "undisciplined."

[20]Anonymous, Tlaltizapán, to Aarón Sáenz, August 24, 1918, Archivo de Emiliano Zapata, Universidad Nacional Autónoma de México (cited hereafter as AZ), 30/20/360; Casarín to Secretaría de Relaciones Exteriores, April 11, 1917, ASRE-119, L-E-803, Leg. 2; Vicente Fuentes Díaz, *Los partidos políticos en México*, p. 204; Amado Aguirre, *Mis memorias de campaña: Apuntes para la historia*, p. 305; Jorge Prieto Laurens, *Cincuenta años de política mexicana: Memorias políticas*, pp. 82–83.
[21]Villarina to Carranza, May 31, 1918, DRM-18, pp. 39–42; Portes Gil, *Autobiografía*, pp. 239, 241.
[22]Sánchez Pontón, interview, PHO/1/20, pp. 32–34; Aguirre, *Mis memorias de campaña*, p. 302.

Carranza even ceased to fill most cabinet posts, preferring to appoint *oficiales mayores* ("chief officers") rather than secretaries. Frightened by the example of Obregón's power while secretary of war, he did not appoint anyone else to this post during the rest of his tenure.[23] Further, despite his attempts to influence the 1918 elections for congress, the country had again elected a majority that favored the P.L.C. and its opposition to Carranza's policies,[24] although other parties were emerging and cutting somewhat into the P.L.C.'s absolute majority. The P.L.C. hegemony was becoming less clear-cut, but the support for Obregón in the congress continued.

One new party that emerged before the 1918 election was the Partido Nacional Cooperatista (P.N.C.), formed by a group of students headed by Jorge Prieto Laurens and including labor leader Rafael Pérez Taylor. Its first president was General Jacinto Treviño, noted for his campaigns against the Villistas in the oil regions in 1914 and against Villa himself in Chihuahua in 1916. Though Treviño was no great supporter of Obregón, most of the members of the P.N.C. and especially Prieto Laurens himself were. The unifying theme of the party was cooperative economic democracy, and some of the points of its program were the nationalization of land and of the large public service industries, the creation and improvement of irrigation facilities, the elimination of the army and its replacement with civil defense units, the fostering of public education with autonomous universities and technical training centers, the suppression of the death penalty and the reform of the penal code, and the strict observation of the principle of nonintervention in international affairs.[25]

Still another party emerged in 1918: the Partido Liberal Nacionalista (P.L.N.), formed by the Carrancistas to draw off support from the P.L.C. Its creation was particularly fostered

[23]Sánchez Pontón, interview, PHO/1/20, pp. 32–34. For Carranza's opinions on Obregón, see Mena Brito, *Ocho diálogos*, pp. 55–56, 70–75. That Carranza did not appoint another secretary of war because he did not want further potential challenges from this direction is an interpretation based on the available evidence.

[24]Cumberland, *The Mexican Revolution*, p. 374.

[25]Fuentes Díaz, *Los partidos*, pp. 206, 207.

by Carranza's secretary of government, Manuel Aguirre Berlanga, whose close friend, Senator José G. Reynoso, became the president of the party.[26] Despite the use of the newspapers favorable to the government to stress its supposed popularity in the election, it never gained significant support.[27] Aguirre Berlanga, however, became yet another *bête noire* for the P.L.C., which attacked him constantly until Carranza's fall in 1920.[28]

A number of labor parties also ran candidates in 1918. In Mexico City alone, four labor-affiliated parties participated: the Partido Nacional de Trabajo, the Centro Obrero Independiente y Estudiantil Unidos, the Partido Liberal Nacionalista Ferrocarrilero, and the Partido Liberal Obrero. None gained significant support alone, although as a group their showing was more impressive. Some of these groups later joined the first important labor party, Partido Laborista Mexicano (P.L.M.), which had been formed by Luis Morones and the Confederación Regional Obrero Mexicana (C.R.O.M.) in late 1919 to support Obregón for president in 1920.[29] Others became associated with the P.L.C. before the 1920 election.[30]

Another major source of support Obregón was building in this period was a regional power base in northwest Mexico, especially in the states of Sonora, Sinaloa, and Chihuahua. He had not always controlled these areas, and up until late 1915, when he had returned to Sonora to chase out the Villistas and secure control for Plutarco Elías Calles, even his home state had been in doubt. Chihuahua, of course, had been Villa's home

[26]Ibid., pp. 216–217.

[27]On support for the P.L.N., see *El Universal* (Mexico City), July 28, 1918. The P.L.N. would nominate Ignacio Bonillas, the Carrancista candidate for president running against Obregón in 1920, in an abortive effort to impose an official candidate.

[28]The attacks in the P.L.C. press were published almost daily in 1919. See, for example, *El Monitor Republicano* (Mexico City), December 10, 1919.

[29]*El Universal* (Mexico City), July 29, 1918; Fuentes Díaz, *Los partidos*, pp. 207–210.

[30]For example, in late October, 1919, the Partido Obrero Independiente began meeting with the P.L.C., and four of its members were added to the board of directors (*El Monitor Republicano* [Mexico City], November 1, 1919).

territory. Sinaloa was also questionable, with both Obregonistas and Carrancistas operating in the area.

In 1915, when Calles and the Constitutionalists were becoming established in Sonora, supporters of Obregón and Carranza were eliminating the Villistas in Sinaloa as well. Shortly before José María Maytorena gave up the battle in Sonora and went to the United States in September of 1915, his close associate, former Sinaloan governor Felipe Riveros, was defeated by the Constitutionalists and run out of Sinaloa. Despite financial help from Villa in Chihuahua, he was unable to reestablish himself, and control passed to Generals Ramón Iturbe and Angel Flores, who had fought with Obregón against Huerta.[31]

After his resignation as secretary of war, Obregón's travels through Sinaloa doing business for his Society of Producers of Garbanzo had made it possible to keep political fences mended in that area. He consulted regularly with Flores, who was considered by that time to be Obregón's man.[32]

Obregón was particularly interested in Sinaloa, the scene both of his years as a mechanic at the sugar mill at Navolato and of some of his major victories in the fight against Huerta. During the gubernatorial contest of 1917, six candidates ran, four of them calling themselves Obregónistas. Ramón Iturbe, who had fought alongside Obregón but was considered a Carrancista, won the election to the accompaniment of accusations of fraud from the losers.[33]

Obregón's friend Angel Flores was one of the defeated candidates, and for a while there was a possibility that Flores might actually take arms against the new governor. Eleven municipalities declared against Iturbe but began backing down under heavy pressure from the central government. Obregón

---

[31]Francisco R. Almada, *La Revolución en el estado de Sonora*, pp. 181–182.

[32]Simpich to Department of State, January 11, 1918, USDS 812.00/21690. Obregón's resignation had the additional effect of shaking the adherence of many on the west coast to the Carranza government. See Special Border Report, March 22, 1917, 8536–199, MID/RG 165.

[33]U.S. Consul, Mazatlán, to Department of State, August 1, 1917, USDS 812.00/21201; Hector R. Olea, *Breve historia de la Revolución en Sinaloa*, pp. 93–95.

himself went to Sinaloa to mediate in the situation, although it
was unclear whether or not he had Carranza's authorization to
do so. In any case, he was successful in getting Flores to accept
Iturbe for the time being. In fact, Obregón had relationships
with various other Sinaloan politicians, and throughout the
period his advice to them was to avoid an open political break.
As a result, Iturbe, though he never renounced Carranza, never
effectively fought against Obregón either. When Obregón
finally broke openly and publicly with Carranza in 1920, Flores
controlled the state within a week.[34]

Chihuahua, of course, continued in a state of turmoil
through 1919 as a result of the Villista raids. The federal military proved unable to defend ordinary citizens in the state,
and a number of local militias called Defensas Sociales were
formed to protect against Villista depredations. General Ignacio
E. Enríquez, who had commanded one of the Red Battalions
that had fought under Obregón at Celaya, served for a short
time as governor and then directed the auxiliary forces and
Defensas Sociales in the state. General Arnulfo González was
also governor of the state for a few months. Other military men
who had commands in Chihuahua were Generals Eugenio Martínez, Joaquín Amaro, and Alfredo Rueda Quijano. General
Francisco Murguía, who had replaced Jacinto Treviño in charge
of the anti-Villista effort in Chihuahua in 1916, was later transferred to Tamaulipas as a result of a dispute with the state
civilian authorities. Up until the time of the Plan of Agua Prieta
in 1920, constitutional government had not been restored in
Chihuahua, and elections had not taken place. Martial law prevailed during most of the period up to 1920. Thus within Chihuahua, the military remained preeminent, despite the appointment of a civilian governor.[35]

Within Sonora itself, Calles had been proceeding with an
extraordinarily radical program and was frequently at logger-
heads with Carranza's central government. Calles had con-

[34]Ibid., Gastélum, interview, PHO/4/43; U.S. Consul, Mazatlán, to
Secretary of State, April 16, 1920, USDS 812.00/23599.
[35]Francisco R. Almada, *La Revolución en el estado de Chihuahua*, 2:331–
349.

tinued the program of land distribution that he had begun in 1915 and 1916 with the division of properties expropriated from those he considered enemies of the Revolution.[36] This action was taken in spite of Carranza's decree of September 4, 1916, in which he attempted to stop the provisional grants of land that the governors had been making. Calles had further carried out a radical anticlerical program, expelling all priests from the state in 1916.[37] He had passed radical labor legislation and had pursued a program of distributing land to striking workers to give them alternative means of support and also to permit the working of unused lands to contribute to the economic recovery of the state. He had further cancelled the contract of the Compañía Richardson, the large U.S. land and irrigation company that controlled much of the land around the Río Yaqui, although this action caused litigation that was to last for years.[38] Despite Carranza's efforts to slow him down, he had proceeded in an energetic manner to put his program into practice, sending off an occasional note to the president describing what he was doing and citing Carranza's own announced programs of December, 1914, and January, 1915, as legal bases for his actions.[39]

De la Huerta also continued these reforms energetically. He established a labor chamber in the state, which was charged with the study of matters relating to the working class. This

[36]Calles to Soriano, June 6, 1918, PHS/69; León to Calles, January 28, 1918, PHS/68; Plutarco Elías Calles, Ley Agraria del Estado de Sonora, July 3, 1919, PHS/70.

[37]Venustiano Carranza, Decree, September 4, 1916, PHS/64; Calles to Moreno, March, 1916, Moreno to Calles, March 21, 1916, both in PHS/66; Aguirre Berlanga to Calles, July 16, 1917, and Calles to Aguirre Berlanga, August 18, 1917, both in PHS/67.

[38]Calles to Aguirre Berlanga, July 9, 1917, PHS/66; Calles to Aguirre Berlanga, July 11, 1917, and Calles to Lawton, July 13, 1917, both in PHS/67; Calles to Carranza, February 28, 1916, PHS/61; Calles to Gobernador Provisional del Estado, April 24, 1918, PHS/69; Calles to Presidente Municipal, Cocorit, April 11, 1919, PHS/71; Calles to Rouaix, November 27, 1919, PHS/72.

[39]Typical is Calles to Carranza, February 28, 1916, PHS/61, in which Calles announced the abrogation of the Compañía Richardson concession, which, he pointed out, was in accordance with Carranza's program announced on December 12, 1914, against concessions and monopolies.

chamber was to study systems for improving the lot of this class, to render judgments in cases of compensation for injury, and to suggest solutions in labor conflicts, among its other duties. At the same time, he established a labor code including the eight-hour day, a minimum wage, and regulations against child labor.[40]

Obregón did not entirely support these efforts, and when Serrano replaced Calles as military commander of the state he saw as one of his principal duties the slowing down of social change. As he described it to a North American, Obregón's administrative policy, which he would carry out, would ameliorate de la Huerta's "visionary and . . . utopian plans for the rule of Mexico by the masses. . . ." On the contrary, he would restore "an attitude of fairness to Americans and their interests" and "make every effort to reestablish public confidence." These efforts would include the establishment of a monetary system that would permit free circulation of Mexican and American gold and silver; increased production, commerce, and foreign trade; and a vigorous campaign against corrupt officials, bandits, outlaws, and hostile Indians.[41] However, as mentioned above, Calles and de la Huerta maintained effective control of the state, and Obregón was forced to work with them. Despite the rumors of disagreements and jealousies between them, they worked together for the next several years. These rumors, however, may have led Carranza to misjudge the strength of Obregón's Sonoran support.

Other members of Obregón's group of close associates were also keeping the lines of communication open. Jesús M. Garza and Francisco Serrano, who had served on Obregón's staff throughout his military campaigns, had returned to Sonora after Obregón's resignation as secretary of war, as had Aarón Sáenz, although neither Garza nor Sáenz was a Sonoran. Benjamín Hill had moved, more or less permanently, to Mexico City, where he not only maintained close contact with the

[40]Ravola to Gompers, October 17, 1916, 8536–131, MID/RG 165; Antonio G. Rivera, *La Revolución en Sonora*, pp. 482–484.
[41]Special Report, October 30, 1916, 8536–133, MID/RG 165.

P.L.C. but allowed it to use his home as its headquarters.[42] Garza and Serrano, going into business together, also formed a local political party, the Partido Revolucionario Sonorense, which supported de la Huerta for governor in the 1919 campaign. They later became affiliated with the growing Partido Nacional Cooperatista.[43] Garza himself had a direct relationship with the Mayo Indians, whom he had helped recruit in 1913.[44] He had been important as well in the later contacts between Obregón and organized labor, speaking for Obregón in contacts with the Casa del Obrero Mundial as early as 1915, and serving as emissary between the candidate and the C.R.O.M. in 1919 when the Convenio Secreto (the C.R.O.M.'s secret agreement to support Obregón for president) was arranged.[45] Sáenz was also an important liaison with other groups, having served in the 27th Congress as a member of the P.L.C. and having been approached by the Zapatistas in 1918 in search of an alliance with Obregón.[46]

Garza, Sáenz, Hill, and Calles had all been members of the military and thus had many friends still a part of that body. De la Huerta, for his part, kept in close contact with the Yaqui Indians, arranging a truce with them in 1919, and the Yaquis would stick with him and adhere to the Plan of Agua Prieta in 1920. Further, he maintained contact with other independents

[42]Prieto Laurens, *Cincuenta años de política mexicana*, p. 82. The P.N.C. also maintained close contact, Hill sending P.L.C. deputy Manuel García Vigil to rescue Prieto Laurens when he was attacked by members of an anti-Obregón faction of the P.N.C., which was supported by a group of Mexico City police.

[43]Ibid., p. 75; Juan de Dios Bojórquez, *Jesús M. Garza, abanderado del gremio agronómico*, pp. 5, 13, 15; Luis N. Ruvalcaba, ed., *Campaña política del C. Alvaro Obregón*, 1:200.

[44]Bojórquez, *Jesús M. Garza*, p. 8.

[45]Luis Morones, "Morones habla claro," *El Universal* (Mexico City), June 11, 1956.

[46]Anonymous, Tlaltizapán, to Sáenz, August 25, 1918, AZ 30/20/360. This letter was also an approach to the P.L.C. itself and began: "The conduct of the members of the P.L.C., which has contrasted notably with that of the servants of the government, has prompted me to send them my cordial congratulations, and because you are a member of the P.L.C. and one of the most distinguished in the work of the Revolution, I am directing this letter to you so that you can make it known to them."

and revolutionaries, such as José Vasconcelos, and, when the Agua Prieta "Revindicating Revolution" was about to be declared, he sent Vasconcelos funds to come to Sonora to join the effort.[47]

Thus, among Obregón's closest associates, he had connections to the labor movement, to the two major political parties, the P.L.C. and the P.N.C., to the military, especially in the northwest region, to the Yaqui and Mayo Indians, and to the Zapatistas—who in turn had been cultivating extensive relationships with other dissident groups since 1918. In short, he had available a number of bases of support, none of which was all-powerful in and of itself but which taken together formed an unbeatable combination in 1920.[48] When the pressure from Carranza became too great and all groups understood his intention to impose Ignacio Bonillas as president, these groups, under the leadership of the Sonorans, would coalesce into a strong political base. It was a combination that Obregón and later Calles would carry, albeit with considerable friction, into their presidencies and that would enable them to make the Mexican presidency a powerful institution.

Meanwhile, Obregón was directing his own efforts toward a practical reconstruction of the garbanzo industry in Sonora and Sinaloa. During the period after his resignation and before the presidential campaign, his own approach to the problems of the *campesinos* was oriented to higher production, better credit, and most of all, organization among producers to exact better prices from potential buyers. Like his approach to labor, his approach to agriculture was one of modernization and rationalization, rather than radical change. A case in point was his formation of the Sonora y Sinaloa Sociedad Agrícola Cooperativa Limitada. He himself had grown garbanzos on his Quinta Chilla, and he knew that the producers had substantial problems with credit. Although the garbanzos of Sonora and Sinaloa were well known as being the highest quality in the world and

---

[47]José Vasconcelos, *La tormenta*, pp. 567–568.

[48]For the Zapatista alliances, see chapter 13, below, and John Womack, Jr., *Zapata and the Mexican Revolution*, chapter 10, "The Resistance Reforms," pp. 288–330.

therefore commanded high prices in the areas where they formed a major portion of the diet, such as Spain, Cuba, and Puerto Rico, the price that the Sonoran and Sinaloan farmer received was far lower. Farmers were usually forced to borrow money from the buyers of the garbanzo in order to meet the costs of planting and harvesting, and in order to get credit they would have to sign agreements to sell all their produce at a fixed, below-market price. This price in general was between $7.00 and $8.00 (U.S.) per hundred kilos.[49]

After his retirement as secretary of war, Obregón proceeded to organize the cooperative to extend credit to the growers and to market their produce. The stated aims of the cooperative were to help members finance their needs, to augment production, to sell directly to the principal markets, to avoid commissions to second persons, to improve the seeds, and to study systems of packing and start a factory to perform this function.[50] The producers pledged to sell their entire production to the cooperative, which in turn advanced them the money they needed for planting and harvesting.

Obregón himself, having gone into the import-export business,[51] arranged for the entire sale of the crop and received $0.50 (U.S.) a bag as a commission. Almost all the *garbanzeros* in Sinaloa and Sonora signed with the new organization. Partly due to the war in Europe and partly because of the united stance of the producers, the price soared to $15.00 (U.S.) a bag, and Obregón, handling all the arrangements for sale and shipping, sold the entire crop to W. R. Grace. In this case he realized a goal that he had articulated as secretary of war: "make money off the war." He himself realized more than $50,000.00 (U.S.) on the transaction in 1918, when 112,430

[49]Fernando Torreblanca, interview, July 19, 1974; Luis L. León, interview, July 18, 1974. Torreblanca and León vary slightly on the figures; the Torreblanca account is given here, since he worked directly with Obregón on the cooperative.

[50]Alvaro Obregón, "Proyecto de la Escritura Constitutiva y de los Estatutos de la 'Sonora y Sinaloa Sociedad Agrícola Cooperativa Limitada,'" June 21, 1918, PHS/69.

[51]Obregón to Gobernador Interino del Estado de Sonora, September 18, 1917, PHS/67.

sacks were sold. The *garbanzeros* received almost double the usual price, and post-Revolution prosperity came briefly to southern Sonora and northern Sinaloa.[52] Unfortunately for Obregón and the *garbanzeros*, the price dropped again in 1920, and the cooperative went into debt to Grace. Obregón assumed the debt himself, and it was still unpaid at the time of his death.[53]

The cooperative was typical of Obregón's agricultural projects, both public and private. Although Obregón was interested in land reform and social change, he was also interested in obtaining larger production through better methods and improved varieties and in obtaining for the producers a larger share of the profit from that production through improved marketing methods. He had earlier invented machinery for cultivation of garbanzos. He was, above all, a modernizer and organizer.

Therefore, between May, 1917, when he resigned as secretary of war, and June, 1919, when he announced his candidacy for the presidency, Obregón had established support, both potential and actual, throughout the country and had managed to perform a more practical task in the reorganization of at least one portion of Sonoran agriculture. He had improved his visibility in the United States, and was generally well regarded there. He had, in addition, begun to establish a personal economic empire, which would continue to grow until his death.

[52]Special Border Report, April 6, 1917, 8536–217, MID/RG 165; Obregón to Calles, September 18, 1918, PHS/70. Jean Meyer, in *La Revolución Mejicana* (p. 76), claims that in 1918 alone Obregón made $1,500,000 (U.S.) in commissions on the 1917 and 1918 garbanzo exports, which he claims had a value of $45 million (U.S.). The author has found no substantiation for this claim, nor does Meyer offer a source. It seems quite unlikely, as the figure for the total garbanzo exports from Mexico in 1919 was only 482 metric tons, as estimated by the U.S. Department of Commerce, *Commerce Yearbook*, *1922*, p. 591.

[53]Bursley to Secretary of State, August 8, 1928, USDS 812.00/Sonora/4.

CHAPTER 12

The Presidential Campaign
and Repression: 1919–1920

As 1919 began, it was clear that Obregón was preparing to challenge Carranza for the presidency in 1920. Obregón's challenge was to be political, not military, as he felt that in a fair election, he would sweep into presidential office. He had been carefully building political support for years, and his popularity was unquestioned. Nevertheless, he continued to avoid direct confrontation with Carranza.[1] He still believed that Carranza would finally acquiesce in his succession to the presidency.

However, Carranza never intended to turn the government over to his popular former secretary of war. He admitted to a former Obregonista that he had only named Obregón to that post under the pressure of the threat of a North American invasion of Mexico, because Obregón "at any moment can inspire the enthusiasm of the multitudes and carry them to triumph." But he went on to say that Obregón as president would mean chaos, because Obregón had no preconceived plan for governing and no understanding of national problems, nor did he have the virtues most necessary for governing.[2] Carranza, a self-important man of rigid principle, probably meant that Obregón, unlike himself, was to willing to compromise to achieve a partial end, too willing to accept or tolerate the views of others, and too willing to mediate between groups rather than to command. It was, however, precisely these qualities

[1] Obregón to Sáenz, August 7, 1917, quoted in Roberto Quiros Martínez, *Alvaro Obregón: Su vida y su obra*, p. 97.
[2] Bernardino Mena Brito, *Ocho diálogos con Carranza*, pp. 74–75.

which would enable Obregón to govern post-revolutionary Mexico and the lack of them which would lead to Carranza's ouster and death.

Nevertheless, Carranza was implacably opposed to Obregón's possible succession to the presidency, and he used what power he could command to prevent it. He had been putting his own supporters into office whenever he could, particularly in the military. He also moved early to control the telegraph, with Mario Méndez as director, the railroads, run by Paulino Fontes, and other systems of communication.[3]

Carranza had also done what he could to influence both state and national elections. Although he never was able to control the congress in any real sense, after 1918 the power of the P.L.C., known to support Obregón, was somewhat reduced. Worse, by the end of 1917 Carranza had been able to secure the election, by fair means or foul, of fourteen governors of his choice. Only five governors were not closely linked with him, and of these only three were clearly oppositionist.[4] One of the latter was removed by being arrested on a trumped-up charge while he was in Mexico City. One of the two remaining was Calles, and Carranza believed that Calles, being a man of strict principle like himself, would eventually break with Obregón.[5] He would himself turn to winning Calles over in the latter part of 1919.

What Carranza did not realize was that his own power rested on a very shaky base. If he had men of his own in the top posts in the railway and the telegraph system, both agencies were shot through with Obregonistas at all levels, and even the upper-level management people were loyal to Carranza only so long as he controlled their jobs. The army, though superficially controlled by Carranza, was likewise filled with Obregón sup-

---

[3]López Cotilla to Alberto Pani, February 14, 1916, AC; Report, May 24, 1919, Departamento de Telégrafos, Archivo de Amado Aguirre, private collection of Professor Alvaro Matute, Mexico City (cited hereafter as AAA-DT). Barragán in San Luis Potosí was constantly accused of political repression (see, for example, El Demófilo [San Luis Potosí], April 22, 1919).

[4]See the analysis in Charles C. Cumberland, Mexican Revolution: The Constitutionalist Years, pp. 370–372.

[5]Mena Brito, Ocho diálogos, p. 75.

porters who might or might not follow their commanders in a given instance. The congress did not support him, much of the populace felt dissatisfied with his administration, at no time during his tenure was the country completely pacified, and even his support from the state governors might fall away in the face of a challenge to his authority that looked likely to prevail. It was precisely this kind of challenge that Obregón would be able to mount. Carranza had been able to establish no sort of institutional support for himself and his administration, and his attempt to control the country by the arbitrary use of what power he had was eroding the aura of legitimacy his government had enjoyed after the Constitutional Congress.

In January, 1919, Carranza felt sufficiently threatened to issue a warning to Obregón. In a manifesto to the nation, he pointed out that elections for federal office were still almost two years away and that the "political effervescence" in the countryside was therefore likely to cause trouble. He went on to say that the "anticipation of the electoral struggle causes citizens, especially men of certain political prestige in their respective regions, to extract premature promises before they have had time to reflect sufficiently. . . ." He further urged that only those individuals who had public support, rather than the backing of a few friends, should run for national office.[6]

The manifesto was aimed directly at Obregón, and not surprisingly confirmed Carrancistas and others who opposed him hastened to support it. Jacinto Treviño, who had been an enemy of Obregón's ever since he was removed by him as chief of operations against Villa, said publicly that the Partido Nacional Cooperatista would support Carranza's suggestions, and José J. Reynoso, the head of the Partido Liberal Nacionalista, pledged his party's support. Pablo González, considering his own candidacy, suggested that the manifesto was worthy of attention and consideration.[7] At this time in early 1919, Obregón was so clearly the front-runner for the presidential office that all potential opponents must have felt it to be to their ad-

[6]*Excelsior* (Mexico City), January 15, 1919.
[7]Ibid., January 16 and 17, 1919.

vantage to keep him out of the spotlight for a little while longer.

It seems likely that Carranza had already at least considered raising the issue of militarism, which he was to use against Obregón later in the campaign. In early January, it was discovered in the Department of Defense that Obregón's letter of resignation was missing. It was apparently not located in time for the issuing of the manifesto, despite a tremendous flap involving both the Defense Department and the Department of Foreign Relations.[8] In any case, Carranza saved the militarism versus civilism issue for a later time, and Obregón himself had largely dispelled the question by the time Carranza raised it.

The year 1919 was to be a difficult year in Mexico apart from its political problems. It was a year of economic crisis, resulting in widespread strikes, some of which were put down with considerable violence. It was also a year of a virulent epidemic of so-called Spanish influenza, which claimed many lives and particularly afflicted the armed forces. Further, the countryside still suffered from sporadic but widespread violence, which usually took the form of banditry against trains and travelers and against small settlements unable to defend themselves.[9] The country was stricken, and Obregón looked to the populace like the man who could put it right. His message was a message of consolidation, reunification, and working together to solve common problems, and it was a message that appealed to people at all levels. Moreover, he seemed to be the one person who was capable of pacifying and reunifying the country, the one person with the confidence of the masses. Politically, the Carrancistas would have to combat this appeal if they were to retain control of the country after Carranza's presidency.

After the president's opening salvo, his close associate and secretary of finance, Luis Cabrera, took up the cudgels. In a publicly circulated letter dated March 14, 1919, he announced

---

[8]Ríos to Pérez, December 28, 1918, Pérez to Ríos, January 3, 1919, Ríos to Pérez, January 6, 1919, all in ASRE–125.

[9]A summary of conditions is in Jesús Romero Flores, *Anales de la Revolución Mexicana*, Vol. 2: *La Constitución de 1917 y los primeros gobiernos revolucionarios*, p. 105.

his intention, quite probably spurious, of leaving office after Carranza's presidency terminated, despite the fact that he had friends dependent on him for offices or for political protection. He regretted that they would be subject to injustices as employees and abuses as partisans when he would no longer be able to defend them. He denied that he had ever used his political power to make friends, but indicated that there were some revolutionary leaders who knew how to do this very well by dispensing jobs and favors. Then, raising the military-civilian issue that had been a problem between Cabrera and Obregón since before Aguascalientes, he said that there were some military men who knew how to make friends—Obregón and Pablo González among them—and some civilians who could do the same thing. They therefore had *lastres políticos* ("political ballast or ties") that prevented them from acting in a disinterested way. Cabrera himself, of course, according to the letter, had always behaved in a disinterested fashion, which was losing him friends rather than making any.[10] As a result of this letter, he no doubt lost a few more, and Obregón, realizing that the battle lines were already being drawn, was moved to reply.

Taking the pseudonym Clemente Reynoso, he published a letter in answer to Cabrera on April 29, 1919. He began by commenting on their friendship from infancy and indicated his hope that he would not be among those friends forsaken by Cabrera, in spite of the fact that he did not form part of his *lastre político*. He went on to criticize Cabrera's analysis of the political situation as groups of hangers-on circulating around individual leaders waiting for favors, pointing out that Cabrera had "absolutely ignored Public Opinion as a factor of stability in government." Obregón, of course, knew that public opinion was precisely the advantage he had over all other candidates. He then went on to attack Cabrera directly, asking if it were he or Carranza who had prevented him from making friends in office, insinuating that Cabrera would have dispensed favors

[10]Luis Cabrera, Letter to unnamed friend, March 14, 1919, in *Campaña política del C. Alvaro Obregón, candidato a la presidencia de la República, 1920–1924*, ed. Luis Ruvalcaba, 1:22–31.

and bought friends if he had had the power. Finally, as did nearly everyone else, he questioned Cabrera's sincerity about leaving office, saying, "They never believe what you say because you never say what you believe."

Then Obregón went on to Carranza himself. In an extended metaphor based on Cabrera's use of the term *lastre*, which means ballast, he attacked both Carranza and Cabrera acidly. He pointed out that Carranza's desire to put off political campaigning arose from the fact that the political movement that was in motion did not suit his ends. Although he did not explicitly state it, Obregón was referring to the movement in his own favor for the office of president. Carranza was simply hoping to buy time to construct his own "shipyard" to save his political "ballast." Carranza was looking around for a new and friendly ship on which to unload this political ballast before arriving at the port in which the ship presently in use would have to change pilots. Obregón accused Cabrera and Carranza of self-serving hyprocrisy in an attempt to save themselves. According to him, "The country and I believe that according to you, nothing that flatters you is premature and nothing that wounds you is timely."

Cabrera had urged that the campaign be based not on the popularity or prestige of the candidate, but on the political program presented by each one. This was a clear sign to Obregón of the Carrancista intention to impose a candidate of their own manufacture, designed to save their own political skins. Obregón warned that public opinion would never accept an imposed candidate and suggested that the attempt to eliminate Obregón himself as a presidential possibility would fail.[11]

He was right, of course. Everyone in the country knew it already, except possibly Carranza. The president's advisers, however, knew the strength of the challenge they would have to face, although they were probably not completely honest with Carranza himself.

With this exchange of letters, the struggle between Carranza and Obregón became open and definitive. What had

[11]Alvaro Obregón (pseud. Clemente Reynoso) to Luis Cabrera, April 29, 1919, in ibid., 1:32–39.

been obvious to almost every political observer was at last admitted publicly. Carranza would oppose Obregón's accession to the presidency in every legal way he could; he might also use other methods. Certainly his associates, particularly those who recognized the power of Obregón's popularity, were not reluctant to use whatever means they could to slow down the momentum of Obregón's political movement.

In May, a week after the Clemente Reynoso letter, the director of the telegraph office cancelled the permits that had been issued to many former military leaders and took away the individuals assigned to them as telegraph operators in order to prevent them from communicating with their supporters. New permits would have to be ordered by the president, would be only for official purposes, and would not permit the use of codes. These regulations would, of course, make it possible for Méndez' department to monitor all communications by telegraph throughout the country, and in many cases the new telegraph operators would be spies for the central government. Meanwhile Méndez met with Palavicini, Carranza's long-time associate, to assure him that his newspaper, *El Universal*, would continue to get good service.[12] The P.L.C. paper, *El Monitor Republicano*, would be hampered throughout the campaign by interference with news dispatches from correspondents.

Meanwhile, the political effervescence that Carranza had feared had come to a full bubble. Obregón began to be deluged with offers of help from individuals and from political groups who hoped that he would be their candidate in the coming presidential elections.

The parties that could be expected to support Obregón for president in 1920—the Partido Liberal Constitucionalista (P.L.C.), the Partido Nacional Cooperatista (P.N.C.), and the Partido Laborista Mexicano (P.L.M.)—were not really dependent on Obregón himself, although he was an enormously attractive candidate and all these groups realized the benefits of supporting him. He himself, however, recognized the label of oppositionist that had begun to stick to the P.L.C. and was

[12]Reports, May 24 and 29, 1919, AAA-DT.

unwilling to be the candidate of just one party, particularly when he wanted to run as the unifier of the revolutionary ranks behind one program.

Although by mid-1919 he had given up any expectation of being Carranza's choice for president, he still hoped that a demonstration of overwhelming popular support would force Carranza to acquiesce in his election. The P.N.C. was not sufficiently strong or unified to serve as a political base, despite Prieto Laurens' open support, and the Partido Laborista Mexicano was not formed until Obregón's campaign was well underway and gaining momentum. Therefore, rather than waiting for a party nomination, he declared his own candidacy in Nogales in June, 1919, and took that opportunity to attempt to create a political base that might eventually be used to form a national party of the Revolution controlled by him and his associates. Moreover, he was eager to take advantage of the popular support, unattached to any political party, that his revolutionary victories, his agrarian policies, and his help to labor had acquired for him.

His self-nomination was a brilliant political stroke. He invited the people of the country to form one party, the Gran Partido Liberal, which would support his candidacy. In this way, calling on the public itself to unite directly behind him, he avoided the problems of internal politics within the existing parties, such as they were. Moreover, it was still possible for the parties to join his movement without his having to make any promises or deals. He suggested that the mechanism for supporting him should be the formation of clubs of five people or more, each one of which would eventually adhere to the Gran Partido, which would then hold a national nominating convention. Ultimately, the P.L.C. itself took charge of the convention, which was held in February of the following year. Hundreds of little clubs were subsequently formed throughout the country to support his candidacy, and the P.L.C. was reorganized to handle its new role as manager of this aspect of Obregón's campaign.[13]

[13]For example, see reports of letters of support in *El Monitor Republi-*

Obregón's justification of his self-nomination reflected his own view of Mexican society and politics. According to Obregón, there was at that time only one real political party, the Partido Liberal (note that he does not say the Partido Liberal Constitucionalista but refers to a much more generalized concept of party), which was divided by small differences of detail into an infinity of groups. Previously, there had been only two political parties: the Conservative, composed of the rich, the high clergy, and foreigners, and the Liberal, composed of rural and urban workers, professionals, farmers, small ranchers, and small industrialists.[14] In short, the difference between Liberals and Conservatives was that the former worked for a living and the latter did not.

The Liberals, in a number of armed struggles, had won power only to lose it in the political arena, as carelessness, greed, and divisiveness on the part of the winners had repeatedly permitted the reaction, led by the Conservatives, to prevent any of the real reforms for which the Liberals had been fighting. Therefore, the deed that would rescue Mexico would be the reunification of revolutionary forces with strict attention to the will of the people as expressed through free suffrage.

Obregón then went on to detail the anxieties from which the Mexican people were suffering under the Carranza administration. They were, first of all, afraid that free suffrage would be subverted.[15] According to him, they were afraid that the goals of the Liberal Party, won in the Revolution, would be

cano (Mexico City), September 7 and 29, November 1 and 26, and December 5, 1919.

[14]A better term for what he meant to express might be artisans or perhaps small businessmen, but he stated *industrialists*.

[15]Various incidents in many states were testimony that their fears were real (see Cumberland, *Mexican Revolution*, pp. 360–372). For early Mexico City incidents, see *El Universal* (Mexico City), July 29 and 30, 1918. Rumors even circulated in Mexico City in the month after Obregón's announcement that congressional elections might be skipped "this ONE time," ostensibly because of the unrest in the country (Report, July 10, 1919, AAA-DT). In December, 1919, the P.L.C. had to delay the planned Obregonista convention because of government persecution, especially from Secretary of Government Manuel Aguirre Berlanga (*El Monitor Republicano* [Mexico City], December 16, 1919).

once again ignored, as those in power, corrupted by their material gains, would permit the Conservatives to destroy incipient reforms. Moreover, they were afraid that civil war might again break out if the desire of the people for relief from their suffering was again frustrated. They were afraid that their civil rights would be violated. They were afraid, finally, that the present administration, unsatisfied with its work, would "not permit the country to liberate itself from its liberators." Therefore, Obregón called on public opinion to support him as an opposition candidate and thus avoid these dangers. He proclaimed himself candidate for the presidency of the Republic in the next presidential election, emphasizing that he had "no obligations of any kind, either inside or outside of this country."[16]

Significantly, he referred only briefly to the economic problems of the country, saying that these problems could be solved only within the context of peace throughout Mexico. In calling for free suffrage, for peace within the country, and for politics free from repression and from secret agreements among individuals, Obregón was both indicting the Carranza administration and responding to the anxieties caused by the years of violence suffered by the country. In short, he was making a broad popular appeal, and he proceeded to back it up by planning an extensive whistle-stop campaign through the country.[17]

If the P.L.C. was not altogether delighted at being thus bypassed, it nevertheless hastened to aid Obregón with his campaign. Not only did the party organize and hold the Gran Convención Obregonista in early 1920 to permit adherents to Obregón's cause to come together to confer in Mexico City itself, its members also carried on intensive recruiting activities in other parts of the country.[18] P.L.C. member Rafael Martínez

---

[16]The complete text of the manifesto is in Ruvalcaba, *Campaña*, 1:40–59.

[17]The best source for details of the campaign is *El Monitor Republicano* (Mexico City) from September 29, 1919, when he began his campaign tour, until April, 1920, when the newspaper was closed as a reaction to government harassment (see *El Universal* [Mexico City], April 15, 1920).

[18]For a description of these activities in Nuevo León, for example, see report on P.L.C. member Juan C. Zertuche's activities from Governor José Santos to Carranza, December 22, 1919, DRM-18, pp. 353–355. Zertuche had formerly been a member of the Confederación Revolucionaria.

de Escobar frequently traveled with Obregón during his campaign, as did Emilio Portes Gil, along with Jorge Prieto Laurens of the P.N.C. Further, Obregón was in constant contact with José I. Novelo, who had taken over as president of the P.L.C., and many of his telegrams discussing the course of the campaign were printed on the front page of the P.L.C. newspaper, *El Monitor Republicano*. Close to half of the members of the directorate of the Centro Director Obregonista were P.L.C. members.[19]

Another crucial group of potential supporters was the military, which, as Obregón recognized, was divided. In his manifesto of June 1, 1919, launching his own candidacy for the presidency, he warned the army against supporting a candidate of the right in the coming campaign, indicating that in such a case the army would find itself functioning in the "role of executioner used to suppress public opinion." Obviously, this warning would apply obliquely to other political figures, such as Carranza, who might attempt to subordinate the people's will to their own by misusing the military. He further invited all members of the army, "from the most modest soldier to the highest official," to join the political campaign in favor of one who "anxiously desires to make the army a respectful and respected institution," i.e., himself. He called on them to abstain absolutely from using their position to intimidate private citizens who did not adhere to his manifesto.[20]

Obregón already feared repression from the armed forces against his campaign, and his public repudiation of any attempts to help his campaign through military force was well received in the country. It would contrast strongly with Carranza's later use of the military in an attempt to intimidate Obregón himself.

[19] Jorge Prieto Laurens, *Cincuenta años de política mexicana: Memorias políticas*, pp. 83–84. For examples of telegrams printed publicly, see Obregón to Novelo, November 17, 1919, in *El Monitor Republicano* (Mexico City), November 18, 1919. Members of the Obregonista directorate are listed in J. W. F. Dulles, *Yesterday in Mexico: A Chronicle of the Revolution, 1919–1936*, p. 21. Prieto Laurens of the P.N.C., Luis Morones and Samuel Yúdico of the labor movement, and long-time Obregón associates Plutarco Elías Calles, Jesús M. Garza, and Luis L. León were also included.

[20] Alvaro Obregón, "Manifesto," June 1, 1919, reprinted in Alvaro Obregón, *Ocho mil kilómetros en campaña*, pp. 554, 560–561.

Moreover, Obregón recognized that he would not need to use force to win if the election were allowed to proceed freely. His stand in favor of a free election won him still more citizen support, especially among those who had been offended by the use of the military loyal to Carranza to influence the gubernatorial and congressional elections in favor of his candidates.[21]

He further attempted to change his own image from that of a military man to that of a civilian leader as the campaign progressed. While articles appeared constantly in the P.L.C. organ *El Monitor Republicano* reminding the public of his glorious military services to his country, the paper additionally printed reports pointing out that Obregón was conducting his campaign as a simple citizen, not "throwing his weight around" like the usual military man. One column by-lined by Djed Bórquez emphasized that Obregón was traveling on ordinary trains during his campaign, walking from car to car greeting friends. Bórquez referred to him aptly as a "verbo-motor," who always had to have someone to talk to.[22] He was also doing some very effective campaigning.

On October 4, 1919, the P.L.C. newspaper carried a message from Obregón clarifying his military status. Reprinted were copies of his request to resign as of January 29, 1917, the date on which the revised and strengthened Article 27, on land reform and property relationships, was submitted to the Constitutional Congress, with the signing of the constitution easily in sight. Also printed was his final resignation of May 1, 1917, in which he completely renounced all military rank and privileges. A long explanation of Obregón's fight against militarism and his own vision of himself as a civilian followed.[23]

---

[21]This repression is detailed carefully in Cumberland, *Mexican Revolution*, pp. 362–375, on the basis of documents in the Archive of the Secretaría de la Defensa Nacional. Cumberland notes (p. 363) that Carranza was sometimes unable to use military force, as he did not control the loyalty of certain members of the military. This problem was one Carranza was constantly trying to solve.

[22]*El Monitor Republicano* (Mexico City), September 2 and 7, 1919. Bórquez is the pseudonym of Juan de Dios Bojórquez, Obregón's close collaborator.

[23]Ibid., October 4, 1919.

Although his sincerity in this regard might well be doubted, the very facts of his resignation as secretary of war and of his renunciation of military rank made a good impression around and outside the country. Other newspapers began to pick up his antimilitarist stance and to comment favorably upon it. The *San Antonio Light* on October 18 commented that "if Obregón is elected—and all signs indicate that he will be— there is a real hope that Mexico will unchain herself from that militarism which has long been so damaging to her political life, leaving the military subordinate to the civilian element."[24]

Obregón increased the credibility of his antimilitarist stance in a major statement made on December 3, 1919. He again described the military's role as one of safeguarding the nation's institutions and stressed the need for absolute morality and strict discipline in the armed forces. He went further, however, to suggest specific reforms for the army: the reduction of forces to no more than 50,000 men in times of peace, the absolute separation of the administrative function from military command, the establishment of uniform retirement and pension standards (important in the reduction of the size of the army), the abolition of the practice of putting criminals into the army as punishment, the establishment of rigorous health and medical standards and services, the reform of the system of pensions for widows and orphans of soldiers and for those men disabled in the military along with their complete separation from active duty, and the guarantee of complete political rights for those members of the army who had been retired or given unlimited leave.[25]

These reforms would make it easier to retire men from active duty and also to assure that they would be equitably provided for as a reward for their revolutionary services. The reduction in the size of the army without antagonizing those relieved of duty and the division of administrative and command functions were the major goals toward which his reforms were

[24]*San Antonio Light* (n.d.), reprinted in ibid., November 1, 1919.
[25]Speech, December 3, 1919, in *El pensamiento político de Alvaro Obregón*, ed. Narciso Bassols Batalla, pp. 153–154.

directed, with the idea of the removal of the military from politics always explicit. Later in December, Obregón further strengthened his position in regard to the military when he requested the P.L.C. to undertake consideration of radical reforms in the army in order to safeguard the national honor and sustain Mexico's political institutions.[26]

Carranza, for his part, tried to discredit Obregón by attacking both his image as military hero and his supposed devotion to civilian rule. He initially tried to claim that Obregón's military rank was only that of lieutenant colonel and that his appointment as general had never been confirmed, thus making him ineligible for military honors during his campaign. The pettiness of this position was obvious to everyone, even Carranza's closest supporters. Obregón, on the other hand, replied that he was not a member of the army at all and asked that his permanent release from the army be recognized.[27] The Carrancistas were caught without a response.

The matter was referred to congress, and the senate informed Obregón that it would not ratify his military rank, thus leaving him permanently a civilian.[28] Obregón was delighted, and he made a major point of his civilian status in his campaign. His military exploits were sufficiently well known to be beyond question, and he could now campaign freely as the civilian choice of the people.

Carranza did not cease to attempt to use the issue, although it had been rendered virtually ineffective. Luis Cabrera, now Carranza's secretary of finance, commented rather acidly that he still considered Obregón a general, regardless of what the senate chose to proclaim. "He is a general because . . . of his character, his temperament, in short, everything about him. . . . Even though the senate takes away his rank, he will continue to be one, as I will continue to be a lawyer, unfortunately."[29] Nevertheless, Obregón was able to present himself as a civilian

[26]*El Monitor Republicano* (Mexico City), December 19, 1919.
[27]Ibid., October 4, 1919.
[28]Ibid., December 4, 1919.
[29]Ibid., December 14, 1919.

candidate, while retaining all the charisma of his military victories.

He was also marshaling the support of organized labor. When he launched his campaign to follow Carranza in the presidential chair, he was approached by Luis Morones and the Confederación Regional Obrero Mexicano (C.R.O.M.), which had risen from the ashes of the defunct Casa, offering their support in return for a series of quid pro quos in their favor. The C.R.O.M., which had been founded with encouragement from the Carranza government in 1918, was the only major national labor organization at that time, with the exception of the railway unions. It had immediately begun to operate independently of the government, and its activities were coordinated through the Grupo Acción, a group of eighteen labor leaders that had been founded by Morones principally from the former membership of the Casa. Contact was made through Jesús M. Garza, Obregón's aide who had spoken to the laborers of Mexico City in his behalf in March, 1915.[30]

On August 6, 1919, in what has become known as the Secret Pact, or Convenio Secreto, Obregón had promised, should he become president, to set up a separate labor department to be headed by an individual who was identified with the labor movement and who understood the "moral and material necessities" of the workers. Until this department could be installed, a person identified with labor would become secretary of industry, commerce, and labor, an already existing department. Further, the secretary of agriculture and development would also be someone with a special understanding of agrarian problems. All of the secretaries mentioned above would be subject to prior approval by the political party that would be formed by the signers.

Obregón promised to support the labor law after its promulgation with the full force of the government, and he further promised to recognize the central committee of the C.R.O.M. as a legal entity, which could deal directly with the secretary

---

[30]Luis N. Morones, "Morones habla claro," *El Universal* (Mexico City), June 11, 1956; Marjorie Ruth Clark, *Organized Labor in Mexico*, pp. 60–63.

of labor and with the president himself. Contact between the labor department and the C.R.O.M. was to be constant, with one day a week set aside for this purpose. Further points in the agreement made it clear that the C.R.O.M. would be consulted in all matters having to do with labor, giving it a quasiofficial role in the government.[31]

Partially as a result of this pact, the Partido Laborista Mexicano, known as the P.L.M., was formed. As agreed before, they supported Obregón in the electoral campaign of 1920. Luis Morones, leader of the C.R.O.M. and a long acquaintance of Obregón, considered Obregón both trustworthy and the best man for the job—that is, the best man who actually had a chance at the job. Morones, like all other leaders of groups that were politically active, considered himself the best choice, but he knew that an exclusively labor candidate had no possibility of winning. Meanwhile, he reserved the right to turn against Obregón should he prove "unfaithful."[32]

El Monitor Republicano, the organ of the Partido Liberal Constitucionalista, which was also supporting Obregón for president, noted the formation of the new party with great pleasure. It reported that the new party had been inspired by a group of French and Catalán syndicalists who had recently visited Mexico and had suggested that the labor movement might well gain from a party made up exclusively of workers and directed by the enlightened element of the labor movement, those "pervaded with advanced ideas." The newspaper went on to announce that the new party would be supported by the C.R.O.M., which, according to them, contained the most worthwhile part of the labor movement.[33]

The platform of the new Partido Laborista Mexicano contained demands for broad rights not only for labor but also for the agrarian movement. Although the support of the

[31]A copy of the Convenio Secreto appeared in the Mexico City newspapers of August 22, 1930, after Luis Morones, stung by accusations that he was implicated in Obregón's assassination, decided to make it public (*El Universal*, August 22, 1930).

[32]J. H. Retinger, *Morones of Mexico*, pp. 59–60.

[33]*El Monitor Republicano* (Mexico City), December 28, 1919.

C.R.O.M. and urban and organized labor was significant, Mexico, not yet an industrialized country, did not at this time have a large labor force to form a stable power base for a presidential candidate. One estimate placed the number of workers in 1910 at 195,000 and of artisans at 500,000, out of a total population of about 15,000,000.[34]

The violence of the Revolution itself had prevented much further industrialization up until 1919. Therefore, the labor organizations, in order to gain membership, were forced to join with agrarian organizations as well as to appeal to individual *campesinos*, from small proprietors to the rural proletariat. The first plank in the P.L.M. platform reiterated the resolutions of former labor congresses urging the division of land as a basis for the welfare of the *campesino* and of the society in general. The next three planks had to do with making tools and other needs available to the *campesino* for working the land, the free use of the water in rivers for all, and the establishment of agricultural schools and experiment stations. The organized labor movement, and Obregón as well, recognized that a really popular mass movement would have to be based on the masses themselves, and they were neither industrial laborers nor even in the cities. They were the people of the countryside.[35]

However, despite organized labor's weakness, the P.L.M. did not hesitate to ask for benefits for the workers themselves. Along with insisting on the fulfillment of those guarantees to labor provided by the constitution, they emphasized the right of the worker to choose his place of employment, the duty of the government to provide machines and capital to the workers, the granting of unused factories to the workers themselves, the

[34]Jean Meyer, *La Revolución Mejicana, 1919–1940*, pp. 16–17.
[35]Platform of the P.L.M., *El Monitor Republicano* (Mexico City), January 3, 1920. The term *campesino* is used in preference to the term *peasant*, which is very misleading in the Mexican context. *Campesino* is used here to include those individuals, ranging from small landowners to rural proletariat, who made their principal living from the soil. Many of these, particularly in northern Mexico, earned a portion of their income working in mines, in agriculture-related industry, or even across the border in the United States in any of these pursuits. Therefore, the term *peasant* cannot be applied in any strict sense. See a somewhat different justification of this point in John Womack, Jr., *Zapata and the Mexican Revolution*, p. x.

right of association, and the inviolability of the meeting places of workers' groups.[36] The party adopted this platform on December 30, 1919, and Obregón's tacit agreement with its demands was indicated by his acceptance of the P.L.M. nomination for president on January 4, 1920. Although illness prevented him from accepting the nomination in person, Jesús M. Garza again represented him, while Luis Morones spoke for the P.L.M.[37]

Morones later emphasized the importance of the P.L.M. to Obregón's candidacy, claiming that it had been difficult to get workers to participate in the campaign until the actual formation of the party. However, help to Obregón's campaign from workers was by no means confined to the C.R.O.M. and the P.L.M. A confused melange of smaller labor organizations was proliferating all over the country, some of them establishing independent Obregonista groups and parties and others adhering to the Partido Liberal Constitucionalista, which also supported Obregón for president in the 1919–1920 campaign. Moreover, many offices and factories formed Obregonista clubs among their employees.[38]

As early as September, 1919, a group of five hundred employees in the Fundición Nacional de Artillería, in the Fábricas de Cartucho #1 and #2, and in the adjunct Laboratorio Químico had formed an Obregonista club, announcing their intention of joining the P.L.C. and supporting Obregón for president.[39] The formation of this club was of particular significance, as these were military industries, and the employees were subject to government reprisal.

In October, President José I. Novelo of the P.L.C. called a general meeting to form a new board of directors, and the attendance of the Partido Obrero Independiente was so significant that four of their members were added to the board. By December, a rally for the candidate in Bucareli Hall featured

[36]Platform of the P.L.M., *El Monitor Republicano* (Mexico City), January 3, 1920.
[37]*El Monitor Republicano* (Mexico City), January 4, 1920.
[38]Morones, "Habla claro."
[39]*El Monitor Republicano* (Mexico City), September 1, 1919.

members of the P.L.C. along with the Partido Sindicato del Trabajo and the Centro Obrero Independiente together on the platform.[40]

The danger of losing the labor movement to another political party was recognized by the P.L.M., which, at the time of its formation shortly after its general meeting, included a plank in its platform warning workers not to join groups formed by professional politicians "alien to our class." The P.L.C., undeterred, continued to court the labor vote. Juan de Dios Bojórquez, under the pseudonym Djed Bórquez, published frequent articles in *El Monitor Republicano* about the contributions of labor to the Revolution, and Rosendo Salazar, one of the leaders of the Casa del Obrero Mundial who had signed the original pact with the Constitutionalists, had a regular column in the paper called "Sección Obrera."[41]

One of the earliest groups to adhere to Obregón's candidacy in 1919 was Felipe Carrillo Puerto's Partido Socialista Yucateco, itself principally a labor group. Later, when a Gran Convención Obregonista was held in Mexico City, organized by the P.L.C. but for the purpose of uniting all those groups supporting Obregón, one of the two vice presidents chosen was Felipe Carrillo Puerto.[42]

Throughout the campaign, *El Monitor Republicano* was careful to mention the workers' presence in the crowds cheering Obregón and the workers' groups that had chosen him as their presidential candidate. Obregón himself made a point of visiting mines and factories in each area where he stopped to campaign, and workers were prominently featured on the programs of the rallies in favor of his candidacy. In one day in Coahuila, for example, Obregón visited six separate mines speaking to the miners—a "brilliant tour," according to *El Monitor Republicano*. On another occasion he was presented with a red sash by the

[40]Ibid., November 1 and December 6, 1919.
[41]Platform of the P.L.M., ibid., January 3, 1920. For Salazar's column, see, for example, ibid., September 3 and December 3, 1919.
[42]*El Universal* (Mexico City), July 14, 1919, reprinted in Ruvalcaba, *Campaña*, 1:130–131; *El Monitor Republicano* (Mexico City), February 1, 1920.

working women of three factories in Tulancingo. He, of course, put it on immediately to great acclaim.[43]

He was constantly approached by workers' groups expressing their support, and he received them with attention. Frequently they came to request that he visit them in their own cities and towns, which seemed to give them local prestige. Certainly the number of local leaders who were willing to work with the popular masses was increasing, at least partly as a result of the ability of these groups to organize in support of the Sonoran candidate.[44] Correspondents from *El Monitor Republicano* and *El Universal* both confirmed what Obregón supporters consistently emphasized: that the meetings, dinners, and rallies for Obregón were attended by "all social classes."[45]

Moreover, in most localities in which he appeared the local political parties included at least one group that represented the workers. For example, one meeting in Morelia, Michoacán, was organized by the local parties Reformador, Nacionalista, and Laborista Michoacana. Luis León, speaking to this group, received strenuous applause when he emphasized that Obregón had no commitment to any special group or political party. In a list of groups supporting Obregón's candidacy in Sonora, one organization, listed as Agrupaciones Políticas del Río Mayo, stated that it was formed of two workers' clubs, four farmers' groups, and one businessmen's club. In Saltillo, Obregón was greeted by the Partidos Socialista Obrero y Agricultores Coa-

[43]*El Monitor Republicano* (Mexico City), March 9, 1920, and December 5, 1919.

[44]For example, ibid., November 10, 1919, and February 17, March 4, and April 2, 1920; Prieto Laurens, *Cincuenta años*, p. 83. *El Universal*, January 3, 1920, describes Obregón's interview with one Señor Moreno, a labor leader in Morelia, Michoacán. *El Monitor Republicano* and *El Universal* were the only Mexico City newspapers that reported Obregón's campaign in any detail. *El Monitor Republicano* was an open advocate of Obregón's candidacy, of course, but *El Universal*, run by Obregón's old enemy Palavicini, gave him much more limited coverage, although it confirmed the enthusiastic reception he was getting.

[45]See, for example, *El Universal* (Mexico City), January 4 and 10, 1920; *El Monitor Republicano* (Mexico City), November 14 and December 5, 1919; Prieto Laurens, *Cincuenta años*, p. 83.

huilenses, which claimed to be an association of forty-three separate clubs.[46]

It was no surprise that the Carranza government tried to repress the workers' enthusiasm for the candidate. As early as October of 1919, the Partido Liberal Obrero of San Luis Potosí was requesting Benjamín Hill to ask Obregón to use his influence to guarantee their right to political activity, described as "brutally obstructed" by the local authorities. During the campaign, many attempts were made by the police to prevent or disrupt rallies in Obregón's favor, both in Mexico City and in other localities, including San Luis Potosí. As the campaign gained momentum, intimidation occasionally got out of hand, as in the assassination of the secretary of the Club Liberal Obrero de Zinepecuaro, who was killed by federal forces under Primitivo Ramírez. The Comité Liberal Obrero of Michoacán protested to Carranza, but with no results.[47]

The repression was, for the most part, ineffective, and the rallies in Obregón's favor continued and grew. As repression increased, some labor groups were able to help the candidate in a direct way, especially the railwaymen, who ignored or defied orders from the director of the railways, Paulino Fontes, to hold up the trains on which the candidate was traveling. Obregón was, to a degree, protected by his habit of taking ordinary passenger trains, a habit enforced not only by the political situation but also by the lack of funds that beset the candidate and his supporters.[48]

Carranza, for his part, began to work on the Sonorans, particularly on Calles. In view of Calles' constant problems with Carranza's central government, it is surprising that Carranza believed that Calles could be won over to his side. Never-

[46]*El Universal* (Mexico City), January 4, 1920; *El Monitor Republicano* (Mexico City), December 5, 1919, and February 16, 1920. Other examples in *El Monitor* appeared November 19 and December 1, 1919.

[47]Davila and Mendoza, Partido Liberal Obrero, to Hill, October, 1919, in Ruvalcaba, *Campaña*, 1:240; *El Monitor Republicano* (Mexico City), November 24 and December 25, 1919, February 11 and 13 and March 16, 1920.

[48]Obregón to Hill, November 23, 1919, in *El Monitor Republicano* (Mexico City), November 24, 1919; Prieto Laurens, *Cincuenta años*, p. 75.

theless, in September, 1919, after Calles had passed the gubernatorial office on to his successor, Adolfo de la Huerta, Carranza
called him to Mexico City to be his secretary of industry, commerce, and labor.

Since Obregón's candidacy had been launched the previous
June and thus was already underway, both Calles and Obregón
hoped that the appointment would enable Calles to persuade
Carranza to accept Obregón as his successor. Calles also hoped
to use the position to help organized labor, with which he had
long been associated and which had been repressed by Carranza,
but probably his major reason for accepting was to be able to
keep an eye on developments within the Carranza government
and to maintain contact with potential allies in Mexico City.
Calles spent a great deal of time with members of the congress,
especially the so-called Bloque Revolucionario Independiente,
which was made up of the more radical members of the various
parties, including the P.L.C. and the Partido Nacional Cooperatista, as he felt that this group was the most likely to support
Obregón.[49]

However, it became obvious that Carranza would not support Calles' attempts to secure more benefits for labor, and
Calles himself felt that he could be of more use to Obregón
if he returned to Sonora. He eventually resigned, dealing a
considerable blow to Carranza, who had counted on separating
him politically from Obregón. He then became vice president
of the Centro Director Obregonista, which was managing the
campaign.[50] He took upon himself the task of maintaining contact with labor leaders, especially Morones of the C.R.O.M.
and Felipe Carrillo Puerto of Yucatán, with leaders of the
various political parties in Mexico City, and with potential
supporters, both political and military, throughout the country
but especially in the north and northwest.[51]

[49]Calles to de la Huerta, October 27, 1919, and Calles to de la Huerta,
December 26, 1919, both in *Sonora y Carranza*, comp. Clodoveo Valenzuela
and Amado Chaverri Matamoros, pp. 72, 74.

[50]Calles to de la Huerta, February 1, 1920, ibid., pp. 76–77; *El Monitor
Republicano* (Mexico City), February 5, 1920.

[51]Carrillo Puerto to Calles, March 10, 1920, Calles to Carillo Puerto,
March 17, 1920, Calles to Morones, April 7, 1920, Cruz to Calles, April 5,

Meanwhile, Obregón was conducting an extensive whistle-stop campaign, starting down the west coast of Mexico, more or less following the same route by which he had defeated Huerta. He drew enormous crowds, to the consternation of the Carrancistas. He continued to travel on regular trains, not having the funds for a special one, and was greeted by supporters at every station, whether or not he had scheduled stops. Financing the campaign was a constant problem, although each of the small groups supporting him financed itself, and an attempt was made by Francisco Serrano, under the auspices of the Partido Nacional Cooperatista, to sell bonds to finance Obregón's candidacy.[52] Although Obregón's telegraph and railroad passes had been taken away, he managed to keep the campaign going.

As he traveled south, the attempts at repression continued, and he was forced to skip a planned visit to Tepic when he was warned that members of the army had orders to assault his train. Even in the state of Michoacán, controlled by Pascual Ortiz Rubio, a governor friendly to his cause, there was considerable fear for Obregón's safety.[53]

At the same time, the success of Obregón's campaign impelled Carranza to launch Bonillas' candidacy quickly. By late November, 1919, Obregón had come to the capital of Mexico itself, and it was no longer possible for Carranza's advisers to pretend that Obregón's campaign was failing; the evidence was under Carranza's nose. Obregón arrived in the capital on November 23 to a tumultuous reception, characterized by *El Monitor Republicano* as representing "all social classes." Indeed, the photographs reflect that the enormous crowds were composed of all kinds of people, from *campesinos* who had come into town from the surrounding countryside, to the urban

---

1920, Aguirre to Calles, April 6, 1920, Topete to Calles, April 8, 1920, Calles to de la Huerta, February 1, 1920, all in Valenzuela and Chaverri Matamoros, *Sonora*, pp. 78, 81, 82, 84, 93–97, 76–77.

[52]*El Monitor Republicano* (Mexico City), November 6, 1919; Prieto Laurens, *Cincuenta años*, p. 75.

[53]Fernando Torreblanca, interview, July 18, 1974; Vicente Estrada Cajigal, interview, PHO/4/12, p. 51.

poor in great numbers, to elegantly dressed men and women.
The crowd had remained at the station despite a delay of six
hours at Irapuato, where the train had been detained by order
of Paulino Fontes, the director of railways. The rumor in the
station in Irapuato had been that the order to keep the train
waiting had come from the president himself.[54]

The demonstrations of Obregón's popularity continued in
full force during his stay in the city. On his entrance to the
city, he was led triumphantly to his hotel, and the march in his
support continued, despite attempts by the police to break it up.
The night of his arrival in Mexico City, two police captains
wearing anti-Obregón buttons were almost lynched after a dispute with a worker at the popular Díaz de León Theater. On
the night of November 25, the candidate presided as a member
of the party at a meeting of the P.L.C.[55]

On November 26 he received more than one hundred
mutilated veterans of the Revolution, along with a large number of workers, at the Hotel Saint Francis, where he was
staying. According to the press report, he invited his visitors to
come in immediately, greeting them with the "same words of
fondness and affection as during the struggle and anguish of
past times." Then he led them all outside to be photographed
with him. The picture appeared on the front page of El Monitor
Republicano the next day.[56]

For the following week he met with groups of supporters,
attended meetings of the myriad parties that were offering him
their support, and presided at banquets in his honor. Wherever
he went, crowds of people gathered around him. His last night
in Mexico City, after a dinner in his honor given by Deputy Antonio Valadez Ramírez of Jalisco in the name of the Bloque
Liberal Revolucionario, he decided to walk back to his hotel
accompanied by the mass of people who had been waiting out-

[54]El Monitor Republicano (Mexico City), November 24, 1919. See also
reports and clippings: Meade Fierro to Medina, November 28, 1919, article
from San Antonio Light, November 28, 1919, and article from Waco Times-
Herald, November 28, 1919, all in ASRE-119, L-E-803R, Leg. 7.
[55]El Monitor Republicano (Mexico City), November 25, 1919.
[56]Ibid., November 26, 1919.

side the Abel Restaurant to see him.[57] His relaxed and accessible manner made an enormous impression in the capital.

Carranza now had real cause for concern. His hope that Pablo González would emerge as a strong candidate to counter Obregón and that they would then neutralize each other so that he could impose Bonillas had not materialized. Indeed, Don Pablo seemed likely to come to some sort of agreement with the man who was now regularly referred to as "the people's candidate." Furthermore, the lower ranks of the army seemed to be more and more evidently Obregonista, and some of the commanders as well. One report quoted northern leaders as saying, "Here we are all neutral, but the first so-and-so who moves against Obregón will be killed."[58]

The Partido Nacional Cooperatista and the Partido Laborista Mexicano had now joined the P.L.C. in supporting Obregón, and the number of other organizations—of workers, of *campesinos*, of overtly political regional groups—who would support Obregón was growing dramatically, despite arrests, violence, and even assassination of a few local leaders.[59] A further danger to Carranza was the possible alliance of Obregón with other groups, particularly the Zapatistas. It was even claimed that Zapata's assassination in 1919 had been ordered by Carranza because he feared such an alliance, and the opposition of Pablo González, the man considered Zapata's murderer, to Obregón could only strengthen Obregón's popularity with that group.[60]

Obregón's triumphal campaign continued into January, when Carranza officially launched Bonillas as his own candidate. Obregón was unimpeded by the colorless unknown who had

[57]Ibid., November 30, 1919.

[58]Report, January 27, 1920, AAA-DT. González had earlier attempted to come to a public agreement with Obregón that would have permitted them both to run as presidential candidates; Obregón was not interested (González to Obregón and Obregón to González, in *El Universal* [Mexico City], June 4 and 11, 1919).

[59]*El Monitor Republicano* (Mexico City), November 10 and 14, 1919; Report, September 26, 1919, AAA-DT.

[60]Antonio Díaz Soto y Gama, *La revolución agraria del Sur y Emiliano Zapata*, p. 235; Fernando Torreblanca, interview, July 19, 1974.

played only a minor part in the Revolution itself. Even his old enemy Palavicini now publicly announced that he considered Obregón the most viable candidate. At a party in Palavicini's honor, the honoree proposed a toast to the three candidates: Obregón (applause), González (silence), and Bonillas (laughter).[61]

By February, the Gran Partido Liberal, organized by the P.L.C. to coordinate the more than three hundred groups now working for Obregón, was meeting in Mexico City. At the same time Calles and Amado Aguirre left the government to participate in the Obregón campaign. Carranza, for his part, called a meeting or conclave of governors, in the hope of strengthening this arm of his support. Most of the governors had been chosen by him, and most of them had been generals in the Revolution. Carranza hoped for a strong statement supporting Bonillas and assurances that the governors would control the military forces at their disposal and prevent their use by Obregón. All he got from the nervous governors was the guarantee of a free election, but this fact did not prevent *El Monitor Republicano* from complaining that the governors were conspiring to prevent exactly that.[62] The situation was grave, and the Carrancistas began to react with panic.

Obregón was traveling meanwhile in areas that were controlled by Carranza partisans, and the repression was increasing accordingly. In mid-February, after opening the meeting of the Gran Convención Obregonista, Obregón went into San Luis Potosí, which was controlled by Carranza's faithful supporter Juan Barragán. Two days after his tumultuous arrival, *El Monitor Republicano* headlined: "The Authorities of San Luis Potosí Do Not Respect Political Rights." The state police had forcefully prevented a meeting organized by Obregón's supporters in the Partido Liberal Obrero. According to *El Monitor*, this repression was the first fruit of the governors' conclave. Obregón himself, undaunted, had gone on to meet with the workers at the local metallurgical factory.[63]

[61]*El Monitor Republicano* (Mexico City), January 19, 1920.
[62]Ibid., February 1 and 11, 1920.
[63]Ibid., February 13, 1920.

The next day the Potosino police had to resort to violence to break up the Obregonista demonstration; a large number of people were wounded. Obregón himself had been walking at the head of the crowd, and he saw the police arresting his followers. When he asked them to stop, the police refused, although Obregón then stopped the demonstration to prevent possible bloodshed. Meanwhile, the telegrams coming out of San Luis Potosí were being censored to prevent news of the repression from reaching the capital.[64]

Obregón, speaking to the Potosino crowd, strongly protested the repression. Referring to the governors' conclave, which supposedly had guaranteed the free exercise of political liberty, he said, "It seems to me that for the governors of Guanajuato, San Luis Potosí, and Querétaro to prepare a program to guarantee effective suffrage is like the criminals who are confined in the Islas Marías studying a program to guarantee property and prevent theft. . . ."[65]

The worst repression was yet to come, however. In late February and early March, Obregón was taken ill while in Saltillo, in Carranza's own territory of Coahuila. The campaign languished for a couple of weeks but then was renewed with enormous political rallies in Saltillo itself. Bonillas, arriving shortly thereafter in the Coahuilan capital, was greeted with cheers for Obregón.[66]

By the end of March, when Obregón arrived in Tampico, which had been a stronghold of the labor movement for several years, he was greeted by a large crowd of oil workers, railway men, and stevedores. They had come from a meeting that morning of a Convención Obrera that had voted to support Obregón for the presidency. The vote had been 1,082 for Obregón, 15 for González, and 3 for Bonillas, a distribution that seemed to be fairly typical for those groups. Workers were not the

---

[64]Ibid., February 14, 1920.

[65]Ibid., February 15, 1920.

[66]Ibid., March 21, 1920; Report, March 19, 1920, AAA-DT. U.S. observers confirmed the reports of repression detailed in *El Monitor Republicano* (see Summerlin to Secretary of State, March 17, 1920, USDS 812.00/23523).

only ones on hand, however, as people of all social classes came out to greet the candidate. He himself had left the train in the small town of Doña Cecilia on the edge of Tampico to greet the crowds and to proceed into the city by car. By the time he arrived in the center of town, the plaza was in a virtual state of siege. Three hundred dragoons armed with loaded Mausers were stationed in front of the Hotel Terminal where the candidate was to stay. General Murguía himself was on hand in his own train nearby, complete with machine guns on the roof trained on the hotel.

As Obregón's party entered the plaza, Chief of Police Orozco made threatening gestures to Congressional Deputy Aurelio Manrique, one of Obregón's companions. The crowd, estimated at 15,000, stopped in front of the Hotel Continental to hear the speeches, with Obregón declaring openly in Orozco's hearing that there were not enough Orozcos in the country to impose Bonillas against the popular will. After the speeches, two of the speakers, Manrique and Rafael Martínez de Escobar, were arrested and taken away. The rest of the Obregón party went to their hotel, only to be stopped at the door by a group of about thirty men who, according to observers, intended to make an attempt on the life of the candidate. He was immediately surrounded by supporters anxious to protect him, and his attackers, thinking perhaps that discretion was the better part of valor, dispersed to await another opportunity. Obregón and Jorge Prieto Laurens, the head of the Obregonista faction in the P.N.C., walked to the municipal jail, while the rest of Obregón's companions went to their room in the hotel, where they were again attacked and more of them arrested by Orozco's men. The crowd continued to protect Obregón.[67]

When Obregón got to the prison, he found that Manrique and Martínez de Escobar had been beaten. On leaving, he was threatened again by Murguía and his staff, who had by now left their train and were waiting in front of the jail. Obregón, according to Prieto Laurens, then said in a loud voice that he

[67]El Monitor Republicano (Mexico City), April 4, 1920; Obregón to Comité Obregonista, reprinted in Emilio Portes Gil, Autobiografía de la Revolución Mexicana, p. 285; Prieto Laurens, Cincuenta años, p. 84.

would not leave Tampico until his companions were released. As the intention of the entire incident seemed to be to prevent Obregón from continuing his campaign, Murguía and his men were satisfied and retired to the Casino de Tampico to celebrate. Obregón went to the federal judge, who promised to have the prisoners released, and immediately began to make plans to leave town, feeling correctly that his life was in danger. In fact, his telegraph and postal messages were not being delivered, apparently by presidential order, and he was to all intents and purposes isolated. He and Prieto Laurens and four or five others caught the train for Ciudad Victoria, leaving Jesús M. Garza to do what he could to protect the prisoners.[68]

His train was soon detained in one of the small towns. One of the railway men, an Obregón partisan, went into the station to find out what was going on and returned with word that Murguía had discovered that Obregón had left town and was sending a military train to capture him for certain offenses against the president and the army. On hearing this report, Obregón warned the other passengers, among them a carload of tourists, that there might be a fight. The train was converted into a political meeting, and small groups of *campesinos*, alerted by the train's long delay, began arriving to help protect the candidate. When Murguía and his men arrived, they found the train surrounded by passengers and *campesinos* shouting "Viva Obregón! Down with the Imposition!" Realizing that to make any move against Obregón would be dangerous, they let Obregón's train go on to Ciudad Victoria. The candidate had escaped for the time being. Obregón later observed that "whenever someone wants my death sufficiently to give up his own life, I will be a dead man."[69] That time had not yet arrived.

He had escaped from the Carrancistas only momentarily. Carranza had hoped to force him to leave the country, thus disqualifying himself as a candidate for president. Failing this, the plan seemed to be to make it appear that Obregón was in

[68]Prieto Laurens, *Cincuenta años*, p. 85; Report, March 31, 1920, AAA-DT.

[69]Prieto Laurens, *Cincuenta años*, pp. 86–87; Torreblanca, interview, July 19, 1974.

revolt against the central government, which would permit military repression of his movement and probably his own death. However, in spite of constant offers of help from armed groups of *campesinos* in the area of the northeast through which he was traveling, Obregón kept refusing to take any illegal action.[70]

At last, when the candidate was in Matamoros, on the U.S. border, Carranza called him to Mexico City to answer charges of conspiring with the "rebel" Roberto Cejudo. Although he was called before a military court, which had no jurisdiction over him as a civilian, he decided to comply because he was sure that the charges could not be proven and because he wanted to show the people of Mexico that he was not afraid. Therefore, in Matamoros, he made what he referred to as possibly his last public speech, explaining that he was returning to Mexico City to fight the charges against him. An uproar arose as the crowd indignantly responded, some saying that it was time to go to the hills and start the battle, others suggesting that a caravan be formed to accompany Obregón to the capital. Obregón calmed the crowd, explaining that he would go with his small group of companions, but ended by assuring them that "we will continue fighting in defense of the revolutionary postulates: Effective suffrage and no reelection." It was only on the way back to Mexico City that Obregón discovered that Carranza was making preparations to send a contingent of federal forces to the state of Sonora at the same time that Obregón would be answering charges in the capital.[71] Obregón would therefore be a sort of hostage against Sonoran action.

The machinery of government had proved unable to contain the Obregonista movement. Now Carranza was moving directly against what he mistakenly assumed to be the exclusive source of Obregón's power, the state of Sonora.

[70]Torreblanca, interview, July 19, 1974; Prieto Laurens, *Cincuenta años*, p. 87; Report, March 21, 1920, AAA-DT.

[71]Prieto Laurens, *Cincuenta años*, p. 88.

CHAPTER 13

Revolt and Consolidation:
The Plan of Agua Prieta

Ironically, it was President Carranza's pressure on Sonora that would ultimately bring all the elements of Obregón's political network into play against him. Although until this time Obregón had conducted an open political campaign within the limits of the law, the legal attacks made against him and the moves against the state Carranza considered to be Obregón's power base pushed the Sonoran leaders to declare an armed movement against the Carranza government. They were thus able to mobilize individuals and groups who had formerly been acquiescent to a peaceful transfer of power along with those who had remained in rebellion against Carranza. The ease with which this mobilization was carried out illustrates the enormous strength of the political support Obregón and his associates had been building so carefully.

Carranza's campaign against Sonora had begun well before the moment of crisis. In mid-1919, he had declared the Río Sonora to be the property of the federal government and had begun to make plans to divert some of its waters. In a state that was largely desert, this threat was a substantial one. Though Carranza probably had the legal authority to take this step, it was nevertheless a direct slap in the face of the Sonorans, who had been promised control over these waters by Madero himself in 1913. The problem was still unresolved when Calles passed the governorship to Adolfo de la Huerta, elected for the 1919–1923 term despite Carranza's effort to keep him in New York as consul to prevent his campaigning.[1]

[1]Clodoveo Valenzuela and Amado Chaverri Matamoros, comps., *Sonora y Carranza*, pp. 9, 11–12; Antonio Rivera, *La Revolución en Sonora*, p. 504.

Shortly thereafter, Carranza fired the acting director of the Secretariat of War, Juan José Ríos, who had been the leader of one of the Red Battalions under Obregón at Celaya, and sent him to Sonora as chief of forces there. In Sonora, he replaced General Torres, another strong supporter of Calles and thus of Obregón. Calles, in a letter to de la Huerta, urged him to console Torres by explaining the political nature of the appointment. Meanwhile, the Carrancistas were calling Ríos a traitor because he had, according to rumor, been helping out the Obregonistas with money, railroad passes, and other considerations.[2]

A more serious threat was Carranza's refusal to live up to the agreement with the Yaquis, which had been arranged by de la Huerta and Ríos, although many of the obligations were met out of state funds.[3] He then named Manuel M. Diéguez, who had long fought under Obregón but had now definitively thrown in his hand with Carranza, to be military chief of operations in Sonora, Sinaloa, and Lower California, with his headquarters in Hermosillo. Diéguez was known to be an enemy of the Yaquis, and his appointment was viewed by the Sonorans as a direct provocation to the now peaceful Indians to revolt again, weakening the state and giving Carranza an excuse for widespread repression.[4]

By the end of March, it was apparent that Carranza was planning to send a large number of federal troops, principally from Chihuahua and Jalisco, into Sonora. The Sonoran press immediately protested that this action proved President Carranza's intent to force the election of his candidate by controlling the state of Sonora.[5]

It did not take de la Huerta long to react. On April 4, 1920, he sent a message to Carranza protesting the arrival of naval troops in the port of Guaymas, supposedly to put down

---

[2]Calles to de la Huerta, December 26, 1919, in Valenzuela and Chaverri Matamoros, *Sonora*, p. 74; Report, September 10, 1919, AAA-DT. Ríos, however, did not join the Agua Prieta movement against Carranza.

[3]Rivera, *La Revolución*, pp. 509–510.

[4]Ibid., p. 508.

[5]*Orientación*, March 30, 1920, in Valenzuela and Chaverri Matamoros, *Sonora*, p. 114.

the Yaquis, who were not in revolt. Moreover, he accused Carranza of beginning to conspire with the Maytorenistas, who had been thrown out of the state at such effort. The troops, according to de la Huerta, were in fact being sent to Sonora to depose his government because it was suspected of being Obregonista and to substitute another more satisfactory to the central government. He then directly questioned the choice of Diéguez as commander, pointing out that the Yaquis viewed him with "marked hostility," after what they felt had been the betrayal of a treaty Diéguez had made with them in 1915. He ended by explaining that should the Yaquis be forced to move into the Sierra again, where they had no way of making a living, they would be forced to rob again and the federal troops would again pursue them. Thus the cycle of desperate struggle that had for so many years devastated the region would begin all over again. De la Huerta protested that it would be a great shame to destroy the agreement now that the solution to the Yaqui problem was at hand. He closed hopefully: "We await your reply."[6]

The reply was not long in arriving. Carranza stated that he would not explain why he had sent troops into the state and added that "any attempt to interfere with the Federal Army will be considered as a declaration of rebellion." He noted that the matter had become one of state versus federal authority and that he as president had no intention of backing down. He further added that he suspected de la Huerta's motives—in other words, he accused him of planning treason—and emphasized that any difference of opinion or revolt would be de la Huerta's, not his, fault.[7]

In view of this direct challenge, the state legislature of Sonora the following day gave de la Huerta special powers to protect the state against what was described as a "deliberate challenge to its independence and sovereignty." The state itself would assume all powers necessary to its protection so long as the threat existed, and the governor was given extraordinary

[6]De la Huerta to Carranza, April 4, 1920, ASRE-119, L-E-866, Leg. 3.
[7]Carranza to de la Huerta, April 9, 1920, ASRE-119, L-E-866, Leg. 3.

powers over the two most important branches of government, finance and war. Further, the governor was given permission to change the seat of government whenever necessary, a sign that the Sonorans viewed a long-lasting civil war as the possible consequence of their actions.[8] Meanwhile, the Sonorans had been buying arms and ammunition in the United States, from Phelps-Dodge among others, and were recruiting men to meet the threat. Troops were being moved to the Cañon del Pulpito between Chihuahua and Sonora to meet the federal forces attempting to enter the state. The Carrancista consul in Douglas foresaw war within the month.[9]

Meanwhile, the candidate had been called to Mexico City to answer charges that he had been conspiring with the rebel leader, Roberto Cejudo, in planning an armed revolt against the central government. It is quite possible that Obregón had been in contact with Cejudo, and he had definitely been in contact with the *caudillo* of the Tampico oil regions, Manuel Peláez, with whom Cejudo was associated, to assure himself of Peláez' support should he become president. However, it is extremely unlikely that he had urged Cejudo to revolt militarily when his own campaign for office was such a success.

In any case, the circumstances of the charges were strange. Cejudo had made peace with the central government in mid-March after promising to join the government to fight rebels in his own state. The government claimed that as soon as he had received arms and ammunition he revolted against the government again. In any case, he was arrested and disarmed in Jalapa in late March and brought to Mexico City for trial. Cejudo's friends claimed that an intrigue was afoot, as Cejudo had given up without a fight. Reports circulated in Mexico City that Cejudo had been removed from the military jail, Santiago Tlaltelolco, and taken to one of the army installations, where he had been threatened with torture and/or death if he did not make accusations against Obregón. As of April 1, Cejudo had

---

[8]Law #30, in Rivera, *La Revolución*, pp. 522–523.

[9]Arredondo to Subsecretario de Relaciones Exteriores, April 1 and 3, 1920, Arredondo to Carranza, April 7 and 8, 1920, both in ASRE-119, L-E-866, Leg. 3.

refused to be used as an instrument of the political machinations against the candidate.[10] The government's case was built entirely on documents that could easily have been forged.

Although Obregón had been asked to testify before the military judge as a witness, when he arrived on April 6 at the prison of Santiago Tlaltelolco, where the investigation was being held, he was informed that he also was a defendant in the case. He immediately designated Miguel Alessio Robles, Deputy Francisco R. Serrano, and other who were with him to be his lawyers and sent one of them to get an injunction against the court.

The judge, by the testimony of several witnesses, was terribly nervous; apparently he had been shaken when the two Yaqui soldiers who were standing at attention at either side of the tribunal had shouted "Viva Obregón!" when the candidate appeared. By the testimony of several observers, the judge frequently went to the phone to get instructions and was heard to protest that he simply couldn't do what was asked. In his excitement, he even tried to smoke his cigar lighted end first. Obregón remained tranquil throughout, insisting that the court had no right to try him, as he maintained no connection with the military, and he consistently denied that he had ever met Cejudo. He emphasized that he had turned down all offers of military help and was running his campaign in a democratic fashion. When shown a letter that purported to be from Cejudo to Félix Díaz, announcing that Obregón and Guadalupe Sánchez were ready to rise against Carranza, he simply answered that it was a forgery. Finally, the judge dismissed the proceedings for the time being and ordered Obregón to report back the following week.[11]

The same day a number of deputies and senators sent Obregón a telegram congratulating him on the fifth anniversary

[10]*El Monitor Republicano* (Mexico City), March 29 and 30, and April 1, 1920.

[11]This account is based on three eyewitness accounts: on the report in *El Universal* (Mexico City), March 7, 1920, which was given to them by telephone by Francisco R. Serrano during the proceedings; on Fernando Torreblanca, interview, July 24, 1974; and on Jorge Prieto Laurens, *Cincuenta años de política mexicana: Memorias políticas*, pp. 88–89.

of the battle of Celaya, with a copy for the president. The reporter in the Telegraph Department commented: "a well-deserved joke on Carranza." Meanwhile, Mrs. Obregón had not had word of her husband for two weeks, a result of the prohibition on messages to and from the candidate. The reporter added that the Carrancistas planned to use whatever excuse to terminate Obregón's candidacy, that de la Huerta was wiring insistently but had received no response (it would come on April 10), and that the chief of telegraphs, Mario Méndez, was preventing any transmission of the news of the proceedings against Obregón. In fact, the family was unsure of his safety until April 17, when Francisco Serrano was finally able to get a telegraph communication through to Sonora.[12]

For a few days after the hearing, Obregón remained in Mexico City, keeping himself visible despite rumors that his arrest was imminent. Benjamín Hill was also threatened, according to the capital gossip. General Andrés Castro, who had worked closely with Obregón in the Secretariat of War and Navy and in the P.L.C., was ordered picked up for having insulted a sergeant in the military guard at the prison while Obregón was testifying. Meanwhile, *El Monitor Republicano* reported that Obregón would resume his political campaign the following week, ignoring the threats to arrest him.[13]

Obregón was using the week to organize his potential supporters in the capital. On April 11, at the restaurant in Chapultepec Park, he had what was described as a cordial conversation with General Pablo González about the imposition of Bonillas. The support of González' troops would be critical to Carranza if he were to succeed in imposing Bonillas, and this casual meeting, which had been carefully arranged to be both public and publicized, must have given the president some cause for concern.[14]

Also, on the eleventh news arrived from Calles to the effect that the state of Sonora, in view of Carranza's communication of the ninth, would be forced to assume her sovereignty. Obre-

[12]Report, April 7, 1920, AAA-DT. See also USDS 812.00/23567, 23600.

[13]*El Monitor Republicano* (Mexico City), April 8 and 10, 1920.

[14]Ibid., April 12, 1920. See also Hanna to Secretary of State, April 12, 1920, USDS 812.00/23569.

gón, under constant surveillance in Mexico City, remarked to those who were assembled at the home of Licenciado Miguel Alessio Robles, where he was staying, that "Adolfo and Plutarco must have good reasons for what they are doing, but we're caught here in the mousetrap." Working feverishly, he contacted various supporters: deputies, senators, and other political leaders, labor leaders, especially in the C.R.O.M., and, most important of all, the railway workers who had helped protect him throughout the campaign.[15]

Despite Obregón's popularity, it was a moment of extreme peril, as he was followed everywhere by Carranza's men. Escape to the north was obviously impossible; Sonora was too far away and the areas in between insecure. Obregón therefore resolved to go south toward the Zapatistas, with whom he had come to an agreement in March. He began his preparation for flight on April 12.

For help in his escape, Obregón again called on the railway men. Evading Carrancista surveillance by leaping out of his car in the Parque Orizaba and into a taxi hired by railway engineer Margarito Ramírez, Obregón was eventually able to escape Mexico City. Ramírez concealed him in a box car on his own regularly scheduled train for Iguala, Guerrero, which took Obregón close to Zapatista territory. On arrival, the military chief of the region, General Rómulo Figueroa, declared his support for Obregón and contacted General Fortunato Maycotte, who controlled the area between them and Zapatista territory. When Maycotte joined Obregón's cause, the candidate's safety was assured.[16]

Obregón had been in contact with the Zapatistas for some

[15]Prieto Laurens, *Cincuenta años*, p. 89. According to Prieto Laurens, this incident took place on the day of the hearing, but it actually seems to have taken place later, as Obregón did not escape the city until the night of April 12. Benjamín Hill left Mexico City shortly thereafter, after visiting the U.S. Embassy to explain to the chargé that Sonora was in open rebellion but that the majority of federal troops and rebel factions would unite behind Obregón in a revolution that would last at most a few weeks. He also requested Embassy refuge for his family (Hanna to Secretary of State, April 12, 1920, USDS 812.00/23574).

[16]This account is taken from two versions in Valenzuela and Chaverri Matamoros, *Sonora*: those of Margarito Ramírez (pp. 179–183) and Obregón (pp. 183–184).

time, and at least since some time in March he had been sure of their support for his future presidency, as he had not been sure of Maycotte's. In mid-March, his representative, Juan C. Zertuche, had approached Zapata's successor, Gildardo Magaña, who had pledged his help and who had immediately gone into the area of the Mixtec del Valle passes, where Oaxaca, Veracruz, and Puebla meet, to secure the region for Obregón. The anti-Carranza groups in the area were at that time allied for the most part with Félix Díaz, the old dictator's nephew, but some of them had been allied previously with Zapata, and in any case Magaña prevailed in securing their support for Obregón. Meanwhile, in Morelos, other Zapatistas were becoming Obregonistas.[17]

Obregón and the Zapatistas had a considerable community of interest. First of all, the Zapatistas had been trying since 1917 to unite with other revolutionary factions either within or outside of the Carranza movement in opposition to the Carranza government. They were encouraged when Obregón resigned as secretary of war to return to Sonora and from that time forward viewed him as a potential recruit or even leader for their cause. They had come to view the revolutionary struggle as essentially an alliance between agrarian radicalism and urban radicalism against the privileged classes who did not work for a living, very much the same terms in which Obregón himself described the battle.[18]

They had been making attempts to approach urban labor for the purposes of alliance and had even tried to make contact with workers' groups outside the country.[19] They had received all comers to their cause, in much the same uncritical spirit with which Obregón himself welcomed support. They had also made active efforts in late 1918, when they were facing an offensive from Pablo González' troops, to interest in an

[17]John Womack, Jr., *Zapata and the Mexican Revolution*, pp. 357–358; Porfirio Palacios, *Emiliano Zapata: Datos biográficos-históricos*, p. 294. Manuel Sosa Pavón (interview, PHO/1/48, pp. 296–301, 306–312) describes the various efforts to get him to change sides and his own recruiting efforts.

[18]Carlos Reyes Avilés, *Cartones Zapatistas*, pp. 53–57.

[19]Zapata to Amezcua, February 14, 1918, Archivo de Amado Aguirre, private collection, Professor Alvaro Matute, Mexico City.

alliance such revolutionary leaders as J. Agustín Castro, Luis Gutiérrez, Juan Andreu Almazán, Saturnino Cedillo, Antonio Villarreal, J. Inés Chávez, and Roberto Cejudo, as well as Obregón himself.[20] In August, 1918, Zapata had authorized a woman, Dolores Jiménez y Muro, to negotiate a plan with Obregón for the unification of all the authentic revolutionary groups and had also attempted to approach him through the P.L.C. Moreover, the Zapatistas had maintained successful contact with Manuel Peláez, the *caudillo* of the oil regions, who would come to support Obregón. Even Villa and Felipe Angeles, before his own death, had been in contact with the southern leader.[21]

All of these contacts were to be useful to Obregón, and the network of communications that Gildardo Magaña, Zapata's successor, had maintained after Zapata's death was to serve Obregón well during the period immediately following his flight from Mexico City. Obregón had chosen the direction of his flight wisely, as the Zapatistas, delighted with the fall of their nemesis, Carranza, rallied to the man they felt would save the Revolution.

To the north, it was Calles who was organizing the fight for Obregón. Even before his resignation from Carranza's cabinet Calles had been keeping close track of which individuals, regional leaders, and groups might be likely to join a movement in favor of Obregón.[22] When the crisis erupted in April, it was Calles who knew whom to call on. In a rash of telegrams, now being transmitted through the good offices of

[20]Zapatista encampment at Tlaltizapán to Cedillo, September 5, 1918, AZ 30/24/449, to Villarreal, September 30, 1918, AZ 30/26/489, to J. Agustín Castro, September 7, 1918, AZ 30/26/474, to Juan Andreu Almazán, September 5, 1918, AZ 30/26/471, to Luis Gutiérrez, September 5, 1918, AZ 30/26/470, to J. Inés Chávez, September 10, 1918, AZ 30/26/455, and to Obregón, September 17, 1918, AZ 30/26/479.

[21]Palacios, *Zapata*, pp. 253–254; Encampment Tlaltizapán to Manuel Peláez, January 6, 1919, AZ 30/24/420; Villa to Zapata, November 29, 1918, AZ 30/21/388; Zapata to Felipe Angeles, November 21, 1918, AZ 30/21/383.

[22]Calles to de la Huerta, December 26, 1918, p. 74, Calles to de la Huerta, February 1, 1920, pp. 78–79, Carrillo to Calles, March 10, 1920, p. 81, Calles to Carrillo, March 17, 1920, p. 82, and Calles to Morones, March 22, 1920, p. 88, all in Valenzuela and Chaverri Matamoros, *Sonora*.

Obregonistas in the Telegraph Department, he contacted labor leaders, members of the military, regional leaders, and other individuals in Sonora and throughout the country.

And it was Calles who pushed through the adoption of yet another plan to give the Sonoran-led movement a rallying point. In Agua Prieta where he was readying troops for the campaign on the capital, he invited all the chiefs of troops who had arrived to join him, along with a few well-known civilian leaders, to consider the draft of a statement of intention written by Gilberto Valenzuela and sent to Calles by de la Huerta.[23] The document accused the central government of making a joke of popular suffrage, of having violated the sovereignty of the states, and of betraying the principles of the Revolution, already raised to near-sacred status. Therefore, calling themselves the Revindicating Movement, the Sonorans withdrew recognition from the government of Venustiano Carranza, as well as from the state governments of Guanajuato, San Luis Potosí, Querétaro, Nuevo León, and Tamaulipas, which they considered more thoroughly Carrancista than the others. However, they explicitly recognized José Santos Godínez as governor of the west-coast state of Nayarit and also recognized all other state governments except those named above.

These provisions were a good indication of where they did and did not expect help to come from. They further declared Adolfo de la Huerta to be the supreme chief of the army, with all the powers necessary to organize the movement politically, militarily, and administratively. The project was adopted as the Plan of Agua Prieta on April 23, 1920, and signed mainly by Sonorans. Telegrams of support, now being delivered more freely through Obregonistas in the telegraph service, began to pour in from around the country.[24]

To all intents and purposes, Obregón was in control of the country within two weeks. The threat of being cut off by Diéguez' troops in Jalisco to the south of Sonora and in Chi-

---

[23]Gilberto Valenzuela, interview, PHO/4/42; Rivera, *La Revolución*, pp. 524–526.
[24]Plan of Agua Prieta, TP.

Demonstration in honor of Obregón in Cuernavaca, as he returns triumphantly from the south, where he had fled from Carranza's persecution, May, 1920. *Casasola, INAH*

Obregón with a group of supporters in Cuernavaca, May, 1920. Benjamín Hill (*second from left*) stands beside Obregón (*center*). *Casasola, INAH*

Obregón (*left*) on his arrival at Tacubaya, D.F., near Mexico City, with potential rival General Pablo González (*center*), who had hastened to meet him there, May, 1920. *Casasola, INAH*

General Benjamín Hill (*front left*) and Obregón (*front center*) lead military parade in honor of Interim President Adolfo de la Huerta, summer, 1920. *Casasola, INAH*

General Plutarco Elías Calles, Obregón supporter from Sonora, who was named secretary of war in the cabinet of Interim President de la Huerta. *Casasola, INAH*

Obregón (*seated, holding white hat*) and noted political and military figures at political banquet in Coyoacán, fall, 1920. *Casasola, INAH*

President Obregón (*center*) with his private secretary, Fernando Torreblanca (*left*) and his chief of staff, General Manuel Pérez Treviño, December, 1920. *Casasola, INAH*

huahua to the west never materialized, as Diéguez' own men refused to follow him.

The situation in Jalisco was typical of what was happening all over the country. The troops Diéguez was commanding in Jalisco had fought under Amado Aguirre during the Revolution, and at the moment of crisis Aguirre had returned to Jalisco to try to persuade Diéguez to give up his persecution of Obregón. Diéguez equally intended to convince Aguirre to join him. Neither changed sides, and Aguirre fled into the mountains to the mining region where he had originally organized forces to join Obregón in 1913. There he received news of the Plan of Agua Prieta, which he immediately supported. He later wrote that it "woke great enthusiasm with the popular masses."[25]

Aguirre maintained communication throughout the period with Colonel Isaías Castro, one of Diéguez' younger officers who had fought with Aguirre against the Villistas, and was even in telephone contact with Diéguez at one point, each trying to convince the other to change sides. When Diéguez ordered Colonel Castro to fight the Obregonistas, he and the other officials of Diéguez' army agreed to arrest him and to kill him and his personal staff if they resisted. Diéguez, however, did not resist when he found himself surrounded by armed men shouting "Viva Obregón!" Rather weakly, he simply asked why they hadn't told him frankly how they felt and avoided all this trouble. Castro, then in effect in control of the state of Jalisco, sent a train for Aguirre, who returned to Guadalajara temporarily. Later, Aguirre, at Obregón's request, returned to Mexico City to organize Obregón's now virtually unopposed political campaign.[26]

Those few commanders who remained loyal to Carranza found that in most cases they could not count on the loyalty of their troops. By April 29, Carranza again was preparing to move his government to Veracruz. It may have been that he

[25]Amado Aguirre, *Mis memorias de campaña: Apuntes para la historia*, pp. 314, 320–322.
[26]Ibid., pp. 320–322.

intended to reestablish himself and meet the Obregonista threat; it seems more likely that he knew he was beaten. Pablo González and his troops had refused to support him, and it would be González' troops who first occupied the capital as Carranza pulled out, briefly causing concern that González would try to take over the government himself rather than passing it on to Obregón. However, González was strong only so long as he adhered to Obregón, and some minor attempts by his supporters to intimidate the Obregonistas failed. As Carranza prepared a railroad caravan that was to take him to the coast, more and more of his support melted away. Not even Guadalupe Sánchez, the *caudillo* who controlled the railroad route to Veracruz, could be counted on, and on May 7 word of his defection reached Mexico City, although no one was quite sure if the report were true.[27] On that same day, Carranza left Mexico City, although many of the troops he had counted on did not even join his train. The dust raised by González' troops approaching the capital was visible from the train as it left.

Even those troops who left Mexico City with the president quickly began to defect. Finally leaving the railroad line, Carranza made his way into the mountains, despite repeated offers by Obregón to guarantee his safety should he surrender. His unwillingness to give himself up and admit that his cause was lost probably cost him his life. Betrayed by an officer who had supposedly come to help him, he was attacked as he slept in the little village of Tlaxcalantongo and killed. Obregón was concerned when he heard of the death of his old enemy, as he feared that in martyrdom the first chief would be a more effective political rival than he had been alive, but, as he moved quickly to apprehend and prosecute the killer, this danger faded.[28]

[27]Reports, April 29 and May 7, 1920, AAA-DT; Ramón Beteta, *Camino a Tlaxcalantongo*, pp. 9–11.

[28]There are persistent rumors that Obregón ordered Carranza's death, and the truth is impossible to determine with certainty from the documents at this point, as the possibilities of fraud, falsification, and ordinary lying are obvious. Most interpretations answer the question, "Did he or didn't he?" by determining what they think would have been smart politically. Those who think Obregón would have profited by Carranza's death usually argue that he had him killed; those who feel it would have been foolish think he did not.

Carranza, despite his position as head of the executive power of the nation, had found himself ultimately powerless. He had badly overestimated his own position, judging that he had control of the military, of communications, of public funds, and of the metropolitan police force in Mexico City, against Obregón's popular appeal and possible Sonoran power base. In attempting to move against the Sonorans, he united them and gave the Obregonista movement a rallying point. In attempting to try Obregón on false charges of inciting rebellion, when it was evident to almost everyone in the country that Obregón would easily win any honest election, he precipitated the crisis that led to his own death.

Despite the critical dangers of the few days between Obregón's escape from Mexico City and the collapse of the Carranza government with the evacuation to Veracruz, the movement was almost bloodless, and the campaign that followed, once order had been reestablished, was carried on in a spirit of peace and reconciliation. Although Obregón had an opponent, Alfredo Robles Domínguez, the result of the presidential election was already foregone. Prominent among Obregón's companions during the preelection period were Luis Morones of the Partido Laborista Mexicano (P.L.M.), who had followed him south into Morelos, Antonio Díaz Soto y Gama, the Zapatista agrarian theorist, and Luis L. León, who had been active in the Comisión Local Agraria in Sonora.

The more economically favored classes were not ignored, however; for the period of reconstruction that Obregón wanted, they would have to acquiesce in his presidency. In addition to

---

The interpretation adopted here is that Obregón was genuinely upset on hearing of Carranza's death, as it could only have harmed the efforts for political consolidation Obregón was making. Thus it seems reasonable that he did not have to have him killed and would have lost by it. Some of the testimony that supports this viewpoint may be found in the following sources: Manuel de J. Solís Androaga, interview, PHO/1/17, p. 27; Daniel Cosío Villegas, interview, COHC; *El Universal* (Mexico City), May 9, 1920, reprinted in *Campaña política del C. Alvaro Obregón, candidato a la presidencia de la República, 1920–1924*, ed. Luis N. Ruvalcaba, 4:131; Obregón to Sánchez, May 8, 1920, Sánchez to Obregón, May 11, 1920, Obregón to Sánchez, May 11, 1920, all in PHS/72.

contacts made by his supporters with such organizations as
the Alliance of Mexican Railwaymen, the Chauffeurs' Union,
and the Bakers' Union, visits were also made to the Y.M.C.A.
(the report commenting that these young men were cultured
and more or less intellectual), the Mexican Red Cross, and other
organizations associated with the middle and upper classes.
The reasons given for these visits were first of all to secure
votes for the candidate in the coming September election, but
also to "unify the thinking of the diverse social classes in an
approach to mutual understanding."[29]

De la Huerta had meanwhile assumed the interim presidency, while Calles had become secretary of war. When it
became evident that there was no war, he continued to handle
political relationships for Obregón. Gradually, almost all groups
in Mexican society were reconciled to the Obregón presidency.
Even Villa eventually made his peace with de la Huerta, although Obregón seems to have been opposed to any association
with the Chihuahuan leader. Calles himself had made the first
moves in this reconciliation, instructing the Chihuahua Obregonistas to offer Villa amnesty immediately after the pronounce-
ment of the Plan of Agua Prieta.[30]

The presidential election took place on September 5, 1920,
and was carried out in peace, almost in lethargy, with the exception of a few areas such as Morelia, Michoacán, where the local
representative of the Centro Director Electoral reported that
Obregón's triumph had been "unanimous" despite enemy efforts.
One of the Mexico City polling places complained that an over-
enthusiastic member of one of the workers' unions had thrown
himself on a number of voting booths shouting "Viva Obregón!" and was thus proving himself an embarrassment to the
candidate.[31] This attitude was quite different from that a few
months earlier, when these same workers were being urged to
support Obregón in a situation that might well have meant

[29]F. Sáenz de Sicilia, September 25, 1920, in Archivo de Amado Aguirre,
Centro Director Electoral, private collection, Alvaro Matute, Mexico City
(cited hereafter as AAA-CDE).

[30]Calles to Villa, May 2, 1920, in Valenzuela and Chaverri Matamoros,
Sonora, p. 269.

[31]Election report, Mexico City, no date, AAA-CDE.

risking their lives in a prolonged military struggle. The exhaustion of the Mexican nation was obvious, and the Mexican people were longing to return to a period of peace, perhaps even boredom.

Obregón, a few days after the election, emphasized this aspect of his future government. Foreshadowing what theorist Crane Brinton would say a few years later about the necessary period of recuperation after the fever of revolution, he said in a speech in Yucatán:

Long convalescenses always follow grave illnesses, and, after the struggle we have sustained for ten years to gain our civic rights, it is natural that we should begin the period of national convalescence. We are going to show the world either that we are capable of reconstructing the country we have half-destroyed, in order to guide it in new paths, or that we are only able to destroy and not to reconstruct the country of the future.

He went on to state that this future was in the hands of those who could aid in its reconstruction, and he urged all capable men to help. He added that he was traveling the country precisely so that he would know which individuals were willing and capable of helping with this important national task, but at the same time he emphasized that the local affairs of Yucatán were the exclusive domain of the men of Yucatán. This policy of staying out of local politics was one he would follow during his presidency, when he urged his secretary and undersecretary of government above all to avoid friction with the state governors. As an example of his policy of consolidation, on the other hand, he attended parties offered by the Socialist party, by groups of workers, by the producers of *henequén*, by the Railwaymen's Workers' League, and by the School of Agriculture.[32]

The tempo of the times had slowed down, and Mexico heaved a sigh of relief. She had a new leader, strong enough to begin some of the tasks that the Revolution had set for her: land reform, economic growth, benefits to the workers, education for the masses, modernization. At the same time, the form

[32]*La Revista de Yucatán*, September 8, 1920, reprinted in Ruvalcaba, *Campaña*, 5:165; Valenzuela, interview, PHO/4/42.

of the presidency would echo the earlier institution of a strong chief executive: the Spanish viceroy, the former dictator Díaz. Still, the goals of government had undergone a significant change, and the new president was amenable to alternation in office, even if he would later prove unwilling to give up office entirely. Mexico was about to enter a new political era, an era of mass politics and stability. This combination, in Latin America at least, was to be unique for many years. Mexico had undergone her social revolution; consolidation and reunification under new principles was underway.

CHAPTER 14

Conclusion

Alvaro Obregón's ascension to the Mexican presidency in December, 1920, marked the end of an era of rapid and violent political and social change, an era of armed popular mobilization. A new elite had emerged that would guide Mexico toward a slower, more orderly but at the same time far less democratic period of change within the limits set by this new elite itself, by the circumstances of the Revolution, by the power base the elite had been able to forge within these circumstances, and by the ideology embodied in the Constitution of 1917. Although sporadic violent movements would challenge this new elite's power, Obregón's political activity entered a new phase; up until December, 1920, he had focused on coming to power, while after that date his role was one of administration and consolidation. This study has thus been confined to the period of his rise to power, and, apart from indications of what some of the consequences were of the limitations set during this early period, it will close with his assumption of the presidency.

A number of factors help explain his ability to take power within a dangerous, fluid, factional situation. First of all, he was well-known throughout the country, and his military exploits in the service of the Revolution had taken him to many different areas. News of his exploits had spread, both by word of mouth and by the rapidly developing system of more modern communications—newspapers and the telegraph, in particular—to those areas where he had not been. He consolidated this popular support with his widespread whistle-stop campaign tour through the country in 1919 and 1920. The victories over Orozco and Huerta, both considered traitors to the Revolution by the populace at large, and over Villa, who was feared almost as much as he was admired, had made Obregón a hero who, in 1920, eclipsed all others. Moreover, his practice of distributing land and raising wages in the areas through which his armies moved had provided immediate rewards for those who followed him and had encouraged still others to join him.

The partial martyrdom of losing an arm had contributed even more to his heroic image. Although he lingered on to have his image tarnished somewhat as the principles of the Revolution proved difficult to achieve when confronted with Mexican realities, and although his story was less dramatic than that of either Villa or Zapata, neither of whom was ever finally faced with the task of putting ideals into practice, at the time of the Revolution itself he was the primary revolutionary hero, the embodiment of the Revolution.

He was also extremely shrewd politically, despite his occasional miscalculations, such as trusting Carranza ultimately to acknowledge him as his successor. When he first came into the Revolution, during the fight against Orozco, he was careful to maintain himself as his own man, declining to become a protégé of the governor, José María Maytorena, whom he neither trusted nor respected. During the early fighting in Sonora, he had already had his eye on the national scene, and in inviting Carranza to come to Sonora behind his lines during the critical summer and fall of 1913 he at one stroke had brought himself to the attention of the first chief and had furnished him a much-needed haven. Carranza responded by making him chief of the Army of the Northwest, a power base beyond the confines of Sonora. Obregón was thus able to bypass the Sonoran political struggle and emerge as a leader of national stature. Carranza's frequent efforts to return him to Sonora were uniformly unsuccessful.

Further, his reputation as a reasonable man and a peacemaker was established when he went personally to the Convention of revolutionary leaders at Aguascalientes, dealing with Villa's representatives despite the fact that Villa had tried to have him killed the month before. As the Convention was held close to Villa's lines, Obregón's reputation for courage was enhanced as well. Had his gamble that Villa and Carranza might both be forced to resign in the interest of revolutionary unity materialized, he might well have emerged even earlier as preeminent politically. However, neither Carranza nor Villa had any intention of giving up whatever power he had achieved, and a split was probably inevitable from the start. It is likely that Obregón recognized this, but the stakes were high and the gamble was probably worth taking.

He had further miscalculated, however, in assuming that Villa would be exposed as an irrational bandit and would thus be politically eliminated by the Convention. On the contrary, Villa, and Zapata as well, emerged with strong claims to legitimacy as leaders of the Convention. Once this development became apparent, Obregón, knowing first-hand the dissensions and potential divisions in the Convention, realized that Villa and Zapata could not establish a stable administration for the country. Therefore, he chose his only remaining alternative and joined Carranza, helping form a cohesive and centrally organized campaign against the powerful Villa. As Obregón had expected, Villa and Zapata were unable to pursue a coordinated military effort, and Carranza, Obregón, and the Constitutionalists were able to prevail.

In spite of frequent differences of opinion between Obregón and Carranza over social and political questions, Obregón stayed with the Carranza government until Carranza was forced by the military situation to name him secretary of war. This position, at last, gave Obregón a true national prominence that he used to advantage, maintaining himself constantly in the public eye, giving interviews in the national and foreign press, attending innumerable official functions, moving with energy to modernize the armed forces. He remained with the administration through the Constitutional Convention at Querétaro in 1917, despite considerable pressure from within the administration and from Carranza supporters within the Constituyente. His strong public stand in favor of the radicals, with the unstated but implicit threat to use the armed forces to guarantee the freedom of the delegates, reinforced by the Carrancista attacks against him, made him political friends who would disperse throughout the country after the Constituyente and would influence public opinion in his favor. The articles he was known to favor, covering such areas as land reform, workers' guarantees, and economic nationalism, were already considered to be the heart of the Revolution. He was therefore seen more and more as the protector of revolutionary principles.

His resignation as secretary of war in 1917 after the promulgation of the constitution was seen as a protest against Carranza's unwillingness to put these principles into practice. Moreover, by leaving Carranza's administration, he became acceptable to groups as yet unreconciled to the central administration, notably the Zapatistas.

Obregón wisely watched and waited during 1917, 1918, and early 1919, as Carranza proceeded to burn himself politically. Though constantly traveling in the northwest and consolidating his own support, he made no move to conspire to overthrow Carranza's government by force. When he did announce for the presidency, his announcement was public and legitimate, despite Carranza's opposition to his candidacy. In putting his own name forward, without permitting one political party or group to claim him exclusively as its candidate, he broadened the potential base of his support and avoided political deals that would restrict his action. Moreover, he encouraged the formation of small political groups throughout the country, lessening still further his dependence on any one group. As his public support grew, other leaders and groups quickly joined his movement, eager to support a winner.

Not until it was clear that Carranza would under no circumstances permit Obregón to become president peacefully did he turn to open revolt. By that time, Carranza and his administration had made their intentions obvious to the whole country, through their attempts to impose a political unknown as president, to crush any potential opposition in the state of Sonora, and to bring the candidate to trial on falsified charges of treason. Carranza was unable to discredit Obregón, however, and Obregón was too powerful by April, 1920, to succumb to even the most overt repressive tactics.

Between 1912 and 1920, Obregón had established a five-faceted power base, which would bring him to the presidency. The *campesinos* and laborers of Mexico, mobilized during the violent phase of the Revolution, remained politically aware and were articulated with a more formal political network of emergent political parties and of a few very close personal associates of Obregón, most of the latter either Sonorans originally or resident in Sonora after 1917. The revolutionary army itself had furnished the first linkages of these groups, and associations formed during the battles against Huerta and later Villa would be of major importance to Obregón in consolidating his support.

The strength of this mass-based political network goes far to explain why Mexico was able to reestablish political institutions and political stability despite the widespread violence and chaos of the 1910–1920 period. Mass mobilization alone, though, is an insufficient explanation, as it may easily lead to further violence and political destabilization.[1] However, in the Mexican situation, the interests of the masses in specific reforms and in immediate benefits were at least partially met by the revolutionary leadership, principally at the local level, and the masses came to associate these benefits directly with the revolutionary hero Obregón. More importantly, they associated potential future benefits with the Sonoran leader. This identification

[1]Samuel Huntington (*Political Order in Changing Societies*, pp. 325–334) discusses the Bolivian Revolution of 1952 and suggests that its failure to establish political stability was caused by four factors that differed from the Mexican situation: the lack of a violent phase leading to the exhaustion of the people and the elimination by death of important factional contenders, a leadership without the ability to compromise, the inability of Bolivian leaders to subordinate such autonomous forces as the labor movement to the larger leadership of the Revolution, and the absence of antiforeign nationalism. The second and third of these factors seem to be the most important. As for the first, some potential factional leaders remained in Mexico in 1920, and Pablo González revolted against Obregón almost immediately, but most accepted Obregón's control as inevitable and attempted to secure the best possible position within Obregonista ranks. The fourth factor, antiforeign sentiment, was as apt to be divisive as it was to lead to cohesion, as in the Villa-Obregón disagreement over the evacuation of Veracruz and later, during the Obregón presidency, in the controversy over the so-called Bucareli agreements, which contributed to the de la Huerta rebellion in 1923.

was heightened by his activities during the months of the Constitutional Congress at Querétaro, his resignation from Carranza's cabinet, and his widespread campaign tour, as well as by Carranza's own failure to put the provisions of the constitution into practice.

Further, the developing political parties, their leadership composed in great part of members of the revolutionary army and of civilians closely associated with the Revolution, formed a political network that kept the mobilization alive and functioning within their definition of revolutionary goals, basically as defined by the Constitution of Querétaro in 1917. Obregón himself carefully fostered political organizations that would give him power independent of Carranza: first the Confederación Revolucionaria, then the Partido Liberal Constitucionalista, and finally the Gran Convención Obregonista. He was also conscious of the need to maintain close contact with other emergent political groups, especially the Partido Nacional Cooperatista and the Partido Laborista Mexicano.

The activities of the Twenty-seventh and Twenty-eighth congresses and their frequent clashes with President Carranza over revolutionary reforms maintained the credibility of these politicians with the masses. The common adherence of the major political parties and of the masses to the popular candidate, Obregón, and their ability to work together within the framework of the Gran Convención Obregonista and the Centro Director Electoral gave Obregón the ability to mount an impressive campaign. The immediate action of his closest associates, mostly Sonorans, in accepting Carranza's challenge in 1920 by issuing the Plan of Agua Prieta and calling for help from all groups that supported Obregón furnished the last organizational link needed to enable this diverse agglomeration to work effectively in bringing Obregón to office.

The articulation existing between all five groups was significant in making this cooperation possible. The revolutionary army and the regular military were joined by shared experiences in battle with members of the new political parties, as well as with the *campesinos* and laborers who had fought in the Revolution. Many of the officers who had risen to prominence and who had remained in the army were from the northwest, and many political leaders in the northwest had served in the revolutionary army.

Each group was similarly connected to each of the others. Individual Obregón supporters frequently belonged to three or four of these categories, and themselves formed bonds between the groups. Although the agrarian movement was quite diffuse, it was brought into the political process in a more focused fashion by the parties, by the northwestern leaders, by the labor movement itself in its recruitment of *campesino* members, and by its own leaders, as in the case of the Yaquis and particularly the Zapatistas. All groups could use as a rallying point the Constitution of 1917, which had become at once the symbol and goal of the Revolution itself and was closely associated with the figure of Obregón.

Following Obregón's lead, new rules for the political game were being established. For these groups to work together, they would have to accept Obregón as compromiser and arbiter. Thus a single, secular, national political authority was emerging that would replace more traditional loyalties, such as to family and religion or to local leaders. Obregón himself had already moved to foster this development in his early attempts to curb the power of regional *caudillos*. He would continue this effort during his presidency, and Calles would carry it much further. This shift of loyalties had been enhanced by the formation of the Confederación Revolucionaria during the retreat to Veracruz, the experience of many individuals and groups from many parts of the country fighting together under Obregón in the campaign against Villa, and the achievements of the Constitutional Congress itself. It is not surprising that the members of the Constituyente continued to be active in politics, that they enjoyed a considerable camaraderie, that they actively supported putting the social reforms of the constitution into practice, and that they by and large supported for president in 1920 the man they felt had supported their autonomy in 1917. In fact, at least ten of the twenty-five state chairmen for this 1920 campaign had been members of the Constituyente. Others were members of the P.L.C., and several had served in the Twenty-seventh Congress, which Carranza had found so undisciplined.[2]

Further, Obregón had made significant attempts to reorganize the regular military and to take it out of politics. Although he was by no means entirely successful, he was able to make considerable progress toward rationalizing its administration and in reducing the size of its forces. During his presidency, he would extend this attempt to rationalize administration in many other areas, such as land reform, where the major portion of his highest officials were engineers and agronomists.

Moreover, he wove newly emergent social groups into the political process. His genius was that he was able to consolidate his power while enhancing theirs. Throughout this period, both Mexico's rural population and its emerging laboring class had been involved to one degree or another as actors in the Mexican political process. Far from being merely manipulated, they had exerted real power, sometimes on their own and sometimes through their influence on other political groups. The mass military mobilization of rural and later urban Mexico was at the same time a political mobilization with profound political consequences. The agrarian and labor movements continued to organize and to influence policy, labor being by far the more effective of the two, particularly in relation to its size. Nevertheless, both continued to have influence, and Obregón would use and help both movements during his presidency.

As a result of the wide-ranging support Obregón brought to the office of the presidency, he was able in the next four

[2]The P.L.C. received three times as much campaign material as all the other parties, including the P.N.C. and the P.L.M., combined. The identifiable members of the Constitutional Congress were Enrique Colunga, Guanajuato; Antonio Gutiérrez, Durango; Rafael Vega Sánchez, Hidalgo; C. Rivera Cabrera, Oaxaca; Enrique Contreras, Puebla; Rafael Curiel, San Luis Potosí; A. Magallón, Sinaloa; L. G. Monzón, Sonora; Enrique Meza, Veracruz; and José Concepción Rivera, Colima. This list of state chairmen is taken from a report sent to each from the Centro Director Electoral, no date, listing 144 clubs and parties supporting Obregón, in the state of Veracruz alone (AAA-CDE). It is possible that there were more ex-members of the Constituyente, as some of the names seem to have been misspelled and occasionally a last name was omitted. Aguirre himself had been a prominent member of the Constituyente.

years to establish it as an extraordinarily strong office. It would continue to get even stronger. Moreover, the early attempts to develop a broad-based political party foreshadowed the development of what would amount to an official party in the late 1920's, the Partido Nacional Revolucionario. This party evolved into the Partido de la Revolución Mexicana and finally into the present-day Partido Revolucionario Institucional. The official party would contain those groups which already existed in microcosm in 1920 and which were active in support of Obregón. The party would claim to speak for the Mexican masses, and this claim was based on the mass mobilization of political support, originally for the ideals of the Revolution and their embodiment in Obregón.

Lázaro Cárdenas in 1934 recognized the major bases of this support for the party when he organized it along sectoral lines: the four divisions were military, labor, agrarian, and "popular," meaning unorganized white-collar and proletarian. It was Obregón, along with his principal aide, Plutarco Elías Calles, who had originally performed a major role in bringing these groups together in support for Obregón and for the principles of the Revolution. Calles, of course, would maintain this mass support during his own presidency, and Cárdenas would take it over as his base of support when he himself was head of the Mexican nation. The party has maintained the same sectoral structure until the present day, except for the dropping of the military as a separate section in 1945. This depoliticization of the military had been one of Obregón's goals since 1915.

The revolutionary principles, which had evolved in a pragmatic manner during the course of the fighting, were directed toward practical and immediate ends. The masses in fact received land, higher wages, and more protection from their employers, although many abuses remained and Mexico was to be for many years longer a poor nation. Nevertheless, the ideas of land reform, workers' guarantees, economic growth, and economic nationalism have formed the political culture since the time of Obregón. It should be emphasized that Obregón's own administrative approach to labor, agrarian problems, and economic nationalism was highly practical. He was strongly focused on modernization and increased production, not on radical structural change.

Nevertheless, Obregón had succeeded where Carranza had failed—in establishing himself as a legitimate and unifying governor for the Mexican people. Because he had mass support, reinforced by regional and sectoral leaders and developing political parties, as president he was able to establish a strong executive and to provide for the perpetuation of a Sonoran dynasty and a national government that was becoming heavily interventionist in economic and social matters and in which the proper relationship between the classes was viewed as an organic, cooperative one. Indeed, the government, and especially the chief executive, became the balance wheel between economic, social, and regional interests. Moreover, the president became the interpreter of the Revolution to the Mexican people and the guardian of its principles.

By late 1920, many of the other major leaders of the Revolution were either dead or discredited or both, and Obregón was able to come to terms with those who still lived and to conciliate the supporters of those who did not. Moreover, he moved immediately to include other sectors of the population, particularly professional groups, small businessmen, and the rural middle class, in his government. He also began at once to recoup the toleration, if not the friendship, of the United States. He was constantly working to check potential dangers and challenges to his power.

The groups still frightened of him—the wealthy landowners and industrialists, the former supporters of Díaz and Huerta, and the church—were precisely those groups which were being excluded from power by the Revolution. Significantly, Obregón himself recognized the division of society into only two classes: those who worked and those who paid. The Revolution was to serve those who worked, a class in which he included himself, and he was able to identify convincingly with members of all groups within that stratum. Carranza was fatally unable to identify with the disadvantaged groups and was terrified that the government would lose control of the Revolution and become subject to the rule of the mob. Obregón identified the government with the Revolution and the Revolution with the masses, all within an organic conception of society, a society in theory working as one to achieve the good of all. In so doing, he had gone far toward resolving the dilemma in the Constitution of 1917: he had made the central government the legitimate authority in socioeconomic matters and thus established the basis for widespread government intervention in the society. Using his own charismatic appeal and his close identification with the goals of the Revolution, gained in battle and through his defense of the radicals in the Constitutional Congress in 1917, he was able to bridge the gap between revolutionary violence and political institutionalization. By establishing a powerful central government, which was seen as the legitimate defender and guarantor of the gains of the Revolution as well as the interpreter of its ideals, he had provided a firm basis for the continuing institutionalization of the Mexican government after the Revolution.

Chronology

May 25, 1911	Porfirio Díaz resigns the presidency of Mexico.
August, 1911	Alvaro Obregón elected municipal president of Huatabampo.
November 6, 1911	Francisco Madero is elected president of Mexico.
March, 1912	In Chihuahua, Pascual Orozco revolts against Madero's government.
April, 1912	Alvaro Obregón organizes a force from Huatabampo to combat Orozco in Chihuahua.
September, 1912	Battle of San Joaquín: Obregón's first major victory.
February, 1913	President Madero is assassinated in Mexico City. Victoriano Huerta takes power. Sonoran Governor José María Maytorena flees Mexico.
March 5, 1913	Sonoran congress refuses to recognize Huerta government. Obregón is appointed chief of military section of Sonoran forces.
March 14, 1913	Obregón's forces take Nogales.
March 26, 1913	Venustiano Carranza proclaims Plan of Guadalupe.

May, 1913	Aarón Sáenz sent by Obregón as emissary to invite Carranza to Sonora.
July, 1913	Governor Maytorena returns to Sonora.
September, 1913	Carranza arrives in Sonora. Obregón named chief of the Army of the Northwest.
November 14, 1913	Obregón's forces take Culiacán, Sinaloa.
February 23, 1914	Carranza leaves Sonora for Chihuahua.
June 23, 1914	Pancho Villa takes Zacatecas, then wires Obregón suggesting mutual help.
July 7, 1914	Obregón's army is victorious at Guadalajara, Jalisco. His campaign turns east toward Mexico City.
July, 1914	Difficulties arise between Governor Maytorena and Plutarco Elías Calles in Sonora.
August 13, 1914	Federal negotiators sign capitulation agreement with Obregón in Teoloyucan.
August 15, 1914	Obregón occupies Mexico City.
August–September, 1914	Obregón makes two trips to Chihuahua to confer with Villa. Open warfare breaks out in Sonora.
October 1–5, 1914	Military convention of Constitutionalists in Mexico City.
October 10–November, 1914	Military convention of Aguascalientes.
November 23, 1914	Obregón leads Constitutionalist evacuation from Mexico City to Veracruz.
December, 1914	Carranza issues "Additions to the Plan of Guadalupe."
January 5, 1915	Obregón's forces take Puebla.
January 6, 1915	Carranza proclaims Agrarian Law.
January 28–March 11, 1915	Obregón's forces reoccupy Mexico City. Support of Casa del Obrero Mundial secured for Constitutionalists.

April, 1915	Obregón defeats Villa in two battles at Celaya.
May–June, 1915	Battle of León. Obregón's forces ultimately victorious; he himself is wounded and loses an arm.
October, 1915	U.S. government extends Carranza's Constitutionalists de facto recognition.
March, 1916	Pancho Villa attacks Columbus, New Mexico. Obregón is appointed minister of war. U.S. forces invade Mexico in pursuit of Villa.
April 28–May 10, 1916	Obregón negotiates removal of U.S. forces with General Hugh Scott.
December, 1916–January, 1917	Constitutional Congress of Querétaro. Partido Liberal Constitucionalista founded.
May, 1917	Obregón resigns as minister of war after Carranza takes office as elected president.
Late 1917	Obregón founds Society of Producers of Garbanzo. Obregón settles political difficulties between Ramón Iturbe and Angel Flores in Sinaloa. Obregón travels extensively in the United States.
1918	Obregón traveling in northwestern Mexico for the Society of Producers of Garbanzo. Sells crop to W. R. Grace and Company. Urges garbanzo producers to observe U.S. Enemy Trading Act.
January, 1919	Carranza issues manifesto warning against early political activities by aspiring presidential candidates for 1920 elections.
March–April, 1919	Public exchange of letters between Luis Cabrera and Obregón regarding political situation.
May, 1919	Telegraph Office cancels permits issued to former military leaders.

June 1, 1919	Obregón declares candidacy for presidency of Mexico.
September, 1919	Plutarco Elías Calles appointed secretary of commerce, industry, and labor by Carranza.
October, 1919–April, 1920	Obregón's whistle-stop presidential campaign throughout Mexico.
November 28, 1919	Congress ratifies Obregón's complete separation from the armed forces.
February 2, 1920	Calles and Amado Aguirre resign from Carranza's cabinet. Gran Convención Obregonista takes place in Mexico City.
Late March, 1920	Obregón called to Mexico City to testify in trial of Roberto Cejudo. Carranza readies troops to send to Sonora, ostensibly to put down Yaqui uprising.
April 10, 1920	State of Sonora withdraws recognition of Carranza government.
April 12–13, 1920	Obregón flees Mexico City.
April 23, 1920	Plan of Agua Prieta proclaimed in Sonora.
May 7, 1920	Carranza evacuates Mexico City.
May 9, 1920	Obregón arrives in Mexico City.
May 21, 1920	Carranza assassinated in Tlaxcalantongo.
May 24, 1920	Adolfo de la Huerta becomes interim president of Mexico.
December 1, 1920	Obregón inaugurated as president of Mexico.

Bibliography

BIBLIOGRAPHIC NOTE

The literature on the Mexican Revolution is extensive, and new studies are appearing regularly. I would like to note, with thanks, some of the most important titles that have influenced my approach to the Revolution.

Studies of the early stage include James D. Cockcroft, *Intellectual Precursors of the Mexican Revolution 1900–1913*; Juan Gómez-Quiñones, *Sembradores: Ricardo Flores Magón y el Partido Liberal Mexicano: A Eulogy and a Critique*; and Juan Gómez-Quiñones, "Social Change and Intellectual Discontent: The Growth of Mexican Nationalism 1890–1911" (Ph.D. dissertation, University of California at Los Angeles, 1972). The agrarian movement is considered in Jesús Silva Herzog, *El agrarismo mexicano y la reforma agraria: Exposición y crítica*; and three books by Frank Tannenbaum—*Mexico: The Struggle for Peace and Bread*, *Peace by Revolution: Mexico after 1910*, and *The Mexican Agrarian Revolution*. It is also treated by Manuel González Ramírez, *La revolución social de México*, vol. 3: *El problema agrario*; and Moisés de la Peña, *El Pueblo y su tierra: Mito y realidad de la reforma agraria en México*. An extremely useful new study of the Zapatista movement is Arturo Warman, *. . . Y venimos a contradecir: los campesinos de Morelos y el estado nacional*.

Literature on the labor movement is coming out rapidly, but the classic is Marjorie Ruth Clark, *Organized Labor in Mexico*. Two recent studies of great interest are Ramón E.

Ruíz, *Labor and the Ambivalent Revolutionaries, 1911–1913*, and John M. Hart, *Anarchism and the Mexican Working Class, 1860–1931*. Edwin Lieuwen's *Mexican Militarism: The Political Rise and Fall of the Revolutionary Army 1910–1940* furnishes a quick look at the role of the military and recognizes Obregón's centrality. Another important view of the military after 1920 is in Hans-Werner Tobler, "Las paradojas del ejército revolucionario: su papel social en la reforma agraria mexicana, 1920–1935" (*Historia Mexicana* 21 [July–September, 1971]: 38–79).

Studies of the Revolution in Sonora include the indispensable books by Antonio G. Rivera, *La Revolución en Sonora*, and Francisco R. Almada, *La Revolución en el estado de Sonora*. The best recent study is Hector Aguilar Camín, *La frontera nómada: Sonora y la Revolución Mexicana*. Vicente Fuentes Díaz, *Los partidos políticos en México*, furnishes only a very brief look at political parties in the 1917–1920 era. On the Constitutional Congress, the best secondary sources are Peter H. Smith, "La política dentro de la Revolución: El Congreso Constituyente de 1916–1917" (*Historia Mexicana* 22 [January–March, 1973]: 363–395), and E. V. Niemeyer, *Revolution at Querétaro: The Mexican Constitutional Convention of 1916–1917*.

Notable biographical accounts include John Womack's excellent *Zapata and the Mexican Revolution*; Stanley R. Ross's *Francisco I. Madero: Apostle of Mexican Democracy*; Charles C. Cumberland's *Mexican Revolution: Genesis Under Madero*; and two works by Michael C. Meyer—*Mexican Rebel: Pascual Orozco and the Mexican Revolution 1910–1915* and *Huerta: A Political Portrait*. Charles C. Cumberland's *Mexican Revolution: The Constitutionalist Years* is a very useful description of the events between 1913 and 1917, based in large part on information from the Archivo de la Defensa Nacional, which is normally inaccessible to foreigners. Robert E. Quirk has produced the important study *The Mexican Revolution, 1914–1915: The Convention of Aguascalientes*. The ideology of the Revolution has been discussed most thoroughly by Arnaldo Córdova, *La ideología de la Revolución Mexicana*.

SOURCES CONSULTED
Bibliographies, Reference Works, and Guides

Carrasco Puente, Rafael. *La prensa en México; datos históricos.* Prologue by María del Carmen Ruíz Castañeda. Mexico City: Universidad Nacional Autónoma de México, 1962.

Charno, Steven M., comp. *Latin American Newspapers in United States Libraries: A Union List.* Austin: University of Texas Press, 1968.

González, Luis, comp. *Fuentes de la historia contemporánea de México. Libros y folletos.* 3 vols. Mexico City: Colegio de México, 1961–1963.

Mexico. Departamento de la Estadística Nacional. *Sonora, Sinaloa y Nayarit. Año de 1927.* Mexico City: Imprenta Mundial, 1928.

Muro, Luis. Guide to the materials in the Archivo Histórico de la Secretaría de la Defensa Nacional. Index available at Colegio de México, Mexico City.

Ramos, Roberto. *Bibliografía de la Revolución Mexicana.* 3 vols. Mexico City: Imprenta de la Secretaría de Relaciones Exteriores, 1931–1940.

Ross, Stanley R., comp. *Fuentes de la historia contemporánea de México. Periódicos y revistas.* 2 vols. Mexico City: Colegio de México, 1965–1967.

Ruíz Castañeda, María del Carmen. "El periodismo y la Revolución Mexicana," *Ciencias Políticas y Sociales,* 4, no. 14 (1958): 423–459.

Ulibarri, George S., and John P. Harrison. *Guide to the Materials on Latin America in the National Archives of the United States.* Washington, D.C.: National Archives and Record Service, General Services Administration, 1974.

Ulloa Ortiz, Berta. *Revolución Mexicana, 1910–1920.* Mexico City: Secretaría de Relaciones Exteriores, 1963.

Velásquez Gallardo, Pablo, comp. *Catálogo colectivo de publicaciones periódicas existentes en bibliotecas de la República Mexicana.* 2 vols. Mexico City: Instituto Nacional de Investigaciones Agrícolas, 1968.

Archival Collections
Private

Austin, Texas. University of Texas at Austin. Latin American Collection.

William Buckley Papers. Lázara de la Garza Archive. Mexican Political Parties Propaganda.

Berkeley, California. Bancroft Library, University of California. Sylvestre Terrazas Papers.

Mexico City. Centro de Estudios de la Historia—Condumex. Archivo de Venustiano Carranza.

Mexico City. Private collection of Professor Alvaro Matute.
Archivo de Amado Aguirre, includes: Archivo del Centro Director Electoral; Collection of reports, Departamento de Telégrafos; Archivo del Ejército del Noroeste.

Mexico City. Museo de Antropología.
Archivo de Francisco Madero. Patronato de la Historia de Sonora (microfilm). Serie Sinaloa (microfilm). Serie Sonora (microfilm).

Mexico City. Universidad Nacional Autónoma de México.
Archivo de Emiliano Zapata.

New York, New York. New York Public Library.
Enrique Llorente Archive.

Washington, D.C. Library of Congress.
Hugh Lenox Scott Papers.

Public

Austin, Texas. University of Texas at Austin. Latin American Collection.
U.S. Department of State, Dispatches from U.S. Consuls in Hermosillo, 1905–1906 (microfilm). U.S. Department of State, Records Relating to the Internal Affairs of Mexico, 1910–1929 (microfilm).

Hermosillo, Mexico.
Archivo General del Estado de Sonora. Archivo Histórico del Estado de Sonora.

Mexico City.
Archivo del Departamento de Asuntos Agrarios y Crédito. Archivo General de la Nación: Ramo de Gobernación, Ramo Obregón-Calles. Archivo de la Secretaría de Comunicaciones y Transportes. Archivo de la Secretaría de Relaciones Exteriores.

Washington, D.C. National Archives.
U.S. Adjutant General's Office, Villa's Revolution, #2212358.
U.S. Military Intelligence Division, Record Groups.

Interviews

Columbia Oral History Collection. Columbia University, New York.
Cosío Villegas, Daniel.
Tinker, Edward Larocque.
Personal interviews conducted by the author.
Araiza, Luis. July 30, 1974.
Espinosa, Juventino. July 24, 1974.
Gastélum, Bernardo. April 11, 1973; July 17 and 25, 1974 (PHO/4/43).
León, Luis L. March 8, 1972; July 18, 1974 (conducted with Jean Meyer); July 30, 1974.
Mena Brito, Bernardino. December 16, 1970.
Portes Gil, Emilio. March 10, 1972.
Ramos Praslow, Ignacio. November 16, 1972.
Rivera, Antonio G. June 28, 1973.
Romero Flores, Jesús. April 12, 1973.
Torreblanca, Fernando. March 8, 1972; November 15, 1972; July 18, 1974; July 19, 1974; July 24, 1974; July 28, 1974.
Valenzuela, Gilberto. July 11, 1974 (PHO/4/42); July 16, 1974 (conducted with Jean Meyer).
Programa de Historia Oral. Instituto Nacional de Antropología e Historia, Museo de Antropología, Mexico City.
Alatorre, Julian Adame. PHO/1/32.
Anda, Victor. PHO/1/46.
Baez, José de. PHO/1/34.
Baz Prada, Gustavo. PHO/4/6.
Cervantes, Federico. PHO/1/9.
Clark, Johnny. PHO/5/8.
Estrada Cajigal, Vicente. PHO/4/12.
Fierro Villalobos, Roberto. PHO/1/42.
Gastélum, Bernardo. PHO/4/43.
Hurtado Olín, Juan. PHO/1/30.
Navas Presa, Gilberto. PHO/1/26.
Ramos Praslow, Ignacio. PHO/1/35.
Ruíz González, Alberto. PHO/5/7.
Salinas, Gustavo. PHO/1/11.
Sánchez Pontón, Luis. PHO/1/20.
Solís Androaga, Manuel de J. PHO/1/17.

Sosa Pavón, Manuel. PHO/1/48.

Valenzuela, Gilberto. PHO/4/42.

Published Documents and Collections

Barrera Fuentes, Florencia, ed. *Crónicas y debates de la sesiones de la Soberana Convención Revolucionaria.* 3 vols. Mexico City: Talleres Gráficos de la Nación, 1964–1965.

Fabela, Isidro, comp. *Documentos de la Revolución Mexicana.* Volumes 1–4, Mexico City: Fondo de Cultura Económica, 1960–1964. Volumes 6–25, Mexico City: Editorial Jus, 1965–1972.

González Ramírez, Manuel, ed. *Fuentes para la historia de la Revolución Mexicana.* 4 vols. Mexico City: Fondo de Cultura Económica, 1954–1957.

Mexico. *Crónicas y debates de las sesiones de la Soberana Convención Revolucionaria.* Edited by Florencio Barrera Fuentes. 3 vols. Mexico City: Talleres Gráficos de la Nación, 1964.

———. *Diario de los debates de la Cámara de Diputados.* 2 vols. Mexico City: Cámara de Diputados, 1917.

———. *Diario de los debates del Congreso Constituyente.* 2 vols. Mexico City: Imprenta de la Secretaría de Gobernación, 1917.

Obregón, Alvaro. *Partes oficiales de las batallas de Celaya, 6, 7, 13, 14, 15 de abril de 1915.* Orizaba, Mexico: Confederación Revolucionaria, 1915.

———. *Parte oficial de la batalla de Culiacán.* Douglas, Arizona, 1914.

———. *El problema agrario; version taquigráfica del cambio de impresiones tenido por el presidente electo, con un numeroso grupo de diputados al Congreso de la Unión. Octubre de 1920.* Mexico City, 1920.

Revista del Ejército y Marina: Organo del Departamento de Estado Mayor de la Guerra y Marina. Mexico City, 1915–1916.

Ruvalcaba, Luis N., ed. *Campaña política del C. Alvaro Obregón, candidato a la presidencia de la República 1920–1924.* 5 vols. Mexico City, 1923.

Torre Villar, Ernesto de la; Moisés González Navarro; and Stanley Ross, eds. *Historia documental de México.* Mexico City: Universidad Nacional Autónoma de México, 1964.

U.S. Department of Commerce. *Commerce Yearbook, 1922.* Washington, D.C.: Government Printing Office, 1923.

U.S. Department of Commerce and Labor, Bureau of Manufactures. *Commercial Relation of the United States with Foreign Countries 1909* .Washington, D.C.: U.S. Government Printing Office, 1911.

U.S. Department of State. *Papers Relating to the Foreign Relations of the United States, 1916.* Washington, D.C.: Government Printing Office, 1925.

Periodicals

Acción Mundial. Mexico City. 1916.
Boletín del Partido Liberal Constitucionalista. 1916.
El Comercio. Guaymas, Sonora. 1897–1898.
El Constitucionalista. Hermosillo, Sonora. 1914.
Dallas Morning News. Dallas, Texas. 1914–1915.
El Demócrata. Mexico City. 1914.
El Demófilo. San Luis Potosí. 1919.
Excelsior. Mexico City. 1916, 1919–1920.
Gladiador. Mexico City. 1916–1917.
El Liberal. Mexico City. 1914.
El Monitor Republicano. Mexico City. 1919–1920.
El Nacional. Mexico City. 1916.
El Norte. Mexico City. 1915.
Nueva Patria. Mexico City. 1914.
New York Times. New York City. 1914–1920.
New York Tribune. New York City. 1916.
La Opinión. Mexico City. 1914–1915.
Orientación. Hermosillo. 1919–1920.
La Patria. Chihuahua. 1915.
La Prensa. Mexico City. 1915.
La Prensa. San Antonio, Texas. 1921.
El Pueblo. Mexico City and Veracruz. 1914–1919 (place of publication moved back and forth between the two cities as the Constitutionalist leadership moved).
El Renovador. Mexico City. 1915.
San Antonio Express. San Antonio. Texas. 1919.
San Antonio Light. San Antonio, Texas. 1919.
Los Sucesos. Mexico City. 1915.
El Universal. Mexico City. 1916–1920, 1938.
Waco Times-Herald. Waco, Texas. 1919.

Books and Pamphlets

Aguilar Camín, Hector. *La frontera nómada: Sonora y la Revolución Mexicana.* Mexico City: Siglo Veintiuno, 1977.

Aguirre, Amado. *Mis memorias de campaña: Apuntes para la historia.* Estampas de la Revolución Mexicana, 1953.

Aguirre Benavides, Luis. *De Francisco I. Madero a Francisco Villa: Memorias de un revolucionario.* Mexico City: A. Del Bosque, Impresor, 1966.

――――. *Las grandes batallas de la División del Norte.* Mexico City: Editorial Diana, 1964.

Almada, Francisco R. *La Revolución en el estado de Chihuahua,* Volume 2, *1913–1921.* Mexico City: Biblioteca del Instituto Nacional de Estudios Históricos de la Revolución Mexicana, 1965.

――――. *La Revolución en el estado de Sonora.* Mexico City: Biblioteca del Instituto Nacional de Estudios Históricos de la Revolución Mexicana, 1971.

Alvarado, Salvador. *El problema de México.* San Antonio, Texas, 1920.

Amaya, Juan Gualberto. *Síntesis social de la Revolución Mexicana.* Mexico City, 1947.

Amaya, Luis Fernando. *La Soberana Convención Revolucionaria, 1914–1916.* Mexico City: Editorial F. Trillas, 1966.

Araiza, Luis. *Historia del movimiento obrero mexicano.* 4 vols. Mexico City: Editorial Cuahtemoc, 1964–1965.

Arendt, Hannah. *On Revolution.* New York: Viking Press, 1971.

Barragán, Juan. *Historia del Ejército y de la Revolución Constitucionalista.* 2 vols. Mexico City: Antigua Librería Robredo, 1946.

Bassols Batalla, Narciso. *El pensamiento político de Alvaro Obregón.* 2nd ed. Mexico City: Ediciones El Caballito, 1970.

Beteta, Ramón. *Camino a Tlaxcalantongo.* Mexico City: Fondo de Cultura Económica, 1961.

Bojórquez, Juan de Dios. *Los agríos de Sonora en los albores de 1916.* Mexico City: Ediciones Atenagro, 1953.

―――― [pseud. Djed Bórquez]. *Crónica del Constituyente.* Mexico City: Ediciones Botas, 1938.

――――. *Forjadores de la Revolución Mexicana.* Mexico City: Biblioteca del Instituto Nacional de Estudios Históricos de la Revolución Mexicana, 1960.

――――. *Hombres y aspectos de México.* Mexico City: Biblioteca del Instituto Nacional de Estudios Históricos de la Revolución Mexicana, 1963.

——. *Jesús M. Garza, abanderado del gremio agronómico*. Mexico City: Ediciones Atenagro, 1954.

—— [pseud. Djed Bórquez]. *Obregón: Apuntes biográficos*. Prologue by Luis L. León. Mexico City: Ediciones Patria Nueva, 1929.

Breceda, Alfredo. *México revolucionario*. Volume 1, Madrid: Tipografía Artística Cervantes, 1920. Volume 2, Mexico City: Ediciones Botas, 1941.

Brinton, Crane. *The Anatomy of Revolution*. New York: Vintage Books, 1952.

Bustamante, Luis F. *La defensa de "El Ebano."* Tampico, Tamaulipas, Mexico, 1915.

——. *La historia del movimiento obrero en México*. Mexico City: Almanaque Nacional, 1937.

Calderón, Esteban Baca. *Juicio sobre la guerra del Yaqui y génesis de la huelga de Cananea*. Mexico City: Ediciones del Sindicato Mexicano de Electricistas, 1956.

Cervantes, Federico. *Felipe Angeles en la Revolución. Biografía (1869–1919)*. 3rd ed. Mexico City, 1964.

Chevalier, François. *Land and Society in Colonial Mexico*. Berkeley: University of California Press, 1963.

Clark, Marjorie Ruth. *Organized Labor in Mexico*. Chapel Hill: University of North Carolina Press, 1934.

Clendenen, Clarence. *The United States and Pancho Villa: A Study in Unconventional Diplomacy*. Ithaca, N.Y.: Cornell University Press, 1961.

Cockcroft, James D. *Intellectual Precursors of the Mexican Revolution 1900–1913*. Austin: University of Texas Press, 1968.

Córdova, Arnaldo. *La ideología de la Revolución Mexicana*. Mexico City: Ediciones Era, 1973.

Coser, Lewis A. *The Functions of Social Conflict*. New York: Free Press, 1956.

Cumberland, Charles C. *Mexican Revolution: Genesis Under Madero*. Austin: University of Texas Press, 1952.

——. *Mexican Revolution: The Constitutionalist Years*. Austin: University of Texas Press, 1972.

Davis, William B. *Experiences and Observations of an American Consular Officer during the Recent Mexican Revolutions*. Los Angeles: Wayside Press, 1920.

de la Huerta, Adolfo. *Memorias de Don Adolfo de la Huerta.* Transcriptions and commentaries by Roberto Guzmán Esparza. Mexico City: Ediciones Guzmán, 1957.

de la Peña, Moisés. *El Pueblo y su tierra: Mito y realidad de la reforma agraria en México.* Mexico City: Cuadernos Americanos, 1964.

Díaz Soto y Gama, Antonio. *La cuestión agraria en México.* Mexico City: Universidad Nacional Autónoma de México, 1959.

———. *La revolución agraria del Sur y Emiliano Zapata.* Mexico City: Policromia, 1960.

Dillon, E. J. *President Obregón—A World Reformer.* Boston: Small, Maynard and Company, 1923.

Dulles, John W. F. *Yesterday in Mexico: A Chronicle of the Revolution, 1919–1936.* Austin: University of Texas Press, 1961.

Fuentes Díaz, Vicente. *Los partidos políticos en México.* 2nd ed. Mexico City: Editorial Altiplano, 1969.

Gamio, Manuel. *Forjando Patria.* Mexico City: Librería Porrua, 1916.

Gil, Feliciano. *Biografía y vida militar del General Alvaro Obregón.* Hermosillo: Imprenta de M. F. Romo, 1914.

Gómez-Quiñones, Juan. *Sembradores: Ricardo Flores Magón y el Partido Liberal Mexicano: A Eulogy and a Critique.* Los Angeles: University of California Aztlán Publications, 1973.

González Garza, Roque. *Discurso leido por el C. Coronel Roque González Garza en la solemne apertura de la Convención Militar Revolucionaria de Aguascalientes, la noche de 14 de octubre de 1914.* Impresa Pedroza y Hijos, 1914.

González Ramírez, Manuel. *La revolución social de México.* 3 vols. Mexico City: Fondo de Cultura Económica, 1974–1976.

Gruening, Ernest. *Mexico and Its Heritage.* New York: Century Company, 1928.

Gurr, Ted Robert. *Why Men Rebel.* Princeton, N.J.: Princeton University Press, 1971.

Guzmán, Martín Luis. *Memoirs of Pancho Villa.* Translated by Virginia H. Taylor. Austin: University of Texas Press, 1965.

———. *Memorias de Pancho Villa.* Mexico City: Cía. General de Ediciones, 1951.

Hagopian, Mark N. *The Phenomenon of Revolution.* New York: Dodd, Mead and Co., 1974.

Hart, John M. *Anarchism and the Mexican Working Class, 1860–1931.* Austin: University of Texas Press, 1978.

Hill, Larry D. *Emissaries to a Revolution: Woodrow Wilson's Agents in Mexico.* Baton Rouge: Louisiana State University Press, 1973.

Hobsbawm, E. J. *Primitive Rebels.* New York: W. W. Norton and Co., 1959.

Huntington, Samuel P. *Political Order in Changing Societies.* New Haven: Yale University Press, 1968.

Johnson, Chalmers. *Revolutionary Change.* Boston: Little, Brown, and Co., 1966.

Lenin, V. I. *State and Revolution.* 2nd ed. New York: International Publishers, 1971.

Lieuwen, Edwin. *Mexican Militarism: The Political Rise and Fall of the Revolutionary Army 1910–1940.* Albuquerque: University of New Mexico Press, 1968.

McBride, George M. *The Land Systems of Mexico.* New York: American Geographical Society, 1923.

Marx, Karl. *A Contribution to the Critique of Political Economy.* Chicago: Charles H. Kerr and Co., 1904.

Mena Brito, Bernardino. *Ocho diálogos con Carranza.* 2nd ed. Editores Mexicanos Unidos, 1964.

Meyer, Jean. *La Revolución Mejicana, 1910–1940.* Barcelona: Dopesa, 1973.

Meyer, Michael C. *Huerta: A Political Portrait.* Lincoln: University of Nebraska Press, 1972.

———. *Mexican Rebel: Pascual Orozco and the Mexican Revolution 1910–1915.* Lincoln: University of Nebraska Press, 1967.

Molina Enríquez, Andrés. *Esbozo de la historia de los primeros diez años de la revolución agraria en México, de 1910 a 1920.* 2nd ed. Volume 5, Mexico City: Talleres Gráficos del Museo Nacional de Arqueología, Historia y Etnografía, 1936.

Murillo, Gerardo [pseud. Dr. Atl]. *La importancia mundial de la Revolución Mexicana.* Mexico: Confederación Revolucionaria, 1915.

———. *A los obreros de Puebla.* Escuela de Artes y Oficios del Estado, n.d.

Niemeyer, E. V. *Revolution at Querétaro: The Mexican Constitutional Convention of 1916–1917.* Austin: University of Texas Press, 1974.

Obregón, Alvaro. *Ocho mil kilómetros en campaña.* 2nd reprint. Mexico City: Fondo de Cultura Económica, 1970.

———. *Plan de propios y arbitrios: presupuesto de egresos; y ordenanzas municipales, formado por el ayuntamiento de Huata-bampo.* Alamos, Sonora: Tipografía de V. Hernández, 1911.

Olea, Hector R. *Breve historia de la Revolución en Sinaloa.* Mexico City: Biblioteca del Instituto Nacional de Estudios Históricos de la Revolución Mexicana, 1964.

Palacios, Porfirio. *Emiliano Zapata: Datos biográficos-históricos.* Mexico City: Libro Mex Editores, 1960.

Palavicini, Felix. *Mi vida revolucionaria.* Mexico City: Ediciones Botas, 1937.

Pani, Alberto J. *Apuntes autobiográficos.* 2 vols. Mexico City: Librería de Manuel Porrua, 1951.

Pletcher, David M. *Rails, Mines and Progress: Seven American Promoters in Mexico, 1867–1911.* Ithaca, N.Y.: Cornell University Press, 1958.

Portes Gil, Emilio. *Autobiografía de la Revolución Mexicana.* Mexico City: El Instituto Mexicano de Cultura, 1964.

Powell, Fred Wilbur, *The Railroads of Mexico.* Boston: Stratford Co., 1921.

Pozas, Ricardo. *Juan: The Chamula.* Berkeley and Los Angeles: University of California Press, 1966.

Prieto Laurens, Jorge. *Cincuenta años de política mexicana: Memorias políticas.* Mexico City: Editora Mexicana de Periódicos, Libros y Revistas, 1968.

¿Quién es Obregón? San Antonio: Librería de Quiroga, 1922.

Quirk, Robert E. *The Mexican Revolution, 1914–1915: The Convention of Aguascalientes.* Bloomington: Indiana University Press, 1960.

Quiros Martínez, Roberto. *Alvaro Obregón: Su vida y su obra.* N.p., 1928.

Retinger, J. H. *Morones of Mexico.* London: Labour Publishing Company, 1926.

Reyes Avilés, Carlos. *Cartones Zapatistas.* Mexico City, 1928.

Rivera, Antonio G. *La Revolución en Sonora.* Mexico City: Imprenta Arana, 1969.

Rojas, Basilio. *Un gran rebelde: Manuel García Vigil.* Mexico City: Editorial Luz, 1965.

Romero Flores, Jesús. *Anales históricos de la revolución mexicana,* Volume 2, *La Constitución de 1917 y los primeros gobiernos revolucionarios.* Mexico City: Libro Mex Editores, 1959.

Rosas y Reyes, Román. *Las imposturas de Vicente Blasco Ibañez: Verdades sobre México.* Barcelona: Librería Sintes, 1922.

Ross, Stanley R. *Francisco I. Madero: Apostle of Mexican Democracy*. New York: Columbia University Press, 1955.

Rouaix, Pastor. *Génesis de los Artículos 27 y 123 de la Constitución política de 1917*. Prologue by Antonio Díaz Soto y Gama. Mexico City: Biblioteca del Institución Nacional de Estudios Históricos de la Revolución Mexicana, 1959.

Rueda, Jorge. *Pluma falsa*. Mexico City, 1920.

Ruíz, Ramon E. *Labor and the Ambivalent Revolutionaries, 1911–1913*. Baltimore: Johns Hopkins University Press, 1976.

Salazar, Rosendo. *Carta del Trabajo de la Revolución Mexicana*. Mexico City: Libro Mex Editores, 1960.

———. *La Casa del Obrero Mundial*. Mexico City: Costa-Amic, Editores, 1962.

———. *Líderes y sindicatos*. Mexico City: Ediciones T. C. Modelo, 1953.

———, and José G. Escobedo. *Las pugnas de la gleba*. Mexico City: Editorial Avante, 1923.

Scott, Hugh L. *Some Memoirs of a Soldier*. New York: Century Co., 1928.

Seymour, Charles. *The Intimate Papers of Colonel House*. Volume 1. Boston: Houghton Mifflin Co., 1926.

Silva Herzog, Jesús. *El agrarismo mexicano y la reforma agraria: Exposición y crítica*. Mexico City: Fondo de Cultura Económica, 1959.

Tamayo, J. A. *El General Obregón y la guerra*. Tampico: El Mundo, 1922.

Tannenbaum, Frank. *The Mexican Agrarian Revolution*. Reprint. Archon Books, 1968.

———. *Mexico: The Struggle for Peace and Bread*. New York: Alfred A. Knopf, 1950.

———. *Peace by Revolution: Mexico after 1910*. Reprint. New York: Columbia University Press, 1966.

Tinker, Edward Larocque. *New Yorker Unlimited: The Memoirs of Edward Larocque Tinker*. Austin: University of Texas at Austin and Encino Press, 1970.

Trueba Urbina, Alberto. *La primera constitución político-social del mundo*. Mexico City: Editorial Porrua, 1971.

Turner, John Kenneth, *Barbarous Mexico*. Austin: University of Texas Press, 1969.

Urióstegui Miranda, Píndaro. *Testimonios del proceso revolucionario de México*. Mexico City: Talleres de Argrin, 1970.

Urquizo, Francisco L. *Organización del Ejército Constitucionalista.* Mexico City: Talleres Gráficos de la Secretaría de la Guerra, 1916.

———. *Origen del Ejército Constitucionalista.* Mexico City: Biblioteca del Instituto Nacional de Estudios Históricos de la Revolución Mexicana, 1964.

———. *Páginas de la Revolución.* Mexico City: Biblioteca del Instituto Nacional de Estudios de la Revolución Mexicana, 1956.

———. *Recuerdo que. . . . Visiones aisladas de la Revolución.* 2 vols. Mexico City: Ediciones Botas, 1934.

Valadés, José C. *Las caballerías de la Revolución: Hazañas del General Buelna.* Mexico City: Ediciones Botas, 1937.

Valenzuela, Clodoveo, and Amado Chaverri Matamoros, comps. *Sonora y Carranza.* Mexico City: Casa Editorial "Renacimiento," 1921.

Vasconcelos, José. *La tormenta.* Mexico City: Ediciones Botas, 1937.

Warman, Arturo. *. . . Y venimos a contradecir: los campesinos de Morelos y el estado nacional.* Mexico City: Centro de Investigaciones Superiores del INAH, 1976.

Weber, Max. *On Charisma and Institution Building.* Edited by S. N. Eisenstadt. Chicago: University of Chicago Press, 1968.

Wilkie, James W. *The Mexican Revolution: Federal Expenditure and Social Change since 1910.* Berkeley and Los Angeles: University of California Press, 1970.

Wolf, Eric. *Peasant Wars of the Twentieth Century.* New York: Harper Torchbooks, 1973.

Womack, John, Jr. *Zapata and the Mexican Revolution.* New York: Alfred A. Knopf, 1969.

Articles and Unpublished Manuscripts

Aguilar Camín, Hector. "The Relevant Tradition: Sonoran Leaders in the Revolution," in *Caudillo and Peasant in the Mexican Revolution,* edited by D. A. Brading. Cambridge Latin American Studies, No. 38. Cambridge: At the University Press, 1980.

Angeles, Felipe. "Justificación de la desobediencia de los Generales de la División del Norte, en Torreón, el mes de Junio de 1914." Chihuahua, August 12, 1914. PHS/59.

Cabrera, Luis. "The Mexican Revolution—Its Causes, Purposes,

Bibliography 279

and Results." Annals of the American Academy 69, 1st supplement (January, 1917).
Calles, Plutarco Elías. Tierra y libros para todos! Programa de Gobierno. Nacozari, Sonora, Mexico: Talleres de Imprenta Gregorio Moreno, 1915. Pamphlet reprinted as article in La cuestión de la tierra. Mexico City: Instituto Mexicano de Investigaciones, 1962.
Chevalier, François. "The Ejido and Political Stability in Mexico." In The Politics of Conformity in Latin America, edited by Claudio Véliz. London: Oxford University Press, 1970.
———. "Survivances seigneuriales et presages de la revolution agraire dans le Nord du Mexique." Revue Historique 222 (1959): 1–18.
Dillon, Richard H. "Del rancho a la presidencia." Historia Mexicana 6 (October–December, 1956): 256–269.
Fornaro, Carlo. "General Alvaro Obregón." Forum 55 (February, 1916): 236.
Friedrich, Paul. "Revolutionary Politics and Communal Ritual." In Political Anthropology, edited by Marc J. Swartz, Victor Turner, and Arthur Tuden. Chicago: Aldine Publishing Company, 1966.
Gómez-Quiñones, Juan. "Social Change and Intellectual Discontent: The Growth of Mexican Nationalism, 1890–1911." Ph.D. dissertation, University of California at Los Angeles, 1972.
González, Pablo. "Postrimerías del periódo pre-constitucional." La Prensa, San Antonio, May 10, 1921.
Grajales, Francisco J. "Interpretación de las campañas militares del General Obregón." In Alvaro Obregón, Ocho mil kilómetros en campaña. 2nd reprint. Mexico: Fondo de Cultura Económica, 1970.
Hall, Linda B. "The Mexican Revolution and the Crisis in Naco, 1914–1915." Journal of the West 16 (October, 1977): 27–35.
Hansis, Randall George. "Alvaro Obregón, the Mexican Revolution, and the Politics of Consolidation, 1920–1924." Ph.D. dissertation, University of New Mexico, 1971.
Harris, Charles, and Louis R. Sadler. "The Plan of San Diego and the Mexican–United States War Crisis of 1916: A Re-Examination." Hispanic American Historical Review 58 (August, 1978): 381–408.
Hobsbawm, E. J. "Peasants and Rural Migrants in Politics." In

The Politics of Conformity in Latin America. London: Oxford University Press, 1970.

"El Hospital Militar de Instrucción y la Escuela Médico Militar." *Revista de Revistas* (January 23, 1927): 62–63.

Lasswell, Harold. "The Political Personality." In *Personality and Politics*, edited by Gordon J. DiRenzo. Garden City, N.Y.: Anchor Books, 1974.

Meyer, Jean. "Los obreros en la Revolución Mexicana: Los Batallones Rojos." *Historia Mexicana* 21 (July–September, 1971): 1–38.

Morones, Luis N. "Morones habla claro." *El Universal* (Mexico City), June 11, 1956.

Murillo, Gerardo. "Obregón y el principio de renovación social." In *Obregón, Aspectos de su vida*, pp. 67–90. Mexico: Editorial Cultura, 1935.

Obregón, Alvaro. "El problema agrícola y agrario; conferencia pronunciada en Guadalajara, 11 noviembre 1919." In *El pensamiento político de Alvaro Obregón*, edited by Narciso Bassols Batalla. 2nd edition. Mexico: Ediciones El Caballito, 1970.

Richmond, Douglas W. "Venustiano Carranza's Rise to Power, 1893–1915." Master's thesis, University of Washington, 1971.

Rivera, Antonio G. "Apuntes sobre la vida de Alvaro Obregón." Unpublished manuscript, 1974.

Romero, Rubén. "Alvaro Obregón." In *Obregón: Aspectos de su vida*, pp. 5–36. Mexico: Editorial Cultura, 1935.

Smith, Peter H. "La política dentro de la Revolución: El Congreso Constituyente de 1916–1917." *Historia Mexicana* 22 (January–March, 1973): 363–395.

Tobler, Hans-Werner. "Las paradojas del ejército revolucionario: su papel social en la reforma agraria mexicana, 1920–1935." *Historia Mexicana* 21 (July–September, 1971): 38–79.

Urquizo, Francisco L. "Obregón, militar." In *Alvaro Obregón, Ocho mil kilómetros en campaña*. 2nd reprint. Mexico City: Fondo de Cultura Económica, 1970.

Villarreal, Antonio I. "The Real Story of the Aguascalientes Convention." In *Immediate Causes of the Present Conflict in Mexico*. N.p., 1914.

Index

Abitia, Jesús, 21
Academia del Estado Mayor, 158–159
Acosta, José María, 62, 66
Acuña, Jesús, 161, 191
agrarian dcrees: Jan. 6, 1915, 103, 107–108, 140; Sept. 4, 1916, 197
agrarian reform: in 1917 Constitution: 174, 179–181. *See also* land reform
Agrupaciones Políticas del Río Mayo, 222
Agua Prieta, Son., 31, 35, 42, 61, 200
Aguascalientes (city), 74, 90, 91, 96, 133
Aguascalientes, Convention of, 60, 76–94, 95, 140, 143, 164–165
Aguilar, General Cándido, 99, 172, 173
Aguirre, Amado, 135, 174, 182, 228, 243
Aguirre Berlanga, Manuel, 176, 194
Alamos, Son., 12, 16, 19, 29, 43, 45
Alessio Robles, Miguel, 237, 239
Alliance of Mexican Railwaymen, 246
Almada, Jesús, 22
Almada, Jorge, 22
Almada, Laura Salido de, 22
Almazán, Juan Andreu, 241
Alvarado, Salvador: as military commander, 43, 44, 55, 61, 62, 104; as Obregón's rival, 45, 59–60, 62, 192; as Sonoran, 19, 43; as Yucatán governor, 19, 192
Alvarado Mining Company, 151
Amaro, Joaquín, 118, 129, 130, 196
Angeles, Felipe: Carranza accuses, 74;

at Convention of Aguascalientes, 85, 87; described, 51; military successes of, 104; Obregón's distrust of, 51, 65, 98; supports Carranza, 51; supports Huerta, 51; supports Madero, 47, 51; as Villa's advisor, 47, 52, 64; Villa rejects advice of, 97–98, 123, 134; and Zapata, 241
anticlericalism, 12, 18, 181; of Obregón, 21, 114, 117, 174–176
Apizaco, Tlax., 99
Apolo Theater, 102
Arizona, 17, 63, 154
Arizpe, Son., 16
Army of the Northeast, 56, 64, 92
Army of the Northwest, 50, 109, 127
Arrieta brothers, 74
Atl, Dr. *See* Murillo, Gerardo

Baja California, 28, 74, 184, 234
Bajío, 120, 122
Baker, Newton D., 149, 151
Bakers' Union, 246
Batallón Regional Río Blanco, 116
Barragán, Juan, 228
Benavides, Eugenio, 62, 71, 75, 77–78, 105
Benavides, Luis, 64, 65, 66
Blanco, Lucio, 55
Bloque Revolucionario Independiente, 224, 226, 228
Bojórquez, Juan de Dios (pseud. Djed Bórquez), 141, 160, 182, 192, 214, 221

18, 43; named governor of Jalisco, 53; opposes Obregón, 242–243; as Sonoran general, 51, 92
Division of the North: and Aguascalientes convention, 78; Carranza's lack of support for, 63, 74; at Celaya, 128; loyalty of, 71, 77, 92; Obregón and, 72, 75; Villa and, 93, 99
Dorados, 72
Douglas, Ariz., 35, 42, 236

Eisenstadt, S. N., 8, 166
El Ebano, S.L.P., 99, 122, 129
El Fuerte, Sin., 49
Elizondo, Alfredo, 118, 130
El Paso, Tex., 50, 52, 65, 74, 150, 155
El Paso and Southwestern Railroad, 35
Empleados de Comercio, 128
Enríquez, Ignacio E., 196
Escudero y Verdugo, Manuel, 142
Escuela de Medicina Militar, 158
Estación Sabinal, 31
Estrada, Roque, 101

Figueroa, Romulo, 239
First Division of the East, 129
First National Bank of Douglas, Ariz., 35
Flores, Angel, 195, 196
Flores Magón, Enrique, 16, 28
Flores Magón, Ricardo, 16, 28
Fontes, Paulino, 204, 223, 226
free municipality, 102
Fronteras, 31, 33, 34, 42
Fuller, Paul, 70
Fundición de Sinaloa, 24
Funston, Frederick, 150

Gadsden Hotel, 35
Garza, Jesús M.: characterizes Obregón, 184; and land reform, 160; military schools under, 171; in Obregón's campaign, 198, 217, 220, 231; prevents Obregón's suicide, 134; represents Obregón, 117, 120; in Sonoran politics, 199
Gastelum, Bernardo, 22
Gayou, Eugenio, 29

González, Abraham, 39, 41–45
González, Alejo, 172
González, Arnulfo, 196
González, Pablo, 65, 177; and Aguascalientes convention, 92, 93; as Carrancista military leader, 44, 53, 56, 64, 153, 240; and Carranza, 145, 172, 207, 238, 244; and labor, 161; leads Army of Northeast, 53, 56, 64, 92; as Obregón's rival, 171, 227, 228, 229; and other leaders, 182; in P.L.C., 172, 173; political ambitions of, 205, 244
González, Porfirio, 129
González Garza, Roque, 74, 82, 84, 85–87, 106
governors, conclave of, 228–229
Grace, W. R., 201–202
Gracidas (deputy), 178
Gran Convención Obregonista, 210–212, 221, 228, 254
Gran Partido Liberal, 210, 228
Greene, William, 11
Grupo Acción, 217
Guadalajara, Jal., 54, 55, 97, 141, 243
Guadalupe, Zac., 81
Guaje, Guan., 125
Guanajuato (state), 229, 242
Guaymas, Son., 10, 20; Carranza's troops in, 234; federal troops in, 48, 49, 121; landholdings in, 16; Masonic movement in, 15; revolutionary leaders from, 12, 24, 41; siege of, 60
Guaymas Club Antireeleccionista, 12
Guerrero (state), 99
Gutiérrez, Eulalio, 90–93, 105–106, 110
Gutiérrez, Luis, 241
Guzmán, Martín Luis, 64, 137

Hacienda de Guadalupe, 44
Hacienda del Cristo, 107
Hacienda Ojitos, 30
Hacienda San Joaquín, 31
Hay, Eduardo, 81, 91, 172, 191–192
Hermosillo, Son., 31; Angeles forced to leave, 52; armed forces in, 42; Carranza in, 48, 50; Junta de Notables in, 25; Madero mourned in, 43; Maytorena in, 43, 50, 60; Obregón in, 29, 35, 41, 45, 51; revolu-

Siquisiva, Son., 20
Siurob, José, 192
Society of Producers of Garbanzo, 190, 195, 200
Sonora (state), 36, 72, 122, 164, 190, 191; anticlericalism in, 12, 15, 18; Carranza and, 144, 196–197, 232, 233–236; commercial activities in, 14, 15, 21; conditions in, 11, 13, 15, 16; factionalism in, 46, 57, 61–63, 66–67, 73–74, 85, 198; garbanzo producers in, 13, 200–202; Indian relations in, 18, 19, 21, 42, 245; national politics in, 11, 12, 17; Obregón's support in, 187, 194, 200, 233–234, 242, 245; opposes Huerta, 42–44; relations of, with U.S., 17; revolts against Carranza, 238–239; role of, in Revolution, 10; U.S. economic influence in, 13, 15, 16–17
Sonora and Sinaloa Irrigation Companies, 18
Spain, 201

Tamaulipas (state), 196, 242
Tampico, Tamps., 99, 129, 141, 229, 230
Tapia de Obregón, María, 149, 168, 189
Teoloyucan, Méx., 56. *See also* Treaty of Teoloyucan
Tepic, Nayt., 52, 55, 60
Terrazas family, 52
Tierra y libros para todos, 108
Tigre Mine, El, 31
Tinker, Edward Larocque, 31, 33–35, 134
Tizapán, D.F., 112
Tlaxcala (state), 99
Tlaxacalantongo, 244
Topolobampo, Sin., 49
Torreón, Coah., 53, 55, 134
Torres, Luis, 12, 234
Treaty of Teoloyucan, 56, 57, 165
Treviño, Jacinto, 155, 156, 193, 196, 205
Tucson, Ariz., 45, 46
Tulancingo, Hidal., 222

Unión Liberal Humanidad, 17

Universal, El, 172, 173, 209, 222
Urbalejo, Francisco, 62, 66
Urbina, Tomás, 64, 65
Ures, Son., 43
Urquizo, Francisco, 159
Urueta, Jesús, 101, 142, 173, 191
U.S. Department of State, 127
U.S. Enemy Trading Act, 190
U.S. Food Administration, 190
U.S. Infantry, 188

Valadez Ramírez, Antonio, 226
Valderrain family, 23
Valenzuela, Gilberto, 242
Vanguardia, 141, 142
Vasconcelos, José, 200
Velasco, Ernesto, 162
Veracruz (city), 255; Carranza's retreat toward, 243; Constitutionalists in, 99, 101–102, 104, 107, 116, 118, 126, 128, 132, 133, 141; U.S. troops in, 70–71
Veracruz (state), 108, 164, 240
Vieyra, Epifanio, 16
Villa, Francisco ("Pancho"), 27, 35, 38, 83, 86, 89, 99, 104, 164, 170, 241, 253, 255; at Aguascalientes convention, 76, 77, 78, 80, 84, 87–88, 90, 91, 95; alliance of, with Maytorena, 51; alliance of, with Zapata, 85, 96, 97, 132; amnesty for, 246; Angeles and, 47, 52, 97–98, 123, 134; background of, 39, 44; in Bajío battles, 122, 123, 124–127, 128, 129–131, 137; border raids by, 145, 146; breaks with Carranza, 74, 93; under Carranza, 44–45, 52, 53, 61, 63, 69; characterized, 19, 39, 44–45, 98; compared with Obregón, 19, 82, 92, 137, 165; early battles of, 53–54; finances of, 52, 129–130, 131–132; hostility of, toward Obregón, 51, 69, 70, 93; in León battle, 131, 134–137; Obregón confers with, 64–68, 71–73, 75; as Obregón's subordinate, 50–51; overtures of, toward Obregón, 54; psychology of, 104, 105, 123–124, 126, 133–134, 137–138; supporters of, 60, 63–64, 71, 75, 77, 81, 82, 105, 106; threatens Obregón's life, 72–73, 75;